INTRODUCTIONS TO THE LESSONS

Mike Stone

Introductions to the Lessons

A RESOURCEBOOK FOR LECTORS

NOTES AND INTRODUCTIONS TO THE BIBLE READINGS
ACCORDING TO THE REVISED COMMON LECTIONARY
AND THE COMMON WORSHIP LECTIONARY

the columba press

First published in 2000 by
the columba press
55A Spruce Avenue, Stillorgan Industrial Park, Blackrock, Co Dublin

Cover by Bill Bolger
Origination by The Columba Press
Printed in Ireland by Colour Books Ltd, Dublin

ISBN 1 85607 304 1

Acknowledgements

My very grateful thanks to the many good friends with whom, over many years, I have been able to share in group Bible Study. They have taught me more than I could ever have discovered alone, and we have always been able to mix profundity and laughter. Among them, special thanks to Christine, who conceived this particular approach to helping others, and watched it through its infancy.

I acknowledge also the kindness of The Revd Bennett Barnes, of the Episcopal Church of America, for allowing me to see in draft his doctoral thesis 'Incipits for lectionary use'. This helped clarify the rationale for the task and the principles of this genre. It also contains suggested material for Year B. Ben will recognise some of his phrases here.

Contents

Note: RCL and CWL

The Revised Common Lectionary (RCL), the ecumenical and international pattern for the public reading of scripture, is in widespread use. But some churches modify its provisions for their own purposes. The Church of England has approved the Common Worship Lectionary (CWL), and its choices for Principal Services sometimes vary from RCL, mainly in the Epiphany season and before Advent. There are also some 'calendar' differences, in the names given to Sundays.

This book covers both RCL and CWL, using those abbreviations to indicate where an entry is unique to one or the other.

Other churches which apply different variations, particularly in those seasons whose length varies from year to year according to the date of Easter, can use the Index at the back of this book to identify introductions which apply to their readings.

Introduction

This book is a tool, and a resource, for those whose ministry is to read lessons in church. Following the Common Lectionary, it provides a short introduction to each set reading, to give the listening congregation some brief information before the reading itself.

Such introductions are sometimes known as 'incipits', and for brevity I use that word in what follows. An incipit is provided here for every Bible reading of the Sundays and major Holy Days in the Revised Common Lectionary (RCL) and the Common Worship Lectionary (CWL).

The material offered covers such things as the context of a reading, its relationships to other readings (on the same or other Sundays), and a brief indication as to what the reading is 'about'. There is sometimes a general statement of its place within God's scheme of things for making himself known through the Bible. I have always tried, though, to avoid pre-empting or circumscribing what the preacher may find as inspiration in seeking the Lord's word in his Word.

The need for incipits

Knowledge of the Bible among churchgoers is nowhere near so deep as it used to be. Today's Christians did not have the Bible read to them as children, and their encounters with it through formal education were probably minimal. Things which, for generations, everybody 'knew' something about, such as Samson, David and Goliath, the Good Samaritan, are no longer part of our given cultural heritage. And within the churches, except those few which week on week foster a steady diet of biblical teaching, one cannot expect to find people saturated in the narratives, the imagery, and the language (ancient or modern) of the Bible.

This being so, the many resonances which every reading carries will be unknown mental territory to most hearers. And – dare one say – those whose ministry is to read the Word of God in worship may be no more familiar with the text than the listeners. An abundance of modern translations, while undoubtedly valuable in many ways, also removes the other possibility of well-known words lodging and echoing in the mind. All this unfamiliarity with the texts argues for some effort to be undertaken.

There is, then, a challenge to those responsible for the conduct of worship to make as meaningful as possible the character and purport of each passage read from the Bible. Some of this, some of the time, for some of the readings, will be accomplished by the preacher. But on those occasions when the three readings for the day have no internal connection, one cannot envisage three mini-sermons. And always, the formal nature of liturgical reading gives no sense of whether the passage is a letter, a saga, a theological reflection, a poem, or another literary form. Unmediated readings can be baffling. A congregation perplexed is one for whom the Word of the Lord does not speak plainly.

Incipits, being short explanatory introductory sentences, attempt to put readings into context, both as to their place in the liturgical calendar and the over-arching dynamic of scripture. My experience, since CWL came into common use in the Church of England, is that many churches have quickly realised the need for incipits – in particular, because the former lectionary (of the Alternative Service Book) with its thematic approach seemed to make the meaning of every reading self-evident. Whether or not that was true, the very different lectionary system of the 'Common' lectionaries compels new reflection on the presentation of the Word. And local attempts are being made to create incipits. However, where the composition is left to the lector, the quality is bound to be variable; where it is done by the priest or minister, a new task is added to the weekly workload – with no clear resource.

Structure of entries in this book
I am aware, of course, that my words will not suit all occasions nor all approaches to the scriptures. Some will wish to construct their own incipits. Therefore, as well as providing a form of words which can, if desired, be used 'as is', I try to help by offering in every case a brief note of the 'context' of each reading, and some of the 'ideas' contained in it.

I do not claim my words as the best that could be said, and certainly not (because brevity is vital) all that could be said; but I offer this work to all churches of all denominations with the promise that all the prayer poured into the doing of it will continue for those who use it.

Year A: The First Sunday of Advent

Isaiah 2:1-5
CONTEXT: A collection of the speeches of 'Isaiah of Jerusalem' (Chs 1-39), during the period when Assyria had conquered Israel and constantly threatened Judah.
IDEAS: Mount Zion as the ultimate holy place; a day of peace will come, for it is God's will.

The Bible tells us much about God's past dealings with his people. All our readings in the Advent Season speak of the future in God's ultimate will. Even for Isaiah, in turbulent times, there is expectancy and the hope of peace, when all people shall come together to worship the one who comes to us in holiness.

Romans 13:11-14
CONTEXT: Christian lifestyle in a secular world.
IDEAS: The passage of time; last days; fitting behaviour.

Isaiah and all Israel expected a new age of the Messiah. For Paul's readers as for us, the new time has come – not yet in its fullness, but begun in the coming of Jesus Christ. Our behaviour must therefore be suitable to these decisive times, nearer every day to the Christ who will come again.

Matthew 24:36-44
CONTEXT: Jesus's warnings about the end of all things.
IDEAS: Any moment may be his moment of coming – be prepared.

In this new church year, the Gospel on most Sundays will be from that of Matthew. Here, Jesus has some warnings for his disciples about the final coming of the Son of Man. His kingdom will mean a separation between those who are expectant and those left unprepared. God may refuse those who eternally refuse him.

Year A: The Second Sunday of Advent

Isaiah 11:1-10
CONTEXT: Prophecies over the fate – and the saved remnant – of Israel.
IDEAS: Universal harmony under God; a new (Davidic) King will achieve this.

Many ancient prophets foretold the day of the Lord's coming. He will be within the dynasty of Jesse's great son David, and once again there will be peace and harmony. All peoples, and all the natural world too, will be reconciled.

Romans 15:4-13
CONTEXT: A section of the letter that deals with relationships.
IDEAS: Concede to the weaker, as Jesus did; search the scriptures for encouragement.

Paul quotes the scriptures for evidence that Jesus always considered others before himself. So let all Christians now agree in a common hope, joy, and perseverance.

Matthew 3:1-12
CONTEXT: John and Jesus now adults: the preaching begins.
IDEAS: Repentance; 'Elijah' precedes the Messiah (Mt 17:10); scathing denunciation of evil ways.

The last of the old prophets, the one whom Jesus called greatest in his kingdom, was John the Baptist. John, like Paul, quotes Isaiah, to explain his function of preparing the way for the Lord's coming.

Year A: The Third Sunday of Advent

Isaiah 35:1-10
CONTEXT: Assurance that Yahweh will destroy Israel's enemies, and restore her.
IDEAS: All nature's wildest places and all unhappy people healed; returning to the Lord.

Today's Gospel refers to this prophecy. Isaiah's poetry speaks of a world transformed when prisoners are freed, the sick healed, the hungry fed, and all nature bursts with life, as God in person comes to save.

James 5:7-10
CONTEXT: Miscellaneous injunctions about Christian life.
IDEAS: Patience while awaiting the Day of the Lord.

We know from our Old Testament how the Jews longed for the Lord's coming. And we know Christ has come, Christ will come again. James urges us never to despair or lose faith in this time of waiting.

Matthew 11:2-11
CONTEXT: The Twelve have been commissioned to share Jesus's work.
IDEAS: The work of the Messiah; how is it to be recognised?

The friends of John the Baptist had expected their Messiah to come with political power, but for them and for us the evidence of Christ's presence is found in our individual lives as he comes constantly to transform us.

Year A: The Fourth Sunday of Advent

Isaiah 7:10-16
CONTEXT: King Ahaz of Judah threatened by an alliance of Israel and Syria.
IDEAS: God's voice through prophets; signs and wonders; the young woman (or 'virgin')
and child a 'messianic' figure (we cannot be sure what Isaiah originally meant).

A young woman will give her son the name Immanuel, meaning 'God is with us'. Isaiah's words were meant as encouragement to King Ahaz in dangerous times, but for us they will always have the profound meaning fulfilled in Mary and the birth of Jesus.

Romans 1:1-7
CONTEXT: Paul writing to Christians he had not met.
IDEAS: Paul's credentials; Christ born of David's line; greetings between Christians.

On the last Sunday before Christmas Day, we hear a reminder from Paul of the content of the Good News: that prophecy is fulfilled, that Christ is born a son of David, that he died and rose again – and calls us into his company.

Matthew 1:18-25
CONTEXT: The Gospel begins with the wonder of the Incarnation.
IDEAS: A unique pregnancy; angelic messengers; ancient hopes now become reality; Joseph's consternation.

Mary conceives a child by divine grace, and to the worried Joseph there appears a dreamlike messenger with strange words of assurance. This strange circumstance is safe in divine hands. '... and she will call her son Immanuel.'

Year A: CWL: Christmas Eve (morning)

2 Samuel 7:1-5, 8-11, 16
CONTEXT: King David has defeated all the warring neighbours, and set up the Ark in Jerusalem.
IDEAS: A worthy place for God (cf. the stable); the king will bring peace; God will secure David's dynasty.

King David is told that God is content to dwell in the humblest of places. God has always been present, leading and guiding, and can always be trusted to guide and bless. All Jewish hope rested on the promise of a king like this, born of David's line.

Acts 13:16-26
CONTEXT: A synagogue sermon in Galatia.
IDEAS: God's chosen people; David and his succession; now the Saviour has come.

Paul was invited to speak at a synagogue in Galatia. His Jewish audience heard him briefly review their history under God, and the promise of a Davidic King. The way was prepared, he says; now – to us – Jesus our Saviour has come.

Luke 1:67-79
CONTEXT: Luke's stories and songs declaring two wondrous births.
IDEAS: Zechariah released from dumbness for praise; all God's promises come true; the Lord's herald.

Now the hope of centuries is satisfied, and there is nothing left but praise – the praise of old Zechariah whose own son John will usher into the world the one who is the light of the world.

Year A: Christmas Day

SET I

Isaiah 9:2-7

CONTEXT: Judah will suffer defeat by Assyria – but God will deliver.
IDEAS: Poetry of praise; visions of God's wonders; names of the child.

The Bible readings in Advent have prepared us to celebrate the coming of the Lord. His people longed for him, and we know the joy of living with him here and now. So, we understand Isaiah's prophecy as greeting the birth of a child whose new kingdom of righteousness will last for ever.

Titus 2:11-14

CONTEXT: Pastoral instruction to an established church leader in Crete.
IDEAS: God's grace; Christian 'discipline' (= training, learning); vision of a future more perfect age; Jesus (unusually for the Bible) is called God.

The new morning of the world has dawned, says this writer. As we learn how to live in this bright new light, in gratitude for the first coming of Jesus who has made us his own, we await the greater glory when Christ will come again.

Luke 2:1-14 [15-20]

CONTEXT: Luke intertwines the birth stories of Jesus and John.
IDEAS: Dating the birth; Bethlehem and its history; no welcome; another angelic sign.

Luke, the master storyteller, gives us pictures we shall never forget, of the humble birth at Bethlehem of the Saviour of the world, and the shining glory which brought shepherds to worship the Lamb of God.

SET II

Isaiah 62:6-12

CONTEXT: Third Isaiah (post-exile); promise of a new Jerusalem.
IDEAS: Jerusalem (and Israel) restored and protected; renewed by God to be holy people.

The prophet proclaims that the news of God's deliverance will reach every corner of the world, to call all his people back to himself. He will redeem them, and make them his holy ones.

Year A: Christmas Day, continued

Titus 3:4-7
CONTEXT: See SET I above.
IDEAS: Grace; generosity; saved by faith to eternal life.

Christ has come to bring a new dawn, says this writer. Now we know we are not saved by our good deeds, but by grace alone. The divine mercy makes us heirs of eternal life.

Luke 2:[1-7] 8-20
See SET I above for details.

SET III

Isaiah 52:7-10
CONTEXT: Songs of encouragement and the victory to come.
IDEAS: Good news of deliverance; return to the holy city.

In typical Hebrew style, the prophet sings of a glorious future as if it had already happened. For us, God has indeed visited and redeemed his people, glory to Israel and light for the Gentiles.

Hebrews 1:1-4 [5-12]
CONTEXT: The culmination of all God's self-revelation is in Jesus.
IDEAS: Christ present in creation; now revealed to us; his work of salvation.

In this anonymous essay, the writer contrasts the partial revelation given in times past with the outpouring of God's word in his glorious Son. [*If 5-12 is read:* with whom even the angels bear no comparison.]

John 1:1-14
CONTEXT: The divine disclosure in the Word made flesh.
IDEAS: Christ as Logos - Word, present in creation; seen on earth, rejected by many but new life for all believers.

In so few but wonderful words, John captures the majesty and the mystery of God disclosing himself; his divine Word is made flesh. Christ was from the beginning, is now, and all who believe this are children of God.

Year A: The First Sunday of Christmas

Isaiah 63:7-9
CONTEXT: God alone has saved his people, hence this hymn of praise.
IDEAS: Prayers of thankfulness for God's actions; he acts directly for our sake.

The prophet's hymn of praise emphasises that it is always God himself, no intermediary or other, who is the redeemer of his people in his love for them.

Hebrews 2:10-18
CONTEXT: An exposition of the nature and the work of Jesus.
IDEAS: Jesus human and divine; he shared our humanity so we share his divinity.

This unknown writer explains that because God in Christ shared all the experiences we humans suffer, he is able to bring us with him into the Father's glory.

Matthew 2:13-23
CONTEXT: Unique to Matthew, the 'Wise Men' visitation and Herod's plotting.
IDEAS: Rival kings; refugees; Jesus is saved.

We shall hear at Epiphany-tide how important men from the East paid homage to the infant Christ. Today's Gospel tells a harsher tale, of Herod's fury at the possibility of a rival king. So the Holy Family become refugees, until the time when it will be safe to return.

Year A: The Second Sunday of Christmas

Jeremiah 31:7-14
CONTEXT: Babylonian exile: a sequence of promises of restoration of the kingdom and the monarchy.
IDEAS: The remnant preserved; gathering together for celebration; gladness; bountiful provision.

Jeremiah speaks God's words, from the perspective when all nations and peoples shall be restored. The passage has many images which only found their full meaning in Christian vocabulary – God as father to his redeemed people, saviour, gatherer, shepherd and deliverer, giver of joy and gladness.

OR *Ecclesiasticus 24:1-12*
CONTEXT: The Apocrypha; in praise of wisdom (a 'person' of God).
IDEAS: God's attributes personified before Jesus came; present in creation, makes his dwelling with humankind; wisdom = Word (v. 3).

Not long before Christ's birth, these writings were collected in books we call the Apocrypha. Wisdom is here described in feminine imagery, personified as one who existed before time began, sent forth as the word of the Lord to dwell with God's people and make her home in their midst.

Ephesians 1:3-14
CONTEXT: The letter opens with a section of praise for God's blessings.
IDEAS: God's eternal purposes and choices; his gifts to us in and through Christ.

This letter begins with a hymn of praise to God for what he has done for us. The phrase 'in Christ' comes again and again: as God was in Christ Jesus, so we are one in Christ. God has made us his children and calls us to glory.

John 1:[1-9] 10-18
CONTEXT: The divine disclosure in the Word made flesh.
IDEAS: Christ as Logos – Word, present in creation; seen on earth, rejected by many but new life for all believers.

In so few but wonderful words, John captures the majesty and the mystery of God disclosing himself; his divine Word is made flesh. Christ was from the beginning, is now, and all who believe this are children of God.

Year A: The Epiphany: 6 January

Isaiah 60:1-6
CONTEXT: Call to respond to the promise of new Jerusalem.
IDEAS: Come and worship; glory dawns; abundance.

In Isaiah's vision of God's light shining into the world's darkness, symbolic gifts are brought to God from East and West as tribute and praise. So our Gospel's Magi visitors to the stable are foreshadowed.

Ephesians 3:1-12
CONTEXT: The 'near' and 'far-off' united; Jew and Gentile now fellow citizens.
IDEAS: God's secrets now revealed; Paul in prison but rejoicing; all are one in Christ.

Riches beyond imagining, says Paul, are found in Christ. Though he is in prison for his faith, his gospel cannot be confined – the good news that God's purposes, once so obscure, are now made clear for Jew and Gentile alike.

Matthew 2:1-12
CONTEXT: Matthew's (unique) nativity story of gifts to Jesus.
IDEAS: The greatest king has come; journeying to him; wisdom honours him; our gifts to him.

Only Matthew tells us how representatives of other strange religions came from the East to offer their homage to the one and only true God, the child who is king for ever over all earthly powers.

Year A: The Baptism of Christ: Epiphany 1

Isaiah 42:1-9
CONTEXT: The first 'Servant Song'; prophetically Israel (or, we may believe, Jesus) is God's agent to deliver the world.
IDEAS: God's call; his delight in those he forms and guides; light for all nations.

This passage links with the Gospel, where we shall hear a heavenly voice declaring God's delight in his beloved Son. Isaiah had visualised that same delight in a spirit-filled nation, or a person, whose vocation would be to serve God unstintingly.

Acts 10:34-43
CONTEXT: Peter's vision of God's call to reach beyond Judaism; he (and friends) respond to a Roman centurion.
IDEAS: The life and work of Jesus; Gospel for Gentiles; forgiveness is effective for everyone.

This reading is a small part of a story. Peter, and some others who share the new resurrection faith, tell a Roman centurion all the events of Jesus's life, and the meaning of it all. For the first time, the Gospel reaches beyond Judaism, and the climax is the surprising conversion of Gentiles.

Matthew 3:13-17
CONTEXT: Matthew's first mention of Jesus since the nativity stories – John is baptising.
IDEAS: Jesus submits to John's baptism; anointing; joy in heaven.

Baptism is a new beginning, and the Lord himself comes to the river Jordan to be baptised by John before he begins his public mission. God delights to declare his Son, upon whom his Spirit rests.

Year A: Epiphany 2

Isaiah 49:1-7
CONTEXT: The 'Servant Songs', proclaiming Israel (or some future individual) the agent of God's activity in all nations.
IDEAS: Light for the world; revelation; vocation.

Epiphany means manifestation. In this Epiphany season, our readings are showing the ways God has revealed himself. For us, Isaiah's poem has come true in a way he could scarcely have imagined, as he anticipates the appearance of God within one who is destined even before his birth to be the bearer of salvation into all the world.

1 Corinthians 1:1-9
CONTEXT: Greeting to Christians and thankfulness.
IDEAS: Affirmation of the work of Christ; spiritual gifts; God keeps faith.

Isaiah's vision of the Lord revealing himself is echoed in this opening greeting from Paul's letter to Corinth. He gives thanks for the spiritual gifts they have received, and shows himself confident that God will strengthen them for the new day of the Lord's appearing.

John 1:29-42
CONTEXT: John the Baptist points people to Jesus, the Chosen One.
IDEAS: John 'reveals' Jesus (v. 31b); baptism by Spirit; directing others to Jesus; Andrew and Peter.

John the Baptist is given an epiphany of who Jesus really is, and declares his own task to be revealing Jesus. So he directs others to follow Jesus, and some men begin to recognise the Messiah.

Year A: Epiphany 3

Isaiah 9:1-4
CONTEXT: The poetic announcement of a new king.
IDEAS: God brings light to the darkness; 'insignificant' Gentile people know God's presence.

Today's first reading includes words which, centuries later, Matthew took as being fulfilled in Jesus. It is a prophetic announcement of deliverance, greeting the one who will establish a new kingdom – the enduring rule of God.

1 Corinthians 1:10-18
CONTEXT: Following the greeting, and affirmation, Paul turns to deal with the internal quarrels.
IDEAS: Christians are to strive for unity; no leader in the place of Jesus.

We continue from last week the opening section of this letter. Paul has expressed his joy in their faith and confidence in their spiritual strength, yet quickly moves to deal with their internal disputes. They are to stop creating factions under different leaders; there is only one Gospel of Christ.

Matthew 4:12-23
CONTEXT: Jesus's ministry begins, after the desert retreat.
IDEAS: Taking over John's mission; Capernaum the base; prophecy fulfilled; disciples called.

Jesus's public ministry began in and around Capernaum, on the shore of Lake Galilee. According to Matthew, this made true the prophecy of Isaiah. Jesus calls men from their daily work to share his mission work.

Year A: Epiphany 4

RCL only: *Micah 6:1-8*
CONTEXT: God as judge of his people – after the hope expressed in Chs 4 and 5.
IDEAS: Remember the Lord's past acts; our approach to God.

This passage contains a phrase which takes us back to those Magi of Epiphany Sunday. 'What shall I bring to the Lord?' asks the prophet, pondering his response to God's saving work. Bring justice, bring humility, answers the Lord.

CWL only: *1 Kings 17:8-16*
CONTEXT: Episodic accounts of Elijah's life and work.
IDEAS: God works with power through his servants; miraculous provision.

Both this story of Elijah and today's Gospel tell of God changing something ordinary into the extraordinary, to meet human need. Here, a widow's life is saved as her last drop of oil and flour become a supply that lasts throughout a drought.

1 Corinthians 1:18-31
CONTEXT: Paul's correctives to congregational disputes.
IDEAS: God's wisdom contrasted with human folly, human wisdom contrasted with revelation.

This reading continues from the past two Sundays. Paul is trying gently but firmly to reprimand the Corinthian Christians for their behaviour in and out of church. He tells them no-one should claim to be cleverer than the rest, because we do not find God by being wise – God simply reveals himself to the simple in heart.

RCL only: *Matthew 5:1-12*
CONTEXT: Jesus's popularity in and around Capernaum; his early ministry of teaching and healing.
IDEAS: The Blessed/Happy (translations vary) are made so by God; challenge to be unpopular; unexpected people enter the kingdom.

In these strange paradoxes we call the Beatitudes, Jesus teaches us who are the holy people in God's sight, the ones who will find his blessings as his kingdom comes.

CWL only: *John 2:1-11*

CONTEXT: For John, Jesus's work begins quietly but significantly.

IDEAS: 'Signs' in John's Gospel; wine (and vines, etc.) in Biblical imagery; superabundant provision of finest quality; hastening the normal process of wine-making!

In the Gospel of John, the miracles of Jesus are signs – of who he is and therefore what God is like. The first sign is almost unnoticed. At a village wedding among his family and friends Jesus made extravagant quantities of water into the finest wine. The ordinary becomes the extraordinary.

Year A: The Presentation of Christ in the Temple: Candlemas

Malachi 3:1-5
CONTEXT: About 500 BC, return from exile but under Persian rule.
IDEAS: Restoration of nationhood and Temple worship; the fate of those who cannot face the Lord's coming.

In today's Gospel, Simeon will greet the infant Jesus in the Temple. Malachi speaks of the Lord coming suddenly; he knows, like Simeon, that to encounter the Lord is a mixed blessing because we have to face his testing and purifying.

Hebrews 2:14-18
CONTEXT: The theology of the humanity and divinity of Jesus.
IDEAS: Christ fully human; he is our help under all trials.

Christ became flesh and blood like us, says this writer, and we shall hear how his parents did the same as for every first-born child in Israel. Jesus fully shared our human condition, so that he could unite us all to God.

Luke 2:22-40
CONTEXT: See Exodus 13:1-2 and Leviticus 12:6-8.
IDEAS: Religious duty; offering; holy waiting; visionaries.

As the Law requires, Jesus the first-born is brought to the Temple with a thanks-offering. Two old and holy people, Simeon and Anna, perceive that this child is the fulfilment of ancient prophecies of redemption, but the glory will not be without pain and suffering.

Year A: CWL Proper 1; RCL Epiphany 5
(3-9 February, if earlier than 2 before Lent.)

Isaiah 58:1-9a [9b-12]
CONTEXT: Third Isaiah. Return from exile. The Promised Land has not given peace and prosperity.
IDEAS: 'Religious' acts and duties must issue in social concern and action.

People ask why God does not reward their faithful attention to religious duties. The prophet's reply is that God's will can only be done in and through people who care about social justice too – obedient people who, in Jesus's words, shed light among their neighbours.

1 Corinthians 2:1-12 [& 13-16]
CONTEXT: Corinth – a racially mixed city renowned for immorality. Paul's own converts, for whom the Christian promise seems not to bring happiness.
IDEAS: Worldly wisdom and logic will not lead us to God; this is the Holy Spirit's work.

To his Christian friends, finding it hard to live with happy pagan neighbours, Paul explains how the joy of God revealed in Jesus Christ does not come from human wisdom or worldly ways, but by Holy Spirit speaking to human spirit. Spiritual perception discloses hidden truths of God's wisdom.

Matthew 5:13-20
CONTEXT: 'The Sermon on the Mount' – Matthew's collected sayings of Jesus.
IDEAS: Salt and light. There is more to holy living than keeping religious law.

Just as Isaiah urged a deep concern for other people, Jesus requires us to go beyond our necessary worship and prayer. God cannot bring in his kingdom except in and through people who shed light to their neighbours, whose motives and intentions are deeper than obedience to religious rules.

Year A: CWL Proper 2; RCL Epiphany 6
(10-16 February, if earlier than 2 before Lent.)

EITHER *Deuteronomy 30:15-20*
CONTEXT: The end of Moses' great discourse before leadership passes to Joshua.
IDEAS: The one great life choice: God, or not God.

Behind all the legal systems God has led us to create, says Moses, each of you has a life-or-death choice: to serve God, or not. We shall hear Jesus describe this as an attitude of mind: your own way for your life, or God's way.

OR *Ecclesiasticus 15:15-20*
CONTEXT: A late (180 BC?) collection of Jewish proverbial wisdom, in the Apocrypha.
IDEAS: Humankind can choose to be faithful to God – and thereby live fully.

Among the books we call the Apocrypha comes a collection of wise words from the second century BC. The writer says God has our life or death within his own wise hands, but still leaves to us an entirely free choice.

1 Corinthians 3:1-9
CONTEXT: New Christians in the wicked city of Corinth.
IDEAS: Infantile understandings of Christian life; their leader (cf. Moses/Joshua) is not important, only God is.

Paul's unruly converts in Corinth found it hard to throw off old habits and discover new ways of Christian living. He wants them to acquire a grown-up maturity in this new kind of life, and most of all to grow out of childish petulance and judgmentalism.

Matthew 5:21-37
CONTEXT: More from Matthew's loosely-connected collection of Jesus's sayings.
IDEAS: Behind all law lies motives; intentions are as significant (to God) as actions.

Laws are necessary in every society; they and the lawyers have authority. Jesus claims an authority greater than theirs, and says anything and everything malicious violates God's way of kingdom living. You have a life-or-death choice to make: life with God or death without him.

Year A: CWL Proper 3; RCL Epiphany 7
(17-23 February, if earlier than 2 before Lent.)

Leviticus 19:1-2, 9-18
CONTEXT: The 'Holiness Code' – cultic regulations for post-exilic people.
IDEAS: Be holy. Negative ways of creating positive social justice.

The detailed Laws in Leviticus prescribe a way of holy living. As Jesus says, all 'Thou shalt not' commandments really point to a generosity of spirit, a concern for the weak, a forgiving and gentle heart. The holy God requires us to be like him, loving every neighbour.

1 Corinthians 3:10-11, 16-23
CONTEXT: Paul's 18-month stay had brought the Gospel to Corinth; others now had to build the church life.
IDEAS: Belonging; God's wisdom seems like worldly foolishness.

Other Christian leaders are now guiding Paul's converts in Corinth. He writes about building up the church, then extends the metaphor to each individual as a dwelling-place for God's Spirit. Because the foundation is Christ, to whom we all belong, there is no room for silly squabbles about who is more important.

Matthew 5:38-48
CONTEXT: Continuing Matthew's collection of Jesus's teachings.
IDEAS: New ways of understanding religious law – positive, not negative.

Jesus speaks of attitudes and intentions being more significant than the details of any particular rules of religion. God's purposes and motives are always for good, and ours are to be like his.

Year A: CWL Second Sunday before Lent; RCL Epiphany 8

RCL only readings. (See following page for CWL only readings)

Isaiah 49:8-16a
CONTEXT: Second Servant Song, of joy in the return from exile.
IDEAS: God hears and answers; God provides; God unites; God loves.

This prophet is always aware of Israel's vocation to be God's light for every nation. The promise of the Lord is a tender love, meeting our every need and smoothing everyone's way.

1 Corinthians 4:1-5
CONTEXT: Apostles, and all Christians, are servants of Christ.
IDEAS: Don't judge (condemn); no place for pride; all our gifts are God's.

This is the last week of several when we have read from this letter. Paul has been writing about the teachers and learners in the church, and now insists that no-one is to be critical of those who lead them, because leadership is service of the Lord.

Matthew 6:24-34
CONTEXT: Sermon on the Mount – collected teachings.
IDEAS: God the creator of birds and plants and people. Worries and frustrations – anxiety; God's concern for us; single-minded pursuit of the kingdom.

Jesus uses picture-language in a lesson about anxiety. Do not get over-anxious, don't let your worries dominate your life. God is the Creator and sustainer of everything there is, and his loving care can be trusted to meet all our deepest needs.

Year A: CWL Second Sunday before Lent; RCL Epiphany 8

CWL only readings. (See preceding page for RCL only readings)

Genesis 1:1-2:3
CONTEXT: The great Creation story.
IDEAS: Maker of heaven and earth, everything seen and unseen – and it is good.

This Sunday's readings all affirm God as Creator and sustainer of every-thing. We begin with the opening lines of the first book of the Bible and their poetic account of the origin of all things in the will of the Creator.

Romans 8:18-25
CONTEXT: Contrasting unspiritual life and the Spirit's transforming power.
IDEAS: Frustrations of physical life; God has created everything with a universal divinely-implanted longing.

In Paul's thinking, the whole created order yearns for perfection just as we humans do. Therefore, he can see that in God's time both we and all nature will be brought to completion in a new kind of glory, free from death and decay.

Matthew 6:25-34
CONTEXT: Sermon on the Mount – collected teachings.
IDEAS: God the creator of birds and plants and people. Worries and frustrations – anxiety; God's concern for us; single-minded pursuit of the kingdom.

Jesus uses picture-language in a lesson about anxiety. Do not get over-anxious, don't let your worries dominate your life. God is the Creator and sustainer of everything there is, and his loving care can be trusted to meet all our deepest needs.

Year A: CWL The Sunday next before Lent; RCL Epiphany 9

(CWL readings: optional in RCL; see next page for the RCL-only alternatives.)

Exodus 24:12-18
CONTEXT: Moses and the elders (v. 9) encounter God, then on the mountain-top the Law is given.
IDEAS: Meeting-places with God; divine law; God's glory in a 'cloud'.

Our Old Testament reading is chosen for its likeness to today's Gospel. On the threshold of Lent we are reminded of the awesome holiness of God. This story of Moses tells how on a mountain-top he had a transfiguring experience, as if taken up into the glory of God.

2 Peter 1:16-21
CONTEXT: A reminder that the reality of God was revealed in Jesus.
IDEAS: Biblical truths – the witnesses and interpretations; the transfiguration of Jesus; the Father's glory given to the Son.

This letter, in the name of Peter, reminds Christians of the second century that Jesus was no ordinary man, but one whom his first disciples had seen transfigured in glory, as God disclosed him to be his Son. All the prophecies had therefore come true.

Matthew 17:1-9
CONTEXT: Jesus determines to go to Jerusalem (16:32); the last stages of his life begin with a new revelation of glory.
IDEAS: Moses and Elijah symbolising Law and Prophets – completed and fulfilled in Jesus; God encountered on mountain-tops; the 'cloud' of God's presence; a few see what all may long for.

The Lord's closest friends see him transfigured upon a mountain-top, in a disclosure of his true identity. In the presence of the figures of Moses and Elijah, a cloud of glory comes upon him and the voice of the holy one is heard.

Year A: CWL The Sunday next before Lent; RCL Epiphany 9

(RCL only; see preceding page for CWL readings, which are alternatives in RCL.)

Deuteronony 11:18-21, 26-28
CONTEXT: A discourse of Moses on the Ten Commandments.
IDEAS: Never forget your obedience to God.

The Lord has given his people through Moses ten basic commandments; keeping them will bring blessing. However, just as all ancient contracts included lists of curses upon those who broke them, Yahweh's covenant has penalties for disobedience. Jesus will similarly speak sternly of those who reject God's way.

Romans 1:16-17, 3:22b-28 [29-31]
CONTEXT: Paul had not yet been to Rome; this is a theological, not a personal, letter.
IDEAS: Faith is everything: all who have it, Jew or not, are put right with God.

When Paul wrote to the Roman Christians, he had not met them but hoped to visit soon. So the letter has no personal touches, but it is a profound document of his mature theology – in which everyone with faith in Jesus is justified before God.

Matthew 7:21-29
CONTEXT: The Sermon on the Mount: Jesus's teachings.
IDEAS: Don't presume upon God's mercy. Good foundations make good buildings.

Matthew, a Jew writing for Jewish Christians, often portrays Jesus's severity towards those who fail to hear and do what he says. The unchanging God of Israel has always been stern but he is also just; those who build their lives on firm foundations will stand firm in the kingdom of heaven.

Year A: Ash Wednesday

Joel 2:1-2, 12-17

CONTEXT: Visionary apocalyptic of the Day of the Lord.

IDEAS: God's coming will be fearsome – yet gracious to the penitent; come together and fast.

The powerful and dramatic words of Joel are a solemn call to public repentance, to realise the divine mercy and goodness. It helps set the tone of the Lenten season as a time for self-examination and spiritual renewal, in preparation for the gifts of Easter.

OR Isaiah 58:1-12

CONTEXT: The restored community are ignoring the ways of God.

IDEAS: Right motives for fasting; right ways of fasting.

The prophet denounces the hypocrisy of people who make gestures of fasting but practice injustice and deceit. Make your fast work for God: he will hear you when you ask what you should do.

2 Corinthians 5:20b-6:10

CONTEXT: An appeal to Christians not to let grace go for nothing, but sustain mutual reconciliation.

IDEAS: God's work of reconciliation; preaching without self-glorification.

Paul calls upon the Corinthian Christians to be reconciled and reconcilers. He offers his own way of life as an example of the way of a peace-maker – to bear suffering, avoid self-aggrandisement, speak the truth in love.

Matthew 6:1-6, 16-21

CONTEXT: Sermon on the Mount – teaching on prayer and fasting.

IDEAS: vv. 2, 5 & 16 reiterate 'when', not 'if'; public and private devotion.

Jesus contrasts those who do religious acts to gain admiration from others with those who are sincere. All our acts of piety, whether fasting or the symbolic use of ashes, are worthless unless they express the spirit of true penitence, embodied in a life of prayer and service.

OR John 8:1-11

CONTEXT: A Passover visit to Jerusalem. (Many scholars regard this as not correctly a part of 'John', but an isolated pericope in the synoptic tradition.)

IDEAS: God infinitely merciful: no punishment. But don't sin again!

In Lent we are reminded of the need for repentance, as we hear again how God in Christ comes to us in forgiving tenderness. Jesus will not allow a sinful woman to be punished; his love offers new life free from sin.

Year A: The First Sunday of Lent

Genesis 2:15-17, 3:1-7
CONTEXT: The Creation stories – the Garden of Eden.
IDEAS: Temptations – succumbing and resisting; who is to blame?

Our readings at the beginning of Lent are all concerned with doing right or wrong, and knowing the difference. In the ancient tale of how evil came into the world, the first human beings in the Garden of Eden succumbed to temptation.

Romans 5:12-19
CONTEXT: The reconciliation accomplished by Christ means the overthrow of sin and death.
IDEAS: Adam (= all humanity) disobeys God and thus sin exists in the world; Jesus the New Man – his gift of salvation.

Paul's words are complicated to hear, as he draws new meaning from the old story of Adam. Humanity has been innately sinful since the beginning of time, but through one new man, Jesus, we are now not condemned for our sins. God's gift of righteousness offers us the possibility of a new and free life.

Matthew 4:1-11
CONTEXT: The temptations Jesus faced before his ministry began.
IDEAS: Jesus tempted; worldly power and glory; sin resisted and overcome; his way took him to a different tree.

In the first garden of the world, Eve could not resist the temptation to please herself and not God. When Jesus faced the temptation to bring in his kingdom by using the levers of worldly power, he was strong to resist. He always chose God's ways, not man's.

Year A: The Second Sunday of Lent

Genesis 12:1-4a
CONTEXT: The descendants of Noah, the migratory people.
IDEAS: 'By faith Abraham obeyed the call' (Heb 11:8).

Last Sunday we heard the sad tale of mankind's first disobedience. This reading is a happier circumstance, with consequences just as far-reaching. God's demand to Abraham is to start anew – to be 'new-born' as Jesus later told Nicodemus. Because Abraham is totally obedient, God's purpose can begin in his chosen people.

Romans 4:1-5, 13-17
CONTEXT: God is one, and for everyone; the example of Abraham's faith.
IDEAS: Faith, not works, justifies us; sheer grace.

Paul uses Abraham as an example of complete faith. It is not through obedience to law that God accepted and used him, and it is not our good deeds which justify us. By the sheer grace of God we too are inheritors of God's promises.

John 3:1-17
CONTEXT: Jesus in Jerusalem for Passover (a visit not referred to by the other gospels).
IDEAS: Spiritual re-birth; 'lifting-up' = crucifixion and glorification; faith brings eternal life.

Jesus seems to demand the impossible – that we be born again. But he means that faith in his redeeming love brings us spiritual re-birth, into a wholly new kind of living.

OR (RCL only) *Matthew 17:1-9*
CONTEXT: Jesus determines to go to Jerusalem (16:32); the last stages of his life begin with a new revelation of glory.
IDEAS: Moses and Elijah symbolising Law and Prophets – completed and fulfilled in Jesus; God encountered on mountain-tops; the 'cloud' of God's presence; a few see what all may long for.

The Lord's closest friends see him transfigured upon a mountain-top, in a disclosure of his true identity. In the presence of the figures of Moses and Elijah, a cloud of glory comes upon him and the voice of the holy one is heard.

Year A: The Third Sunday of Lent

Exodus 17:1-7
CONTEXT: The Israelites in their desert camp between Egypt and the Promised Land.
IDEAS: The biblical image of water; vital to all life.

Lent may mean some abstinence – but even in a desert we need water. This reading tells us how the Israelites were given water in their desert pilgrimage, when they looked to God to meet their need.

Romans 5:1-11
CONTEXT: Faith alone sets us free for life in Christ.
IDEAS: Joy and hope; reconciliation; Christ comes to our sinful helplessness.

Paul's letter to Rome is much concerned with Christian conduct. This passage sets out the foundation for our conduct: our life now is our response to the extraordinary thing God has done for us, through Christ, flooding us with hope, grace, Holy Spirit and love. He calls us to exult.

John 4:5-42
CONTEXT: Jesus returning from Jerusalem to Galilee via Samaria.
IDEAS: Animosity between Jews and Samaritans; Jesus's perceptiveness; living water.

God miraculously provided water for the Israelites on their desert journey. Now we hear of Jesus as living water. Among the Samaritan people whom the Jews hated, he convinces them that he himself is the Messiah, the fulfilment of all their needs.

Year A: The Fourth Sunday of Lent

See next page for CWL readings if this Sunday is kept as Mothering Sunday.

1 Samuel 16:1-13

CONTEXT: King Saul's failings, Samuel seer and judge, David the new king.
IDEAS: God rejects Saul for disobedience (15:11); Samuel's warnings (8:10 ff, esp 19); choice of David, anointing.

All three readings today teach us that God sees things differently from us. When Israel needed a new king to succeed the disgraced Saul, the search took Samuel to Bethlehem, and a family of brothers. The youngest, a shepherd boy, was chosen – because God had seen past the outward appearances to what he could do through King David.

Ephesians 5:8-14

CONTEXT: Christian conduct to be Christlike.
IDEAS: Light and darkness – seeing things properly.

Only God can see things as they really are, yet he allows us to share something of that vision. The Bible calls it light, the light of Christ, and because it is given to us our understanding of the world and of ourselves is illuminated.

John 9:1-41

CONTEXT: Jesus in Jerusalem – controversy with the authorities.
IDEAS: Blindness and sight; healing on Sabbath; the man's energetic explanation of what Jesus did for him.

This is an extended reading so that we hear the whole story. It is telling us much more than just the gift of sight to the blind; the question is, who is this man who is able to make people see things clearly?

Year A: CWL Mothering Sunday

(See previous page if this Sunday is kept as the Fourth Sunday of Lent.)

Exodus 2:1-10
CONTEXT: There are too many Israelites for Egypt's stability: forced labour, and death to all male babies.
IDEAS: Mother's care for child; the eventual hero left to die and rescued.

The mother of Moses worked a deception to preserve her son's life, when the Egyptians were controlling the population by killing every new-born Jewish boy.

OR *1 Samuel 1:20-28*
CONTEXT: Elkanah and his two wives: Peninnah has children but Hannah has none and is mocked for it.
IDEAS: Longing for motherhood; barren wives conceive; God-given child offered back to God's service.

Samuel, that great Old Testament figure, was born to a mother who for years had been unable to bear a son. In thankfulness for God's gift, his mother took him to the Lord's house to give him back to God.

2 Corinthians 1:3-7
CONTEXT: A letter mostly of joy that the crisis in the Corinthian church was now overcome.
IDEAS: God is ever-present in trouble.

Paul writes of the consoling strength of God, the one we can all turn to in trouble, and how this grace we receive enables us to sustain one another.

OR *Colossians 3:12-17*
CONTEXT: Instructions in Christian behaviour – avoid all hurtful ways.
IDEAS: The enduring virtues, all summed up in love.

Paul writes of the compassionate gifts, forgiveness and love. These, received and given always in the name of Jesus, are a vocation for us all.

Luke 2:33-35
CONTEXT: Purification, presentation of Christ in the Temple.
IDEAS: Joseph and Mary's bewilderment; mother's suffering foreshadowed.

Jesus is the son of a human mother, just like us. In the Gospel, his earthly father and mother fade into the shadows as the nature of his life is hinted at. Yet we never forget his home, the love and teaching he received.

OR *John 19:25-27*
CONTEXT: The crucifixion of Jesus.
IDEAS: Jesus's mother sees him die; his love and concern for her.

Mary, who gave birth to Jesus, is there to watch his ugly death. Every mother's heart can suffer with her. In his last agony, Jesus's love for his mother ensures that she is not left alone.

Year A: The Fifth Sunday of Lent
(Passiontide begins.)

Ezekiel 37:1-14
CONTEXT: Our book 'Ezekiel' is not in chronological order; all the visions and oracles relate to the Babylonian exile and hopes for restoration.
IDEAS: Desolation and death. Wind = breath = spirit (Heb: Ruarch). God will give new life.

The thought of God-given new life pervades today's readings. At the time of Ezekiel's vision, Jerusalem was derelict and the land laid waste. He sees nothing but dried-up bones, until the breath of God – the Spirit of God – fills the valley with life. It is a sign that God will give new life to his people Israel.

Romans 8:6-11
CONTEXT: Unspiritual lives are changed by God's redemptive work.
IDEAS: The indwelling Spirit gives life.

Paul says that if the Spirit of God is in you, if the breath of God inspires you, then your whole body contains real life and you can go like the wind instead of wasting away into death and decay.

John 11:1-45
CONTEXT: Jesus in temporary withdrawal from Jerusalem.
IDEAS: He has power even over death; the love of friends; Jesus's own emotions.

This is a longer Gospel reading than usual, so that we miss nothing of the extraordinary event at Bethany. God in Jesus does indeed bring new life, even to the dead, for he raises his friend Lazarus from the tomb.

Year A: Palm Sunday

Matthew 21:1-11
(Within the Liturgy of the Palms, this passage precedes the procession, which is itself a dramatic commentary. It is therefore best read without introduction.)

Isaiah 50:4-9a
CONTEXT: A 'Servant Song' of mission and suffering.
IDEAS: Obedience to God; patient dignity and endurance.

Isaiah pictures a faithful servant of God who is deeply and unjustly humiliated, but remains dignified in suffering. As we contemplate the mystery of the cross, these words take on a profound meaning for us in the Passion of Jesus.

Philippians 2:5-11
CONTEXT: Paul in prison, writing to friends.
IDEAS: The humility of Christ and his exaltation.

It is our faith that 'Jesus Christ is Lord', because he came from God in total self-giving, and overcame the humiliation of death on a cross by rising and ascending. He is indeed worthy of our adoration and worship.

Matthew 26:14-27:66 OR *Matthew 27:11-54*
Traditionally, the Gospel narrative of the passion and death of Jesus has no introduction except formal words such as: 'The Passion of Our Lord Jesus Christ according to Matthew'.

Year A: Monday of Holy Week

Isaiah 42:1-9
CONTEXT: The first 'Servant Song' – Israel is God's servant, but we may read these songs as prophecies of Jesus.
IDEAS: God acknowledges his Servant; quiet bringing-in of justice; light for all nations.

The readings from Isaiah these next three days are appropriately called 'Servant Songs'. Whatever their original application, they speak to us of the Jesus who did not complain as he faithfully walked the way of the cross for the world's salvation.

Hebrews 9:11-15
CONTEXT: The old covenant and high-priestly sacrificial duties.
IDEAS: Christ the new and perfect high priest; his own blood; new covenant.

Christ's offering of himself in his perfect purity, says this writer, completes and transcends all the sacrificial offerings made by the priests. He has procured for us what no other could: our eternal redemption.

John 12:1-11
CONTEXT: Jesus in and near Jerusalem preparing for Passover.
IDEAS: The last week of Jesus's life; company of friends; anointing for burial.

Throughout this week we follow John's account of the way to the cross. The week begins for Jesus in the home of his friends, where Mary of Bethany anoints his feet. Some condemn what they regard as wasteful, but Jesus accepts her gift as foreshadowing his impending death and burial.

Year A: Tuesday of Holy Week

Isaiah 49:1-7

CONTEXT: Second 'Servant Song' – the restoration of Israel from Babylon.
IDEAS: Vocation; revelation; light for the world.

This week's readings are the 'Servant Songs' of Isaiah, each of which speaks of the suffering that accompanies faithful witness. The prophet may have meant that Israel was the Servant, but we read it as the vocation of Jesus who, though he was despised, was true to God's will and brings light to all the ends of the earth.

1 Corinthians 1:18-31

CONTEXT: Paul's corrective to congregational disputes.
IDEAS: God's wisdom versus human folly; human wisdom versus revelation.

The cross of Christ, says Paul, is an offensive folly to most people, yet in reality it displays God's loving wisdom. We must stop trusting in our own wisdom and skills if we are to discern how freedom, salvation and righteousness are found in this cross.

John 12:20-36

CONTEXT: Jesus in and around Jerusalem preparing for Passover.
IDEAS: Death and glory; losing and keeping; light and dark.

In the week before he died, Jesus often spoke of his own suffering as being his glorification, but most people did not understand him. Those who do walk the way of the cross with him will share his light and become children of the light.

Year A: Wednesday of Holy Week

Isaiah 50:4-9a
CONTEXT: Third 'Servant Song' – of mission and suffering.
IDEAS: Obedience to God; patient dignity and endurance.

In this third of Isaiah's Servant Songs we hear of the humiliation unjustly suffered by one who teaches and consoles others. As we contemplate the mystery of the cross, these words take on a profound meaning for us in the Passion of Jesus.

Hebrews 12:1-3
CONTEXT: The great faith shown in past ages.
IDEAS: All the witnesses; perseverance; Jesus changes a cross into glory.

This writer urges us to keep our eyes fixed on Jesus. He was not deflected from his task by the ordeal he faced, and we are surrounded by examples of faithfulness which should strengthen our own resolve.

John 13:21-32
CONTEXT: Jesus in and near Jerusalem; farewell discourses to disciples.
IDEAS: Jesus betrayed; why did Judas do it? Evil turns to good in God's hands.

We are following John's narrative of the week leading Jesus to Calvary. Now and tomorrow the scene is the Last Supper, where Jesus seems to know that Judas will betray him. It was the darkest of moments when, John says, 'Judas went out. It was night.' Yet this passage does not end in despair but in Jesus glorified.

Year A: Maundy Thursday

Exodus 12:1-4 [5-10], 11-14
CONTEXT: The Israelites' hurried escape from Egyptian slavery.
IDEAS: Archetypal salvation event; Passover remembered and celebrated ever since.

At his last supper with his friends, Jesus transformed a Passover meal into our constant remembrance of the salvation we have in him. Appropriately today, we recall the story of the first Passover, the great saving event in Jewish history.

1 Corinthians 11:23-26
CONTEXT: How a divided congregation is to observe the Lord's Supper.
IDEAS: Eucharistic tradition; remembrance and proclamation.

This is almost certainly the earliest account of the Lord's Supper as celebrated by the church. Paul reminds the Corinthians that it was from the Lord that he received this tradition, and handed it on.

John 13:1-17, 31b-35
CONTEXT: Jesus's final meal with his friends at Passover time.
IDEAS: Humble service; the ultimate commandment is to love.

We remember now another event of that night. Jesus washed his disciples' feet, and gave them a new commandment – the word is 'mandate', or 'maundy' – to follow his example in loving service to one another.

Year A: Good Friday

Isaiah 52:13-53:12
CONTEXT: Fourth 'Servant Song' – leading the return from Babylon (52:11).
IDEAS: Humiliation without complaint; despised and rejected for our sake.

This poem of God's Servant facing suffering picks up a theme from earlier readings this week. Although written centuries before Jesus, it has become for Christians one of the most profound meditations on the events and the deep meaning of Good Friday.

Hebrews 10:16-25
CONTEXT: The place of sacrifice in human approaches to God.
IDEAS: Sin forgiven; nothing separates us from God; Christ's perfect priesthood.

The writer of this letter helps our solemn reflection on what Jesus did for us this day. The Jewish sacrificial priesthood could only dare approach God's holiness with offerings and with fear. But in Christ all our sins are forgiven, and we are free to know the new, living, open way to God.

OR *Hebrews 4:14-16, 5:7-9*
CONTEXT: Scripture tells of many partial understandings of God – Jesus perfectly opens to us his intimate knowledge.
IDEAS: The sinless High Priesthood of Jesus; his suffering obedience; our access to God.

By what he did this day Jesus became a greater high priest than there has ever been, making it possible for us to approach God without fear. The work of Christ is the means of our salvation.

John 18:1-19:42
Announce as: 'The Passion of Our Lord Jesus Christ according to John.'

Year A: Easter Eve
For use at services other than the Easter Vigil.

Job 14:1-14
CONTEXT: A theology of innocent suffering; a poetic cycle of speeches.
IDEAS: Transience of human life; in nature, new life follows death.

Job contemplates the fact that every human life ends in death. Plants cut down may rise again, but he knows of no such resurrection when we die.

OR *Lamentations 3:1-9, 19-24*
CONTEXT: Poems of lament over the fall of Jerusalem to Babylonia (587 BC).
IDEAS: Affliction within God's purposes; patient suffering; new mornings.

This writer is filled with anguish for himself and for Israel, but the reading ends in a confident and patient waiting for an act of God's love that comes 'new every morning'.

1 Peter 4:1-8
CONTEXT: Letter to Gentile Christians, probably under (Nero? Domitian?) persecution.
IDEAS: Enduring suffering and abuse; Christ 'descended to the dead'; the end is nigh.

The readers of this letter were enduring Roman persecution. The encouraging reminder here is that it was through suffering that Christ put an end to sin. The writer also hints at the idea of Christ descending to a place of the dead in an act of rescue.

Matthew 27:57-66
CONTEXT: Jesus has died; the body to be decently interred.
IDEAS: Generous act of Joseph; women waiting and mourning; Jewish fears that the story does not end here.

On the evening Jesus died, his body was decently placed in a tomb before the Sabbath. But even in death his influence lives on, as the religious authorities become anxious about what might happen next.

OR *John 19:38-42*
CONTEXT: Jesus has died; the body to be decently interred.
IDEAS: Acts of Joseph and Nicodemus; burial before Sabbath.

Two friends of Jesus, of whom we know so little, take care that his body is reverently placed in a garden tomb, in good time before the Sabbath when such work could not be done.

Year A: Easter Vigil

No introductions are provided for the readings at the Easter Vigil. Churches will wish to make their own choices from the provision of the Lectionary, and may use the opportunity to create a devotional sequence of lessons with psalms or canticles. It may be felt that on this occasion any other introductory material to the readings would be intrusive.

Year A: Easter Day

Acts 10:34-43
CONTEXT: Peter's teaching to a Roman centurion.
IDEAS: The life and work of Jesus; forgiveness effective for everyone.

[*If the readings from Acts will be used as the first lesson throughout the Easter season:*
During the Easter season, in place of the Hebrew Scriptures, we read the witness of the early church to the power of the Lord's resurrection.]

This is a small part of the story of Peter and a centurion of the Roman occupying army, when the Gospel first reached beyond the Jews. The teaching sums up Jesus's old and new life.

OR Jeremiah 31:1-6
CONTEXT: Despite the privations of exile, there will be a restoration, says the Lord.
IDEAS: God saves his people; song and dance in joy; a remnant preserved.

The prophet's vision is of Jerusalem rebuilt after it had been totally destroyed. His song of resurrection fits our mood today, when we know that the life of Jesus was destroyed on Friday but is now raised again to save us and restore us.

Colossians 3:1-4
CONTEXT: Correctives to those still following the habits and rules of other religions.
IDEAS: Christ alone is to be our focus.

It is not just that Christ is risen, says Paul. Our life is now his life, so we too are raised up above much that is earthly, to dwell in God's realm of being.
OR *Acts 10:34-43. See above.*

47

John 20:1-18
CONTEXT: Jesus has died and is buried; after the Sabbath, mourning can resume.
IDEAS: The empty tomb; Peter and (?) John rush in; Jesus unrecognised; incredibly good news.

Mary Magdalene is sometimes called 'The Apostle to the Apostles', for she was the first to see the risen Lord and tell the others. But his appearance had changed, and only love speaking to love made him known to her.

OR *Matthew 28:1-10*
CONTEXT: The tomb tightly sealed and guarded; after the Sabbath, mourning can resume.
IDEAS: Angelic messengers and strange phenomena; news of resurrection; meeting the risen Christ.

The birth of Jesus was announced to Mary by an angel; so now it is angels who tell the two Marys that he is risen to new life. They run to share the good news, and meet him on their way.

Year A: The Second Sunday of Easter

CWL: *If the Old Testament reading is used, the reading from Acts must be used as the second reading.*

CWL *Exodus 14:10-31, 15:20-21*
CONTEXT: The Israelites have just left Egypt, taking the long way round (13:18). Pharoah then regrets the absence of the slaves and sets out after them.
IDEAS: The past was better (vv. 11, 12); a mighty miracle – the Lord acts to save.

Just as Christians continually give thanks for our salvation in Jesus, the Jews continue to this day to give thanks for their deliverance from slavery. At the time of the Exodus, the Lord worked a great saving miracle at the Red Sea.

Acts 2:14a, 22-32
CONTEXT: Jesus's followers remain together, and begin preaching his resurrection; Peter's Pentecost sermon.
IDEAS: God's guiding hand throughout Jesus's life – and now raised to new life.

[*If the Old Testament reading is not used:*
During this Easter season, instead of reading the Hebrew Scriptures, we hear the Apostles' witness to the truth of the resurrection.]

On the Day of Pentecost, a crowd gathered to listen to the Apostles speak of the risen Christ. Peter shows how a Psalm of David can now be seen as proof that everything that had happened was within God's plan of salvation.

1 Peter 1:3-9
CONTEXT: An appeal to stand fast, and encouragement; probably written to Gentile Christians under (Nero? Domitian?) persecution.
IDEAS: Hope and certainty; testing times; believing without seeing.

We begin today a series of readings from a letter ascribed to Peter. It was written to Gentile Christians, and begins with a hymn of praise. Even those who have not themselves seen the risen Jesus still know the joy, love and trust that faith brings.

John 20:19-31

CONTEXT: The evening of Resurrection Day – Mary Magdalene is the only witness thus far.

IDEAS: Disciples keep together for safety; the same Jesus, wounded; commissioning with Holy Spirit and 'sent'; seeing and believing.

On the first Easter evening, Jesus appears to his disciples with his habitual greeting of peace, and a gift of the Holy Spirit. Thomas must wait another week until he can see, believe, and adore.

Year A: The Third Sunday of Easter

CWL: *If the Old Testament reading is used, the reading from Acts must be used as the second reading.*

CWL *Zephaniah 3:14-20*
CONTEXT: Judah and her neighbours to be destroyed for disobedience – but a remnant will be preserved.
IDEAS: The Lord is here – his Spirit is with us; gathered together by God.

This prophet of the 7th century BC sees a time when all will be joy and peace, for God will have saved his people, renewed them in his love, and will dwell in their midst.

Acts 2:14a, 36-41
CONTEXT: Jesus's followers remain together, and begin preaching his resurrection; Peter's Pentecost sermon.
IDEAS: Jesus the expected Messiah; baptism in his name; Christian common life.

**[*If the Old Testament reading is not used:*
During this Easter season we hear of the power of the risen Christ in the early church.]**

This reading is the culmination of a sermon we began last Sunday. Peter has been speaking to the Jews at Pentecost, proclaiming the crucified Jesus as their Lord and Messiah. Those who now respond are baptised and join the believing community.

1 Peter 1:17-23
CONTEXT: An appeal to stand fast, and encouragement; probably written to Gentile Christians under (Nero? Domitian?) persecution.
IDEAS: Saved by Christ's blood; God's eternal plan revealed; resurrection faith.

This letter to Gentile Christians suffering the severest persecution says that our salvation was not won without cost. It is by the suffering and death of Jesus that we are born again to new life in God.

Luke 24:13-35

CONTEXT: The evening of Resurrection Sunday – some disciples stay together (see last Sunday's Gospel, and v. 33 here) – only the women have seen the risen Jesus (vv. 10, 11)
IDEAS: Returning home in sadness; meeting (the unrecognised) Jesus on the journey; revelation in the 'breaking of bread'.

Luke's Easter evening takes us on the road from Jerusalem to Emmaus, where the risen Jesus joins two of his friends as they walk and talk. Only when, at supper, he takes bread, gives thanks, breaks it and shares it, do they come to recognise him.

Year A: The Fourth Sunday of Easter

CWL: *If the Old Testament reading is used, the reading from Acts must be used as the second reading.*

CWL *Genesis 7*
CONTEXT: The world turned wicked; God saves every good thing he made, through Noah.
IDEAS: Truths in ancient (myth) stories; salvation; something of everything is preserved.

This week (and for the next two Sundays) the ancient story of Noah is told. In a wicked world, one person is found righteous, and Noah is the source of salvation for all creation through the cleansing waters that cover the earth.

Acts 2:42-47
CONTEXT: The developing life of the first Christian community.
IDEAS: Regular communion and prayer; power at work; common purpose; church growth.

[If the Old Testament reading is not used:
During the Easter season we are reading about the young church in action, in the power of the resurrection.]

We have heard Peter's first recorded sermon, and its dramatic effect. Now we discover how these new Christians came to develop a new pattern of life and worship together.

1 Peter 2:19-25
CONTEXT: A letter of encouragement, probably to Christians under persecution. Concerning lifestyle.
IDEAS: Undeserved suffering; the example of Christ; what he achieved for us.

We continue on these Easter Sundays to read a letter directed to Gentile Christians. For all those who are humiliated or persecuted for their faith, Jesus is the supreme example and pattern to be honoured and followed.

John 10:1-10
CONTEXT: Jesus in Jerusalem – great controversy over his acts and teaching.
IDEAS: Sheep and shepherds – following; safety/salvation through Jesus.

Jesus uses a familiar image from the Hebrew Scriptures of shepherds and sheep. He is himself the good shepherd; he calls us to follow him, and teaches that he is himself the only way the sheep may be safely gathered.

Year A: The Fifth Sunday of Easter

CWL: *If the Old Testament reading is used, the reading from Acts must be used as the second reading.*

CWL *Genesis 8:1-19*
CONTEXT: Continuing the salvation-story of Noah.
IDEAS: New beginnings; tasks for those whom God saves.

We heard last Sunday the beginning of the ancient saga of Noah in the Ark. He, his family, and two of every creature, have been saved by God from the destruction of the world. Now, as the flood subsides, it is the task of those whom God has saved to revive and renew the world.

Acts 7:55-60
CONTEXT: The growing church in Jerusalem has provoked the authorities to strong action, and Stephen is brought to trial.
IDEAS: The first martyr; visions of glory; Saul/Paul; forgiveness in dying moments.

[*If the Old Testament reading is not used:*

In place of an Old Testament reading, we are hearing about the risen life of Christ at work in the young church, attracting both converts and opposition.]

Stephen was the first Christian to follow his Master to execution. The Jewish leaders found the new teaching, that the crucified and resurrected Jesus is their true Messiah, was even more dangerous and heretical than Jesus's own life had been.

1 Peter 2:2-10
CONTEXT: Continuing this letter: keep firm, faithful and holy.
IDEAS: Stones – foundation, and living; Gentiles now included as God's people.

This writer, after the encouragement we have heard from him since Easter, now directs us to think of Jesus as the foundation stone on which the church is built. Although the resurrection is a stumbling-block to many, we have been chosen by God to proclaim its truth.

John 14:1-14
CONTEXT: Jesus's farewell discourses: promise of future bliss.
IDEAS: Our place prepared; seeing God in Jesus; prayer in Jesus's name.

Jesus taught his disciples how completely he and his heavenly Father are united. We are to believe and trust his promise, that to know him is to know God, and he is our way to the place prepared for us.

Year A: The Sixth Sunday of Easter

CWL: *If the Old Testament reading is used, the reading from Acts must be used as the second reading.*

CWL *Genesis 8:20-9:17*
CONTEXT: Conclusion of the Noah story.
IDEAS: Thankfulness for God's mercy; a new covenant promise, with humankind and all living things; signs from God.

God's safe-keeping of Noah, with two of every creature, has been read these past few Sundays. This is how the story ends happily ever after. God makes a new covenant promise to the survivors, that never again will he destroy everything by such a flood.

Acts 17:22-31
CONTEXT: Paul's second mission, via Cyprus, Galatia, Philippi, Thessalonica, and now Athens.
IDEAS: Teaching opportunities in secular contexts; false gods and the one true God; partial revelation completed in Jesus.

[*If the Old Testament reading is not used:*

During the Easter season, in place of the old Hebrew Scriptures, we are hearing how the first Christians spoke of the risen Christ wherever they travelled.]

Paul's powerful preaching in the synagogues of Athens has made the local government take notice. His speech to the Council proclaims that all the Greek gods are mere shadows of the one true God who created all things in heaven and earth.

1 Peter 3:13-22
CONTEXT: Continuing this letter: the difference in life behaviour for Christians.
IDEAS: Always do the right thing whatever the personal consequences; Christ suffered; the ancient dead are now redeemed.

We have been hearing since Easter Day this writer's encouragement to Christian people, whom he now instructs to be always calm and courteous. If we suffer for our way of life, remember Christ did too, and through his suffering he has brought us, with all the past saints, into his eternal salvation.

John 14:15-21

CONTEXT: Jesus's farewell discourses – his presence here and hereafter.

IDEAS: Jesus absent yet present; promise of the Spirit; evidences of love.

Jesus promises his disciples that although the time must come for him to leave them, the Holy Spirit will be their comforter, and all those who keep faith with him will see him again.

Year A: Ascension Day

The reading from Acts must be used as either the first or second reading.

Acts 1:1-11
CONTEXT: Introduction to Volume 2 of Luke.
IDEAS: Resurrection appearances; waiting for God; final departure.

Luke's account of the divine plan of salvation is in two parts. He ended the earthly life of Jesus, as we shall hear in the Gospel, with the event of the Ascension. Part two is the life of Christ in the church, and it begins as the Gospel ended, with the Lord leaving the earth to his home in heaven.

OR CWL only: *Daniel 7:9-14*
CONTEXT: The second half of this book, a series of visions written in the terrible times of Antiochus Epiphanes (170 BC).
IDEAS: Tyrannical oppressor ultimately overthrown; sovereignty passes to a 'son of man'.

The visionary Daniel in the second century BC sees a human figure from heaven, with all the power and authority of God, becoming the sovereign over every people and nation.

Ephesians 1:15-23
CONTEXT: Probably a general letter to Gentile Christians – about faith and conduct in the church.
IDEAS: Rejoice in the signs of faith; rejoice that Jesus Christ is risen, ascended and now in glory.

The writer of this letter to the churches gives thanks, in one great long sentence of praise in the Greek, for the glory of the risen and ascended Christ – ascended to heaven and therefore empowering his people everywhere. This is the faith of the church.

OR *Acts 1:1-11. See above.*

Luke 24:44-53
CONTEXT: Conclusion of Luke's Volume 1.
IDEAS: The Old Testament has foreseen these things; Gospel for all the world; witnesses; final departure.

Luke ends his life of Jesus with a last blessing, and the commission to go into every nation as witnesses to his suffering, his death, and his resurrection.

Year A: The Seventh Sunday of Easter
(Sunday after Ascension Day)

CWL: *If the Old Testament reading is used, the reading from Acts must be used as the second reading.*

CWL *Ezekiel 36:24-28*
CONTEXT: The prophet, in the role of watchman for the Lord's coming, affirms that God will be merciful to Israel.
IDEAS: Gathering after dispersion; purifying by water; the indwelling Spirit.

We shall hear in the Gospel our Lord's prayer for those he must leave behind in this world. Ezekiel reflects the same tender care of God for his people. His images speak to Christians of Pentecost: cleansing in pure water, the giving of a new heart and an outpouring of the Spirit.

Acts 1:6-14
CONTEXT: Luke's work Volume 2 describes Christ present in the church.
IDEAS: Jesus ascended; he will return; the fellowship continues.

[*If the Old Testament reading is not used:*
During the Easter season, instead of reading the Hebrew Scriptures, we hear how the small Christian community became the church.]

After the disciples knew Jesus had parted from them for the last time, they continued with their prayer together as they waited for the new Spirit he had promised.

1 Peter 4:12-14, 5:6-11
CONTEXT: Christian conduct under hostility.
IDEAS: Persecution for the faith; stand strong; the hope of glory.

Since Easter Day we have read from this letter every Sunday. It has said much about Christian life under persecution, and now ends with a rousing call to steadfastness with the promise of eternal glory.

John 17:1-11
CONTEXT: Farewell discourses and prayer for all disciples.
IDEAS: Jesus's completed work ends in glory; we belong to Christ; he prays for us.

On the night he was betrayed Jesus prayed not so much for himself but for those who would take up his work after his earthly life was over. His glory is now revealed in the world by those he calls his own.

Year A: Day of Pentecost
(Whit Sunday)

The reading from Acts must be used as the first or second reading

Acts 2:1-21

CONTEXT: A hundred or more meet together – the Eleven plus Matthias and women and others; festival of Pentecost 50 days after Passover.

IDEAS: Pentecost and harvest thanksgiving; strange manifestations; awesome power of the Spirit; Gospel in every language.

In Jerusalem, many pilgrims had come for the great Pentecost Harvest Festival. As Jesus had promised, the Holy Spirit of God came upon the gathered company of disciples with great power. They found themselves impelled to proclaim the resurrection Gospel to everyone who would listen.

OR *Numbers 11:24-30*

CONTEXT: The Israelites journeying from Sinai on towards Canaan.

IDEAS: Spirit-giving (sharing); God at work in those not present.

When Moses could no longer carry the burden of leadership alone, the gift of the Spirit was granted to seventy of the Israelite elders, to share God's work on the journey to the Promised Land. Even those not present at this event received an equal measure of the Spirit's inspiration.

1 Corinthians 12:3b-13

CONTEXT: Clarifications on appropriate Christian behaviour, written to an unruly church.

IDEAS: The gifts of the Spirit; all are gifted; all parts of one body.

Paul explains something of the work of the Holy Spirit in our lives: he is active everywhere, inspiring different gifts in different people. All should work together in the unity of the church which is now Christ's body on earth.

OR *Acts 2:1-21. See above.*

John 20:19-23
CONTEXT: The evening of Resurrection Day.
IDEAS: Disciples together; commissioning with Holy Spirit and 'sending'.

John's Gospel is unique in speaking of the gift of the Holy Spirit before the events of Pentecost. Here, Jesus appears to his friends in a locked upper room on the evening of the first Easter; he gives them his peace, a breath of the Spirit and a commission to pronounce forgiveness of sins.

OR *John 7:37-39*
CONTEXT: Jesus in Jerusalem for the great 7-day thanksgiving Feast of Tabernacles; his teaching provokes controversy.
IDEAS: Living water (cf. Jn 4:13ff); gift of the Spirit.

The Holy Spirit is compared by Jesus to the life-giving water he said could be found in him. When he has been glorified, his Spirit will be freely given to all believers.

Year A: Trinity Sunday

RCL only *Genesis 1:1-2:4a*
CONTEXT: The great Creation story.
IDEAS: Maker of heaven and earth, everything seen and unseen – and it is good.

We begin today's readings with the opening of the first book of the Bible and its poetic account of the origin of all things in the will of the God, who is Creator of all that is, seen and unseen.

OR *Isaiah 40:12-17, 27-31*
CONTEXT: Second Isaiah – in Babylon during the Exile.
IDEAS: Humankind can never fully comprehend God; we do know his untiring strength.

This prophet reminds us that we cannot expect fully to understand the mystery which lies at the heart of God. The Israelites' faith was shaken by their enforced exile to Babylon, but here is assurance that at the heart of God is self-giving love; he does not grow faint nor weary, and all who trust in him will find their strength renewed.

2 Corinthians 13:11-13
CONTEXT: Paul's 'foolish boasting' about his apostleship – a concluding appeal to accept him and be reconciled among themselves.
IDEAS: Christians to live in mutual agreement; kiss of peace; Trinitarian blessing.

Paul ends this letter with the full form of his customary blessing. These simple trinitarian words, of grace, love, and communion have been familiar in every church in every century.

Matthew 28:16-20
CONTEXT: After the astonishment of the resurrection, disciples return to the beginning in Galilee where Jesus gives a new commission and promise to the eleven.
IDEAS: Worshipping the risen Christ; mission; baptism in the three-fold name.

Matthew ends his Gospel with the promise that Christ is always with us. The disciples are commissioned to carry Christ's own healing love, to make new disciples, and baptise them as the church has done ever since, in the name of the Holy Trinity, Father, Son and Holy Spirit.

Year A: Day of Thanksgiving for Holy Communion
Thursday after Trinity Sunday (Corpus Christi)

Genesis 14:18-20
CONTEXT: Abram and Lot go separate ways (13:11, 12); Abram goes to the rescue of Lot, defeating the four eastern kings.
IDEAS: Salem (v. 18) = Jerusalem; ceremonial bread and wine; the great priest-king.

Melchizedek is a legendary name from the Israelite past. He was believed to be a priest-king of Jerusalem long before King David made it his capital. In this reading, he acts to seal God's covenant with Abram in an offering of bread and wine, and a blessing.

1 Corinthians 11:23-26
CONTEXT: How a divided congregation is to observe the Lord's Supper.
IDEAS: Eucharistic tradition; remembrance and proclamation.

This is almost certainly the earliest account of the Lord's Supper as celebrated by the church. Paul reminds the Corinthians that it was from the Lord that he received this tradition, and handed it on.

John 6:51-58
CONTEXT: Five thousand fed, and teaching about 'true bread' from heaven.
IDEAS: The bread of life (vv. 34, 48); Jesus's body and blood; eternal life.

To receive the body and blood of Jesus, he says, is to take his eternal life into our very being. This is not an easy truth to understand, yet it is the most profound of all realities.

Year A: Proper 4 (29 May-4 June, if after Trinity Sunday; Week 9.)

Continuous Old Testament: Genesis 6:9 -22, 7:24, 8:14-19
CONTEXT: A series of readings, starting today (or next Sunday, depending on the calendar date) will give us the developing story of Jewish revelation through the great figures of history and legend.
IDEAS: God's merciful judgement; the faithful are preserved.

For the rest of this year, we shall read Old Testament lessons that bring alive for us the great names of early Hebrew times. This is part of the story of Noah, which has parallels in other ancient civilisations. For the Hebrew people its meaning was God's great mercy – he would never destroy his chosen people, nor break off his relationship with them.

Related Old Testament: Deuteronony 11:18 -21, 26-28
CONTEXT: A discourse of Moses on the Ten Commandments.
IDEAS: Never forget your obedience to God.

The Lord has given his people through Moses ten basic commandments; keeping them will bring blessing. However, just as all ancient contracts included lists of curses upon those who broke them, Yahweh's covenant has penalties for disobedience. Jesus will similarly speak sternly of those who reject God's way.

Romans 1:16-17, 3:22b-28 [29-31]
CONTEXT: Paul had not yet been to Rome; this is a theological, not a personal, letter.
IDEAS: Faith is everything: all who have it, Jew or not, are put right with God.

We begin today a series of readings from Paul's letter to the Roman Christians, whom he had not met but hoped to visit soon. So the letter has no personal touches, but is a profound document of his mature theology – in which everyone with faith in Jesus is justified before God.

Matthew 7:21-29
CONTEXT: The Sermon on the Mount: Jesus's teachings.
IDEAS: Don't presume upon God's mercy. Good foundations make good buildings.

The Sunday Gospels now follow through Matthew, a Jew writing for Jewish Christians, always portraying Jesus's severity towards those who fail to hear and do what he says. The unchanging God of Israel has always been stern but he is also just; those who build their lives on firm foundations will stand firm in the kingdom of heaven.

Year A: Proper 5 (5-11 June, if after Trinity Sunday; Week 10.)

Continuous Old Testament: Genesis 12:1-9
CONTEXT: (See Proper 4 note for this weekly series.) Hebrews 11:8. The faith of
Abraham is so significant for Christians and Jews.
IDEAS: Going into the unknown for God; divine plans work through obedient people.

Either (a) if this Sunday is Trinity 1: **For the rest of this year, we shall read
Old Testament lessons that bring alive for us the great figures of early
Hebrew history.**

or (b) if Proper 4 readings were read on the previous Sunday: **Our weekly stories
of God's dealings with his ancient people move on from Noah to
Abraham.**

then the following: **By faith Abraham obeyed the call to start again in a
new country, where his descendants might inherit God's blessings. By his
faith, both he and we become God's children.**

Related Old Testament: Hosea 5:15-6:6
CONTEXT: Israel facing Assyrian menace in 8th century BC. A miscellany of prophetic
oracles, some in verse.
IDEAS: Trust in Yahweh; he is constant in love despite human vacillations.

**We shall hear Jesus quote this passage in today's Gospel. For Hosea, God
is more loving than we can imagine, but does require of us generous and
merciful conduct, not merely religious observances.**

Romans 4:13-25
CONTEXT: In Paul's theology, Abraham is a primary example to us of the way God
embraces as his children all who have faith.
IDEAS: Sheer grace; Abraham's stature derives from his faith, not his obedience to law.

**Our weekly readings from Paul's letter to Roman Christians begin to
unfold his contrast between the rewards of obeying law, and the sheer
grace poured out on the faithful from Abraham onwards.**

Matthew 9:9-13, 18-26

CONTEXT: Matthew now presents Jesus as on a travelling mission.

IDEAS: Jesus calling disciples to follow; his reputation for healing miracles.

If this Sunday is Trinity 1: [**Each Sunday we now read consecutively through Matthew's Gospel.**]

Matthew himself is called from the shabby world of collecting Roman taxes to play his part in Jesus's kingdom work, showing God's active mercy and healing power.

Year A: Proper 6 (12-18 June, if after Trinity Sunday; Week 11.)

Continuous Old Testament: Genesis 18:1-15 [& 21:1-7]
CONTEXT: Over several weeks, readings tell of the faith of Abraham – and God's responses to faith.
IDEAS: The longing to ensure the family line is continued; God's purposes in guaranteeing Abraham's posterity and therefore the promise.

Either (a) if this Sunday is Trinity 1: **For the rest of this year, we shall read Old Testament lessons that bring alive for us Israel's great men.**
or (b) if Proper 5 readings were read on the previous Sunday: **We have heard how the story of Abraham began with his call by God to adventurous living.**
then the following: **God promised mercy to our forefathers – to Abraham and his children for ever. But in Abraham's old age, his hope of having children has faded. Angelic messengers declare there will be a miraculous birth.**

Related Old Testament: Exodus 19:2-8a
CONTEXT: Moses, the pilgrim people's leader, has appointed men to help him; now they are commissioned.
IDEAS: God found in quiet places ('mountain-tops'); God's call into special relationship; shared leadership.

The people of Israel, journeying towards their promised land, have reached Mount Sinai. Moses has just appointed men to share the task God gave him, as we shall hear Jesus do. This passage is a summary of the commissioning from God of those Israelite elders.

Romans 5:1-8
CONTEXT: Faith alone can set us free for life in Christ.
IDEAS: Joy and hope; the astounding work of Christ.
Paul has been explaining how it was Abraham's faith, not his actions, which set him right with God. The Christian faith similarly brings us peace, hope, grace and joy in our union with Jesus. Amazingly, Christ has died for the sake of sinful people.

Matthew 9:35-10:8 [& 9-23]

CONTEXT: On his travelling mission, the demands are too great for Jesus on his own.
IDEAS: Jesus's compassion and authority; even he (and therefore, we learn, God) needs ordinary people to take on special tasks.

If this Sunday is Trinity 1: [Each Sunday we now read consecutively through Matthew's Gospel.]

There are too many people demanding to hear Jesus, and to be healed by him. So he commissions twelve others to share this labour, to work in his name with his authority and power, bringing in the kingdom.

Year A: Proper 7 (19-25 June, if after Trinity Sunday; Week 12.)

Continuous Old Testament: Genesis 21:8-21
CONTEXT: The developing saga of Abraham moves to the fulfilment of one divine promise: he will have descendants.
IDEAS: God's promises to be trusted; family/tribal conflict.

Either (a) if this Sunday is Trinity 1: **The Old Testament lessons this year will bring alive for us the men of early Hebrew history. They begin with the great figure of Abraham.**

or (b) if Proper 6 readings were read on the previous Sunday: **We heard last Sunday God's promise to Abraham was that he would have innumerable children.**

then the following: **In his old age, Abraham is granted a legitimate son at last, as Isaac is born of Sarah. But at once jealousies break out against the son Ishmael whom his slave-girl bore for him. We are assured that God cares for that son too.**

Related Old Testament: Jeremiah 20:7-13
CONTEXT: Jeremiah has been flogged and put in the stocks for prophesying the fall of Israel to Babylon.
IDEAS: The fate of the true prophet. Being angry with God ... turning into praise.

Jeremiah has been subjected to punishment for preaching what he felt compelled to say. So he complains to God who forced him into the situation, while still affirming his trust. Jesus will tell his chosen Twelve that the disciples' task will not make them popular.

Romans 6:1b-11
CONTEXT: The life of the believer is 'in Christ', by faith alone.
IDEAS: Baptism uniting us to Christ, destroying all our sin(s).

Because Jesus Christ came and died, Paul has written, our faith brings God's grace to us. We receive that grace first in our baptism, then by a life in which all sin is conquered – a new quality of life, in Christ and with Christ.

Matthew 10:24-39

CONTEXT: The commissioning of the twelve apostles.

IDEAS: Christian leadership is not a comfortable option, but the blessings outweigh the pains.

[If this Sunday is Trinity 1:
Each Sunday we now read consecutively through Matthew's Gospel.]

Jesus is speaking to the twelve he has chosen to work closely with him. Matthew puts together here several rather contradictory sayings of Jesus about the difficulties of apostolic vocation, alongside its delights. So we hear both warning and encouragement for our own discipleship.

Year A: Proper 8 (26 June-2 July; Week 13.)

Continuous Old Testament: Genesis 22: -14
CONTEXT: The last important sign of Abraham's total trust and obedience.
IDEAS: Another 'unreasonable' word of the Lord (cf. Proper 5). Faith under test; hearing God's voice (through messengers).

In St Paul's roll-call of the saints, Abraham stands as a giant – for Jew and for Christian alike. Through men and women of great faith, ready for whatever God seems to require of them – even the sacrifice of a son – God is able to work out his salvation plan.

Related Old Testament: Jeremiah 28:5-9
CONTEXT: Time of the Babylonian exile. Judah is effectively controlled by Nebuchadnezzar; Jeremiah urges submission while other prophets speak with (false) optimism.
IDEAS: 'Popular' prophets speaking for nationalism and independence. Jeremiah sees God's activity in destruction before rebuilding.

A few verses from the vivid account of controversy between Jeremiah and a more popular prophet. Hananiah has announced that the Lord would soon end the subjection of the nation by the Persian empire. For Jeremiah, prophets preaching optimism have always been wrong; the true prophet, as we shall hear Jesus say, speaks the truth from God whatever the consequences.

Romans 6:12-23
CONTEXT: Paul has reiterated his sense of the Christian's mutual in-dwelling with Christ; he moves on to formulate a Christian ethic.
IDEAS: Sin makes its own demands; we are to reject them, in whole-hearted service to everything good.

The foundation of Paul's ethic is that sin itself has an identity and a power which the Christian must identify in order to combat. Total obedience to God puts obedience to sin out of the question.

Matthew 10:40-42
CONTEXT: Jesus continuing to teach the twelve.
IDEAS: The prophet comes with divine authority.

Jesus tells the Twelve who will act in his name that they are like prophets. Those who speak and work for God in Christ can be assured that he is always with them and working through them.

Year A: Proper 9 (3-9 July; Week 14.)

Continuous Old Testament: Genesis 24:34-38, 42-49, 58-67
CONTEXT: Time for Isaac to marry – but not a wife from the Canaanite people.
IDEAS: Racial/religious purity; immigrants send 'home' for a wife; seeking and finding; signs from God.

From the foreign land where he has settled, Abraham sends a servant back to their own people, to find a wife for his son. This messenger explains his mission to the father of the beautiful Rebecca, and we hear how she became Isaac's wife.

Related Old Testament: Zechariah 9:9-12
CONTEXT: Miscellaneous 'oracles' of (the second) Zechariah, probably as late as 2nd century BC.
IDEAS: The coming of the Messiah – in power and humility.

At least one prophetic voice in Israel associated the Messiah with humility and gentleness as well as with power, and Jesus chose to act out this vision. A king riding on a donkey, so familiar to us, speaks of a strange kind of triumphal entry to take up the kingdom.

Romans 7:15-25a
CONTEXT: Life in Christ, and the inescapable pull of sin.
IDEAS: Even the baptised faithful cannot be wholly spiritual people.

We have heard week by week Paul trying to explain how Christians can say they are free from sin for the service of God, yet still find themselves in a constant battle against sin. Here, he admits this even of himself: how far from perfection he is, doing what he should not and not doing what he should.

Matthew 11:16-19, 25-30
CONTEXT: See Mt 11:1 – Jesus's travelling mission continues. John the Baptist has asked for reassurance about who Jesus is.
IDEAS: Contrasting reactions to the ascetic John and the sociable Jesus; some do recognise the revelation of their Messiah.

Some people were convinced by John the Baptist's stern message; some were convinced by Jesus's more compassionate style and followed him. But many criticised both of them. Who can recognise Jesus as the world's Saviour? Often a simple, childlike heart sees truths which the clever and learned are blind to.

Year A: Proper 10 (10-16 July; Week 15.)

Continuous Old Testament: Genesis 25:19-34

CONTEXT: Abraham's grandsons are born; the later rivalry between Israel and Edom is rooted in those from whom their tribes sprang – Jacob and Esau.

IDEAS: Sagas 'explain' historic enmities; family dissension; active versus contemplative lifestyles.

We have been hearing over recent weeks how God blessed Abraham for his faith. And for a while, all seems well, as God's will is worked out first through a son and now the birth of grandsons. But God's eternal good purpose constantly suffers setbacks through human selfishness and deceit, not least within a family.

Related Old Testament: Isaiah 55:10-13

CONTEXT: The assurance of restoration from Babylonian exile.

IDEAS: God's constancy in nature is paralleled by the certainty of his 'word'.

We shall hear in the Gospel the familiar parable of the seed – the Word of God – sown in different conditions. Isaiah too used the picture of God's word taking root and being fruitful, guaranteeing joy and peace when the time of exile would come to an end.

Romans 8:1-11

CONTEXT: Unspiritual lives are changed by God's redemptive work in us.

IDEAS: Being put right with God; unity with Christ; lives utterly changed.

Paul has discovered that sin is never completely conquered. But the amazing consequence of faith in Jesus Christ is that God does not utterly condemn us. Our lives are quite different, because they are directed to God, and through his Spirit he gives us true life.

Matthew 13:1-9, 18-23

CONTEXT: Matthew's collection of parables.

IDEAS: Seed, God's Word, fruit of the Spirit.

If you have ears, then hear a parable. God's presence and God's word are broadcast everywhere, like seed falling in every kind of soil and climate. To you it has been given to hear and understand and be fruitful.

Year A: Proper 11 (17-23 July; Week 16.)

Continuous Old Testament: Genesis 28:10-19a
CONTEXT: See Proper 9 – the immigrants seeking wives from their homeland.
IDEAS: Racial intermarriage; God is present even in pagan places.

As with Abraham's son, so with his grandson. A marriage is to be arranged by Jacob with a girl from their homeland, not from the local native people of Canaan. We hear how on Jacob's journey, he experienced the presence of Israel's God in a pagan shrine. Everywhere is holy ground.

Related Old Testament: EITHER *Wisdom of Solomon 12:13, 16-19*
CONTEXT: A late (apocryphal) philosophical document.
IDEAS: Monotheism; a just a merciful God.

These few verses are from a long passage in which the writer wrestles with the problem of why God allows evil to continue to exist. Jesus was asked the same question and, as we shall hear, answered with a vivid parable.

OR *Isaiah 44:6-8*
CONTEXT: Conclusion of a (poetic) 'legal case' as to whether God is just.
IDEAS: Alpha and Omega; One God, incomparable.

The Lord God, says Isaiah, is the beginning and the end of everything that ever was or ever shall be. Only someone exactly like him could fully understand his purposes. Jesus's understanding, as we shall hear, is indeed divine – this is both claim and proof that Jesus is Lord.

Romans 8:12-25
CONTEXT: Paul's description of new life in Christ.
IDEAS: Life and death, God's adopted children; everything yearns for God's ultimate resolution of the world's anguish.

Paul has been contrasting law and freedom, right and wrong. The logic leads him to a favourite phrase: God's Spirit makes us God's adopted children, who can use the name Jesus used – 'Abba', Father. Hold on to that, whatever turmoil the world contains.

Matthew 13:24-30, 36-43

CONTEXT: Matthew's collection of parables.

IDEAS: Good and bad allowed to co-exist – but there will come a judgement day.

The parable of wheat and tares seems simple to us, because it is so familiar. But those who first heard it needed the explanation that the evil in this world is allowed by God to exist alongside the good of the kingdom; but there will come a time when only the good survives.

Year A: Proper 12 (24-30 July; Week 17.)

Continuous Old Testament: Genesis 29:15-28
CONTEXT: The search of Jacob for a wife from his own people.
IDEAS: Hebrew customs: 'engagement' and marriage. More deceits.

Our weekly readings have reminded us that Abraham and his family were immigrants, who sent back to their homeland to find wives for their sons. Jacob has met his beautiful cousin Rachel, but her father Laban manages to get his elder daughter married first, according to the custom.

Related Old Testament: 1 Kings 3:5-12
CONTEXT: Solomon has succeeded his father David as king. His legendary wisdom is explained.
IDEAS: Limits of human wisdom; God's gifts; qualities of leadership.

Jesus's teaching in parables reveals that there is only one thing worth having; he called it the kingdom of heaven. King Solomon called it wisdom, and here he prays to God for this above all else. Later Jewish thinkers came to speak of wisdom as a person of God.

Romans 8:26-39
CONTEXT: The nature of life 'in Christ' as children of God means conversations with God.
IDEAS: Our struggle to pray – the Spirit's help. We are one with God.

Paul moves from the ethical teaching we have heard in recent weeks, to rejoice that we who can call God 'Abba', Father, want to talk to him, and his Spirit enables us to pray. We are one vast family of Christian brothers and sisters, and nothing – no created thing whatsoever – can separate this family from God's love in Jesus.

Matthew 13:31-33, 44-52
CONTEXT: More parables of the kingdom.
IDEAS: Luxuriant growth, incomparable worth, unrivalled capacity.

Most of Jesus's teaching about the kingdom of heaven came in parables. Not everyone could instantly understand them, but they were cherished by the first Christians. Here, he gives four such illustrations to show the immense value and the vast size of his kingdom.

Year A: Proper 13 (31 July-6 August; Week 18.)

Continuous Old Testament: Genesis 32:22-31
CONTEXT: Jacob journeys back to the fellow-settlers in Canaan.
IDEAS: Meeting angels unawares. New circumstances and new names.

This is an important and historic moment in the stories of God's dealings with his ancient people. Jacob has married two of his cousins, and when he falls out with his uncle he begins the journey back to Canaan. On the way he has an awesome encounter with an angel, and receives the new name which became that of his descendants for ever: Jacob becomes Israel.

Related Old Testament: Isaiah 55:1-5
CONTEXT: A vision of the Lord's provision after restoration from captivity.
IDEAS: God's invitations; sumptuous provision; Israel's prophetic role to the whole world.

The prophet's promise is that God fulfils more than our basic physical needs. He will satisfy the hungry and the thirsty, as we shall hear Jesus literally doing. Israel's task and ours is to receive and witness to this glorious generosity.

Romans 9:1-5
CONTEXT: A change of tone from previous weeks: Paul's profound concern for his Jewish kindred.
IDEAS: Jews rejection of their Messiah; our inheritance from the saints of Israel.

It almost breaks Paul's heart that his fellow-Jews, whose whole history has been in covenant-relationship with God, have rejected the very Saviour they longed for, the Jesus in whom God has come to this world.

Matthew 14:13-21
CONTEXT: The news of John the Baptist's death leads to a time of reflection for Jesus, then a new revelation of his power.
IDEAS: Retreat before advancing; God's provision; Messianic expectation and the Kingdom Banquet; more than enough for all.

Jesus seeks some peace, but people are too demanding – and the divine generosity can never refuse those in need. Echoing the ancient experience of manna in the wilderness, Jesus provides food for thousands of people – more than they could ever desire or deserve.

Year A: Proper 14 (7-13 August; Week 19.)

Continuous Old Testament: Genesis 37:1-4, 12-28
CONTEXT: Of Jacob's 12 sons (Gen 35:22b ff) only Joseph's story is told at length.
IDEAS: 12 sons, 12 tribes, 12 disciples; sibling rivalry; strange adventures of people when God's hand guides history.

Jacob has been renamed Israel, from whose 12 sons sprang all the tribes. We are now introduced to Joseph, who eventually becomes saviour of the rest. But the story begins with the plot to do away with this dangerous dreamer.

Related Old Testament: 1 Kings 19:9-18
CONTEXT: Elijah in despair – pagan conquest and people's apostasy.
IDEAS: God's presence in bleak times; the still small voice.

For Elijah, the presence and the will of God are found in a quiet voice with an extraordinary commission. Despite the nation's defeat, he is to anoint new kings. Our Gospel will also speak of Jesus going into the quiet before once more doing an extraordinary thing.

Romans 10:5-15
CONTEXT: Continues the theme of Israel's faith being brought to completion in Christian faith.
IDEAS: Use of Scripture in teaching; 'Jesus is Lord', the first Christian creed; imperative to spread the Gospel.

Paul continues to set out his understanding of how Christian faith follows from Jewish faith. Before, there was only law of obedience; now, all who confess Jesus as Lord, Jews and everyone else, are put right with God.

Matthew 14:22-33
CONTEXT: Messianic disclosures – for those who can understand.
IDEAS: Jesus himself needs tranquillity; miracles often happen, and some will recognise their source; Jesus can hold us up when falling.

After miraculously feeding several thousand people, Jesus takes time for renewal and private reflection, then rejoins his disciples in the mystery of walking on water. Surely now they will see who he truly is.

Year A: Proper 15 (14-20 August; Week 20.)

Continuous Old Testament: Genesis 45:1-15
CONTEXT: Culmination of the Joseph story (the lections have omitted so much!)
IDEAS: God's history works through people; the ancestors of the 12 tribes are preserved.

Our weekly unfolding of the great sagas of Hebrew history jumps on from Joseph hated by his brothers to Joseph the saviour of his brothers. They find him in a powerful position in Egypt as they seek famine relief, but at first they do not recognise him.

Related Old Testament: Isaiah 56:1, 6-8
CONTEXT: Warnings and promises to the restored community.
IDEAS: All people will be safely gathered in.

As early as 500 BC, some religious thinkers in Israel had begun to see that the God of their people must in fact be the only God, with the whole world in his hands. So the hope for a time of restoration and peace embraces every nation and race. The Gospel will tell of Jesus reaching out to a woman of another race.

Romans 11:1-2a, 29-32
CONTEXT: How to explain why the Jews, with all their Scriptures, failed to recognise their Messiah?
IDEAS: Does God reject those who reject him? God is the one God for everyone.

If God's salvation is now offered to everyone in Jesus Christ, says Paul, does it mean that the Jews who were once God's chosen people are now rejected? Of course not. They too remain within God's mercy, if they will receive it.

Matthew 15:[10-20] 21-28
CONTEXT: Jesus's ministry of teaching and healing.
IDEAS: [10-20: Teaching by parables.] Jesus apparently surprised that his work included Gentiles.

The Hebrew prophets had a vision of the breadth of God's love reaching far beyond their own race. Matthew here shows us Jesus confronted by a non-Jewish woman who begs his compassion. Perhaps he is surprised by her, or perhaps he presents a challenge to her.

Year A: Proper 16 (21-27 August; Week 21)

Continuous Old Testament: Exodus 1:8-2:10

CONTEXT: The (post-exilic) editors of early material separated the salvation-history ('Exodus') from the beginnings ('Genesis'), but here we have the continuing story of Israel's (= Jacob) sons in Egypt. The period is approx. 1300 BC.

IDEAS: Israelites in Egypt because the Promised Land had failed them. God always calls forth leaders – often unexpected people.

Jacob's sons and their families had escaped famine, thanks to the protection of Joseph in Egypt. Their settlement however turned into miserable slavery. We begin today a series of readings about the great salvation, the Exodus, and the new covenant community formed under Moses.

Related Old Testament: Isaiah 51:1-6

CONTEXT: Poems of future salvation.

IDEAS: The faith of the fathers; hope of glorious salvation.

Isaiah reminds his audience of their origins, using the image of a rock of foundation which we shall hear again in the Gospel. On this rock the Lord will build peace and joy for all.

Romans 12:1-8

CONTEXT: Because God is so great and glorious, 'therefore …'

IDEAS: Serving Christ, in worship and in community; God gives everyone some valuable talent(s).

To serve God is both a duty and a joy, says Paul. Joy, because we are a transformed people, called to share in God's purposes. Duty, because each one of us has some vocation, to use rightly the gift we have: the whole body, church and world, needs the service of every member.

Matthew 16:13-20

CONTEXT: The disciples' difficulty in fully grasping Jesus's true nature.

IDEAS: Son of Man; Son of God; Peter's eyes opened; no publicity!

Jesus questions his disciples about popular opinion – who is the Son of Man? And what do the disciples think of Jesus? The eyes of Simon are opened to the revelation that Jesus is Messiah, and he is given the new name of Peter, with a new commission, to be steady as a rock for Christ.

Year A: Proper 17 (28 August-3 September; Week 22)

Continuous Old Testament: Exodus 3:1-15
CONTEXT: Israel in Egypt; the call of Moses.
IDEAS: Revelation of the Holy Name; holy places; God hears the desperate.

To know someone's name is to know who they are. For the first time in Jewish history, God declares himself by name to Moses, whom he has chosen to save his people out of slavery.

Related Old Testament: Jeremiah 15:15-21
CONTEXT: Jeremiah persecuted, but confident in the Lord.
IDEAS: A prayer of complaint to God answered.

Jeremiah complains to God that his obedience is not giving him an easy life – too many people hating him and maligning him. The word of the Lord comes in consolation and reassurance: God gives strength of purpose and ultimate victory to his faithful ones – Jesus will say the same in the Gospel.

Romans 12:9-21
CONTEXT: Brief injunctions on Christian life, especially relationships within the church.
IDEAS: Love and humility, joy and peace, hope and endurance.

In a series of powerful phrases, Paul describes how to live the Christian life, in which the world's standards of selfishness and success are over-turned. Love is the key, with generosity and humility. Do good always, to everyone, everywhere.

Matthew 16:21-28
CONTEXT: Jesus's joyful mission begins to darken, as conflict becomes inevitable.
IDEAS: Discipleship implies suffering – for us as for Jesus himself; the Way of the Cross begins for him.

As we continue to read Matthew's Gospel, he changes our mood to reflect on the impending events of Christ's suffering and death. The Christian life is never going to be easy; it is hard to give oneself for others. The Lord's promise to those who persevere is kingdom life, where Christ goes before us.

Year A: Proper 18 (4-10 September; Week 23.)

Continuous Old Testament: Exodus 12:1-14
CONTEXT: At last the Exodus from Egypt becomes a reality.
IDEAS: Passover in history and the present; Last Supper and Eucharist; salvation history.

The single most important event in God's work of salvation, before Christ, is the redemption of the Jews from slavery in Egypt. And it begins with the Passover, celebrated ever since, and given new meaning by Jesus. Here is how it all began.

Related Old Testament: Ezekiel 33:7-11
CONTEXT: Babylonian exile – the assurance of restoration.
IDEAS: God appoints heralds of his coming; call to repentance.

Those who see life through God's eyes are bound to confront wrongdoing and call people to repentance and reconciliation. Ezekiel knows he has this responsibility, and does just what we shall later hear Jesus telling us to do.

Romans 13:8-14
CONTEXT: Christian behaviour in the secular world.
IDEAS: All law (religious and civil) is subsumed by love; living in God's new resurrection-time.

Love sums up all commandments and rules of life. As Paul had written to other churches earlier, he now tells the Roman Christians that in this new age, the years of Our Lord, there can be no time wasted on anything that does not feed our spiritual growth.

Matthew 18:15-20
CONTEXT: Several illustrations by Jesus of kingdom life.
IDEAS: Worldly disputes brought into Christian perspective.

Jesus says that we must not be silent in the face of wrong-doing – but try not to make a big fuss about it; seek reconciliation gently. And when Christians are the catalyst for agreement and unity, there Jesus is present in his kingdom.

Year A: Proper 19 (11-17 September; Week 24.)

Continuous Old Testament: Exodus 14:19-31

CONTEXT: The Israelites have escaped from Egypt, and reached an impassible stretch of water.
IDEAS: The (angel of the) Lord travels with his people; miraculous salvation – and movement onwards.

For the Jewish race, in ancient times and today, the deliverance from slavery in Egypt defines the nature of God's protection. Such is his power that he made their escape possible by the mighty miracle of drying up the waters for them to pass over unharmed.

Related Old Testament: Genesis 50:15-21

CONTEXT: Jacob's authority in Egypt – and provision for the family.
IDEAS: All the brother's evils turned to good; unlimited forgiveness.

As the climax to the story of Joseph in Egypt, we are told how he forgives his brothers the wrong they did to him. Because he can now see how God has brought good out of evil, he goes beyond forgiveness to a practical concern for their well-being. In our Gospel, Jesus tells a parable of unlimited forgiveness.

Romans 14:1-12

CONTEXT: Life together in the church.
IDEAS: Accepting other people's foibles and convictions; more harm is done by criticism than by toleration.

Within any church, says Paul, there will be all sorts of people, to whom different things will have greater importance than for others. In all these matters of conscience, never judge who is right or wrong, better or worse, but respect other people's sincerity.

Matthew 18:21-35

CONTEXT: Teaching by Jesus about life in the kingdom.
IDEAS: How much do we – does God – forgive?

A parable of Jesus teaches us what God is like: his whole nature is for-giveness and mercy. And just because he forgives us so much, and loves us so much, we are to show these same graces in our lives.

Year A: Proper 20 (18-24 September; Week 25.)

Continuous Old Testament: Exodus 16:2-15
CONTEXT: Continuing the salvation-history of the Israelite exodus from Egypt.
IDEAS: The good old days were better; blame the leadership; God's miraculous provision for those in need.

The Israelites have been freed from Egyptian slavery, passed over the Red Sea, and are now camped in the desert. Just like people everywhere, they start to complain that the old days were better. But God's proof that he has not deserted them is a miraculous supply: they are given each day their daily bread.

Related Old Testament: Jonah 3:10-4:11
CONTEXT: The short story (history? myth? satire?) of the reluctant prophet disappointed by success.
IDEAS: It is hard to believe God does forgive everyone who repents.

The story is that Jonah was swallowed by a whale, then sent to preach in godless Nineveh. His resentment at being there at all turned to dismay when he found that God does actually forgive people who repent. Jesus will tell his own parable of the God who does not give what we deserve, but an equal measure of sheer grace to us all.

Philippians 1:21-30
CONTEXT: First Christians in Europe; a letter of great warmth, from prison (in Rome?).
IDEAS: Prison does not confine the Gospel (v. 13); life after death will be better than this life.

The first church Paul founded in Europe was at Philippi. Some years later, from prison (probably in Rome), he writes warmly to his friends. Despite his circumstances, and sometimes a longing for his life to end, he believes he can still be useful to God. Let the readers, then, keep faith against all their adversaries.

Matthew 20:1-16
CONTEXT: A parable Jesus told on the way to Jerusalem.
IDEAS: God's generosity; no differential wages in the kingdom.

This well-known parable of the generous land-owner helps us understand how God gives not what we might earn from him, but more than we could ever desire or deserve. In the kingdom of heaven there are no rewards, only grace for all.

Year A: Proper 21 (25 September-1 October; Week 26)

Continuous Old Testament: Exodus 17:1-7

CONTEXT: The Israelites in their desert camp between Egypt and Canaan.
IDEAS: Biblical images of water (e.g. Rev 7:17, Jn 4:10); blame the leaders (see previous week).

In their desert camp, the community had been fed on manna from heaven, and ever afterwards set bread aside in worship as a sign of God's presence. Now they are on the move again, and there is no water. God uses Moses to work another miracle to meet their need – living water from the rocks.

Related Old Testament: Ezekiel 18:1-4, 25-32

CONTEXT: Teaching concerning every individual's relationship to God.
IDEAS: Life and death; personal responsibility; repentance.

It was proverbial in Israel that God punished children and even grandchildren for the ancestors' sins. Not so, says Ezekiel. The Lord is not like that. Every person carries his or her own destiny, and everyone who turns away from sin and turns to God will be given life.

Philippians 2:1-13

CONTEXT: Paul in prison (in Rome?) writing to dear friends.
IDEAS: Christian unity; the humility of Christ, and his exaltation.

Paul is in prison, glad of opportunities to speak of Jesus to his guards. He still feels intimately linked to the Christians in Philippi, and his own humiliating circumstances inspire him to a much-loved reflection on the humility of Christ in coming to share human experience in order to unite us to God.

Matthew 21:23-32

CONTEXT: Jesus in Jerusalem, always teaching the crowds and challenging the religious leaders.
IDEAS: Authority; repentance.

Jesus speaks with more authority than any prophet of former times, and more than John the Baptist. And his message in this Gospel is much the same as theirs, and the same today: every person who turns away from sin and turns to Christ will be welcomed into the kingdom of heaven.

Year A: Proper 22 (2 October-8 October; Week 27.)

Continuous Old Testament: Exodus 20:1-4, 7-9, 12-20
CONTEXT: Three months after leaving Egypt, the Israelites reach Sinai; God appears on the mountain.
IDEAS: Holy places; holy laws; Christian perspectives on Commandments.

Our weekly readings have followed the Israelites on the journey from Egypt towards their Promised Land. God's covenant with them requires faithful obedience to his commandments, which are here disclosed in a sign of great power.

Related Old Testament: Isaiah 5:1-7
CONTEXT: The early Isaiah's prophecies of Judah's downfall because of their disobedience.
IDEAS: Vineyards; good and bad fruit; dereliction is sometimes God's way.

The image of the vineyard is a common one in the Bible. God's people are those he plants, feeds, prunes, renews, and brings to a fine harvest. Isaiah is here warning that because of the people's unfaithfulness and bad leadership, Jerusalem and Judah are about to be over-run by Assyria: it is sometimes the will of God to allow his vineyard to be ruined.

Philippians 3:4b-14
CONTEXT: Paul in prison, making plans and pondering over our destiny.
IDEAS: His respectable background no longer important; yearning for greater knowledge and spiritual perfection.

We have been hearing week by week Paul's reflections in prison. Now his mind turns towards the future. No worldly advantages compare with knowing Christ – that is, a deep experience of his renewing power – and Paul longs to know more and understand more, even though in this life such knowledge can only be partial.

Matthew 21:33-46
CONTEXT: Conflict in Jerusalem with the authorities (see v. 23ff).
IDEAS: Biblical vineyards metaphor; God leaves servants in charge; the son killed.

Jesus takes the familiar metaphor of Israel as God's vineyard, and turns it into a castigation of those with responsibility for tending it. All those whom God sent to guide and direct, even his own son, were reviled and rejected.

Year A: Proper 23 (9 October–15 October; Week 28.)

Continuous Old Testament: Exodus 32:1-14
CONTEXT: After the revelation of God to Israel at Sinai, procedures for worship are established.
IDEAS: Moses 'in retreat'; people without strong leadership; turning to other kinds of worship.

We are hearing each week of the Israelites' journey from Egypt. Their camp is at Sinai, and Moses has taken to spending much time in private prayer – which his people regard as a waste of time. So disquiet turns to frustration which turns to rebellion, in the dramatic episode of the golden calf. But God will not let his people go their own way.

Related Old Testament: Isaiah 25:1-9
CONTEXT: God's future punishment of Israel's enemies will mean the happy restoration of their own fortunes.
IDEAS: Sometimes destruction must precede re-building; feasting; no more tears, only rejoicing.

This reading underlies Jesus's parable about the banquet of the kingdom. The prophet sees that although Jerusalem will be laid waste, within the divine plan of salvation the land will be restored, suffering and death will come to an end, and God and humanity will feast together in joy.

Philippians 4:1-9
CONTEXT: Final personal greetings to dear friends.
IDEAS: Christian friendships; love and mutual concern.

Our weekly readings from this warm and affectionate letter come to an end with some personal messages, and a resounding call to constancy in prayer, to mutual love, and to an intense dedication to all the best things in life within God's peace.

Matthew 22:1-14
CONTEXT: Jesus speaking to the Jewish authorities.
IDEAS: The banquet prepared; invitations refused but everyone invited.

In Jerusalem, Jesus's parable is a lesson for those who oppose him, and for all who do not accept his invitation to join him in feasting in his kingdom.

Year A: Proper 24 (16 October-22 October; Week 29)

Continuous Old Testament: Exodus 33:12-23
CONTEXT: At the Sinai camp, the Tent of Meeting is established where Moses and God meet.
IDEAS: Distinctiveness of the Jews; God's name; seeing where God has been, not face to face (but note v. 11).

At Mount Sinai, the pilgrimage of the Israelites has been at rest. Now it is nearly time to move on again to the Promised Land. Moses seeks a new assurance of God's guiding hand, and receives a new vision.

Related Old Testament: Isaiah 45:1-7
CONTEXT: God affirmed as creator and sustainer of all things, within whose plan Jerusalem will be restored.
IDEAS: Cyrus, King of Persia, agent of God's will; everything is in God's hand.

The Bible always encourages us to think that God's work can be done even through those who do not know him, and that any government may be his agent of good. Isaiah teaches that God will work through Cyrus, the foreign and pagan king of Persia, to free and restore the Jews.

1 Thessalonians 1:1-10
CONTEXT: A very early N.T. writing. The tumultuous circumstances of Acts 17-18 are not reflected in this letter.
IDEAS: Lives have been changed for good; Christian reputations.

This is probably the earliest of all New Testament documents. Silvanus and Timothy had been with Paul on the mission to Thessalonica, and he now reflects on how marvellously the converts' lives had been changed as the Holy Spirit touched them.

Matthew 22:15-22
CONTEXT: Jesus teaching in the Temple – controversies.
IDEAS: Pharisees' (false?) praise; trick questions; secular powers.

We continue to read Matthew's account of Jesus challenged by religious authorities. Here, it is a trick question about secular authority, and where the primary loyalty of a religious person should be directed.

Year A: Proper 25 (23 October-29 October; Week 30)

Continuous Old Testament: Deuteronomy 34:1-12
CONTEXT: The final words and the death of Moses, with Canaan in sight.
IDEAS: Life and work of Moses; dying with the Promise unfulfilled.

We have been following the saga of the Israelite journey, guided by God to their Promised Land under the leadership of Moses. Now they can see the land ahead, but different gifts of leadership will be needed to create a settled people. Moses's life work is done, to be revered by all people for all time.

Related Old Testament: Leviticus 19:1-2, 15-18
CONTEXT: The 'Holiness Code' – cultic regulations for post-exilic people.
IDEAS: Be holy. Negative ways of creating positive social justice.

When Jesus was challenged, as we shall hear, about keeping the Commandments, he quoted the two great positive laws we are never to forget. Love God with all your heart and, as Moses told the Israelites in this reading, love your neighbour as yourself.

1 Thessalonians 2:1-8
CONTEXT: A very early N.T. writing. The tumultuous circumstances of Acts 17-18 are not reflected in this letter.
IDEAS: Unflinching service of the Gospel; no self-seeking.

This reading continues from last Sunday, in Paul's earliest letter. It reminds the Thessalonians that his mission to them had not been like other preachers who did it for profit, but under the gentle compulsion of the free Gospel of God.

Matthew 22:34-46
CONTEXT: Sadducees – who did not believe in resurrection – silenced by Jesus's arguments; the controversy with religious leaders goes on.
IDEAS: Pious authority challenged; Jesus's astute arguments; the command to love God, self and neighbour.

In these conversations with Sadducees and Pharisees we find Jesus turning their arguments upside-down. It was a radical challenge to their authority and to the respect they normally enjoyed. This passage includes the two great commandments of love, which Jesus quotes from the Hebrew Scriptures.

Year A: CWL Bible Sunday

Nehemiah 8:1-4a [& 5-6], 8-12
CONTEXT: Return from exile in Babylon; rebuilding of Jerusalem and the Temple; Nehemiah the governor, Ezra the leading priest.
IDEAS: God's Word/Law highly prized; public reading of Scripture; explanation and instruction.

Jews returning to Jerusalem from exile had repaired the city walls and restored the damaged Temple. Now they must rebuild their lives. Where better to look for direction and inspiration than the holy books of the Law, once lost but now recovered?

Colossians 3:12-17
CONTEXT: Instruction in Christian behaviour.
IDEAS: All virtues summed up in love; instruction in the Gospel; corporate worship – psalms.

The Gospel of Christ can be seen as the rich clothing of our spirit, for it dwells within us. Paul says we are to teach each other its richness of love and peace, as we live and worship together.

Matthew 24:30-35
CONTEXT: Jesus speaking of 'end-time', the world's tribulations and the coming of the 'Son of Man'.
IDEAS: Signs of the times; everything passes away except God's Word.

The Gospel contains some stark warnings about the coming of the Son of Man at the end of time, but Jesus promises that the Word of the Lord will remain for ever.

Year A: CWL Dedication Festival (First Sunday in October or Last after Trinity)

1 Kings 8:22-30
CONTEXT: Solomon's Temple is built and the Ark installed.
IDEAS: God not contained by earthly things; special places of prayer.

Solomon's Temple is completed, and as King he blesses the people gathered for worship. He prays that God, though present everywhere and not confined to a place, will hear his people and watch over the house dedicated to the Lord their God.

OR *Revelation 21:9-14*
CONTEXT: The new heaven and new earth which shall come to pass.
IDEAS: Visions of God's splendour; twelves = completeness; no need of church or temple (v. 22).

In this vision of God's eternal city, there is no need for a Temple because God's glory shines in everything. The new Jerusalem includes all twelve tribes of Israel, and all who have received the Gospel through the twelve Apostles.

Hebrews 12:18-24
CONTEXT: The enduring history of faith; the new perspective in the revelation of God in Christ.
IDEAS: Face to face with God; the city of God; vast crowds come to worship.

In ancient times, to meet God was awesome, and Mount Zion a fearful holy place. By contrast, says this writer, we know Christ brings us the new covenant promises, and we can always come into God's presence without fear.

Matthew 21:12-16
CONTEXT: Jesus's 'Palm Sunday' arrival in Jerusalem among excited crowds.
IDEAS: Right uses for holy places; healing ministry in a place of worship.

In the Jerusalem Temple, built for the glory of God and for prayer, Jesus confronts those who use it to make dishonest profit for themselves. He brings to the holy place his Father's work of compassion.

Year A: CWL Fourth before Advent, RCL Proper 26
(30 October-5 November: Week 31.)

RCL: *Joshua 3:7-17*
CONTEXT: The entry to Canaan and the conquests.
IDEAS: New leader for new situation; the mobile God; Exodus/Red Sea parallels.

When the people of the Exodus at last reached their Promised Land, still they had to cross the River Jordan. In a scene which may remind us of the parting of the Red Sea, Joshua summons the presence of God to hold back the waters.

CWL; RCL alternative: *Micah 3:5-12*
CONTEXT: Messages of judgement – the religious leaders have failed God and their people.
IDEAS: False prophets; God's righteous judgements.

Human nature always wants to know what will happen in the future. Both Micah and Jesus are scathing about professional forecasters, some of whom even claim to speak in the Lord's name. There is, says Micah, no future for those who condition their prophecy to what their employers want to hear.

1 Thessalonians 2:9-13
CONTEXT: Very early N.T. writing, reflecting Paul's mission journey to Thessalonica and its success.
IDEAS: Labour without reward, toil without rest; gentle persuasion.

On these Sundays before Advent we hear from this early letter of Paul. He had not asked payment for his teaching ministry, but brought the Gospel message freely, honestly and diligently. He urges the new Christians in Thessalonica to live in ways worthy of God.

RCL: *Matthew 23:1-12*
CONTEXT: Jesus in Jerusalem – his disputes with the religious leaders.
IDEAS: Practice and preaching; displays of allegiance; all are learners.

In this section of his Gospel, Matthew collects together several of the powerful criticisms by Jesus of the Pharisees. They do not even follow their own teaching; they love public honour; they forget there is always much more to learn about God.

CWL: *Matthew 24:1-14*
CONTEXT: Jesus teaching in Jerusalem; strictures against hypocrisy.
IDEAS: False prophets and misguided leaders; the world in disarray.

As with the prophet Micah, so from Jesus, there are warnings of those who will mislead people in the Messiah's name. Jesus warns us, too, that the world will go its own destructive and violent ways, which the faithful must be prepared to endure until the end of time.

Year A: All Saints' Day
(Sunday between 30 October and 5 November, or 1 November.)

Revelation 7:9-17
CONTEXT: In a vision of heaven, 'seven seals' of a 'scroll' are broken open to disclose the future. This is the sixth.
IDEAS: All Israel safely gathered, then all Christians too; eternal praise; martyrs; ultimate victory of God.

Instead of an Old Testament reading this All Saints' Day, we hear one of the seven visions given to John. He tells of the vast number of holy men and women who served God faithfully in their lifetime and now surround the heavenly throne of glory.

1 John 3:1-3
CONTEXT: A treatise on the reality of the incarnation, and our call to remain steadfast.
IDEAS: Children of our Father in heaven; Christlikeness.

We do not know what our life after death will be like. Our faith is that we shall see and know completely the Christ whom we follow here, and so we shall be like him.

Matthew 5:1-12
CONTEXT: Jesus's popularity in and around Capernaum; his early ministry of teaching and healing.
IDEAS: The Blessed/Happy (translations vary) are made so by God; challenge to be unpopular; unexpected people enter the kingdom.

In these strange paradoxes we call the Beatitudes, Jesus teaches us who are the holy people in God's sight, the ones who will find his blessings as his kingdom comes.

Year A: CWL November 1
(If the All Saints' Day material is used on the Sunday.)

Isaiah 56:3-8
CONTEXT: Warnings and promises to the restored community.
IDEAS: All people will be safely gathered in.

As early as 500 BC, some religious thinkers in Israel had begun to see that the God of their people must in fact be the only God, with the whole world in his hands. So the hope for a time of restoration and peace embraces every nation and race. In the Gospel Jesus will tell us who are blessed by God.

OR *2 Esdras 2:42-48*
CONTEXT: Part of the Christian prefix added later to some Jewish writings of around 100 AD, which are apocalyptic visions ascribed to the ancient priest Ezra.
IDEAS: Vast crowd of the saints surround the Son of God.

This reading comes from a book in our Apocrypha, a collection of Jewish symbolic visions to which were added some Christian passages like this, where all those who acknowledge Christ are gathered round him in his glory.

Hebrews 12:18-24
CONTEXT: The enduring history of faith; the new perspective in the revelation of God in Christ.
IDEAS: Face to face with God; the city of God; vast crowds come to worship.

In ancient times, to meet God was awesome, and Mount Zion a fearful holy place. By contrast, says this writer, we know Christ brings us the new covenant promises, and we can always come into God's presence without fear.

Matthew 5:1-12
CONTEXT: Jesus's popularity in and around Capernaum; his early ministry of teaching and healing.
IDEAS: The Blessed/Happy (translations vary) are made so by God; challenge to be unpopular; unexpected people enter the kingdom.

In these strange paradoxes we call the Beatitudes, Jesus teaches us who are the holy people in God's sight, the ones who will find his blessings as his kingdom comes.

Year A: CWL Third before Advent, RCL Proper 27
(6-12 November. Week 32)

RCL only: *Joshua 24:1-3a, 14-25*
CONTEXT: The Israelite tribes settled in the Promised Land; Joshua's last words and his death.
IDEAS: New covenant for a new generation; life-changing choices.

Joshua has led the people into their Promised Land. He now reminds them of the great things God has done for them, and calls them to an act of commitment, that they will hereafter faithfully serve the Lord and no other.

CWL; RCL alternative: *Wisdom 6:12-16*
CONTEXT: The way of God with his people is wiser than all Greek ideas of wisdom. Chapters 6-8 explain the true nature of Wisdom.
IDEAS: Wisdom personified – recognisable and active.

To religious thinkers of the last century before Christ, wisdom seemed more than just an attribute of God – she was a person of God. This short passage comes from a long section in our Apocrypha, of praise to wisdom and injunctions to seek her.

OR *Amos 5:18-24*
CONTEXT: Israel has denied her Lord by allowing injustice to flourish: punishment is threatened.
IDEAS: Expect the 'Day of the Lord' – but expect harsh judgement.

In Israel in the 8th century BC, Amos sees more attention being giving to religious ritual than to social justice. So, says this fierce prophet, if you expect the Lord's coming, beware that it may not be as delightful as you think. When God comes to his world he comes in righteous judgement.

1 Thessalonians 4:13-18
CONTEXT: A very early N.T. writing. The tumultuous circumstances of Acts 17-18 are not reflected in this letter.
IDEAS: The Second Advent; all equal before the Lord, dead or alive.

This letter is the earliest we have from Paul. The church at that time expected Jesus to return very soon. Paul has encouraging words for those who might die before that second Advent, because every one of us can look forward to life with Christ for ever.

Matthew 25:1-13
CONTEXT: Warnings by Jesus about the end of this age.
IDEAS: Second Advent; being prepared and watching.

Jesus tells a parable about the coming Day of the Son of Man. None of us can know the time of his coming, but we must live as though it might be at any moment, and be prepared to face him.

Year A: CWL Second before Advent, RCL Proper 28
(13-19 November. Week 33.)

RCL only: *Judges 4:1-7*
CONTEXT: The settlement in Canaan – establishment of judges – continuing armed skirmishes.
IDEAS: Women as judges, prophets, leaders; the Promised Land not instantly milk and honey.

All year we have heard stories of Israel's great heroes, from their beginning under Abraham to Joshua and the occupation of Canaan. In this last excerpt in the sequence, a heroine emerges. Deborah encouraged the army to battle against Canaanite forces.

CWL; RCL alternative: *Zephaniah 1:7, 12-18*
CONTEXT: God intends to destroy everything on earth, because of the great corruption he sees.
IDEAS: The Day of the Lord; judgement and purging of the sin.

The Bible has much to say about the anticipated 'Day of the Lord'. For this prophet in the seventh century BC, it would be a time for God to root out all corruption; he will destroy and punish in a sudden outburst of his righteous judgement.

1 Thessalonians 5:1-11
CONTEXT: Anticipation of Christ's return – Christian conduct meanwhile.
IDEAS: Watchful readiness; our destiny to be with Christ.

In this early letter Paul still expected Jesus to return soon and draw all things to an end. He asks the Christians to live with that sense of expectancy, in confidence that the faithful will be taken into the Lord's company when he comes to complete our salvation.

Matthew 25:14-30
CONTEXT: Parables of the end of the age.
IDEAS: The world left in trust to us; the owner/master will return.

Matthew tells another of Jesus's parables about the Day of the Lord. Then, the fullness of the kingdom of heaven will reveal what each person made of the gifts God gave on trust. It is the parable of the talents, and the joy in store for those who are faithful stewards.

Year A: Christ the King (20-26 November)

Ezekiel 34:11-16, 20-24

CONTEXT: Leaders have misled their people; 'the flock' have strayed.
IDEAS: God in search of his sheep; a new David will rule.

David had been the great Shepherd-King, and the Jews longed for another King like him. Today's Gospel will pick up the thought of the King as Shepherd. We hear first from Ezekiel, preparing for a divine intervention into history, speaking of God himself as the gatherer of his flock into safety, under a worthy successor to David.

Ephesians 1:15-23

CONTEXT: The letter has begun with praise to God for the presence of Christ in the church.
IDEAS: Prayer for the church; vast resources and (kingly) power of God; Christ enthroned in heaven.

Paul's great hymn of prayer and praise extols the power of God at work in all the faithful, and the Lord Jesus Christ raised up as king over all things.

Matthew 25:31-46

CONTEXT: Teaching concerning the final coming of the kingdom.
IDEAS: Son of Man is to come; judgement and blessing; service of the king through his subjects.

Jesus speaks about the end of time, and the kingly power that will be seen in the coming of the Son of Man. He reveals what the standard of judgement will be for entry into this kingdom – either we did, or did not, care for him as we find him in the needy.

Year B: The First Sunday of Advent

Isaiah 64:1-9
CONTEXT: The late ('Third') Isaiah; diverse writings from the post-exilic years. Praises and prayers.
IDEAS: Understand God's past to interpret the present; God absent – a plea for his action.

As we begin to prepare once more to celebrate the Saviour's birth, this lesson recalls how God has been known in mighty acts with and for his people. Isaiah pleads for the Lord to come again, and to forgive all their sins.

1 Corinthians 1:3-9
CONTEXT: Opening greeting, from Ephesus, to a church with many problems.
IDEAS: Grace and peace linked; the parousia; God keeps faith.

The Hebrew people anticipated a 'Day of the Lord'. This hope became for Christians the time when the world will know the full presence of Christ in glory. While we wait, there is much to be thankful for as we share God's grace and peace now.

Mark 13:24-37
CONTEXT: Jesus speaking of 'end-time', the world's tribulations and the coming of the 'Son of Man'.
IDEAS: Signs of the times; God's Word lasts for ever; watchfulness.

We begin today a series of readings from Mark's Gospel. Here, Jesus is speaking to his friends about the future and the final coming of the Son of Man. Jesus expects a time of great distress in the world, and tells them to be vigilant and to stand firm.

Year B: The Second Sunday of Advent

Isaiah 40:1-11
CONTEXT: The opening words of Second Isaiah, in Babylon during the captivity –
offering hope of restoration.
IDEAS: Bad things come to an end – even God's punishments; prophetic voices; proclaim
God's coming.

**Be ready, says the prophet, for God is coming soon to Israel, and the people
must prepare to return from exile. Today's Gospel quotes these words, which
became for Christians a prophecy of John the Baptist, proclaiming Jesus and
preparing the way for his coming.**

2 Peter 3:8-15a
CONTEXT: How to live in this last age, near the end of time.
IDEAS: God outside time; deal with the present; how will the world end?

**Like the Jews during their exile, the early Christians wondered why the
Lord did not deliver them from their suffering. But God's time is not like
our time, and we are to be calm in our preparations for the coming 'Day
of the Lord', so that we may be at peace.**

Mark 1:1-8
CONTEXT: The Good News of Jesus begins with John the Baptist.
IDEAS: The Lord is coming; repent and be forgiven; challenge to change.

**Mark's Gospel begins with the mission of John the Baptist, preaching
and baptising for repentance. As prophets had foretold, he is the sign of
the coming of the one who is greater than he.**

Year B: The Third Sunday of Advent

Isaiah 61:1-4, 8-11
CONTEXT: Words of hope to the people restored from exile – under God, places and community will be rebuilt.
IDEAS: Bringing good news; longing for God's salvation; time to rejoice.

All the Advent lessons look towards the coming of the Lord. Here are verses Jesus applied to himself, as the one who brought liberty, justice, and gladness to the world.

1 Thessalonians 5:16-24
CONTEXT: Do not worry about 'The End' – be prepared, but sustain one another.
IDEAS: Support church leaders; live (and work) for each other; constant joy and prayer.

The Advent season rightly has a sombre tone, reflecting our serious preparation and self-examination. But joy keeps breaking in, and Paul ends this letter in that spirit. Waiting for the Lord is a time of joy, prayer, and thankfulness.

John 1:6-8, 19-28
CONTEXT: The coming of the Word into the world – the message and the messenger.
IDEAS: God's witnesses; last and greatest prophet; glad tidings to the lowly.

There was a man sent from God. Before Jesus there came John the Baptist, witnessing to the light of the world, pointing beyond himself to the One who stands among us as God incarnate.

Year B: The Fourth Sunday of Advent

2 Samuel 7:1-11, 16
CONTEXT: King David has defeated all the warring neighbours, and set up the Ark in Jerusalem.
IDEAS: A worthy place for God (cf. the stable); the king will bring peace; God will secure David's dynasty.

The Ark, a chest containing the Ten Commandments, represented the presence of God. The prophet Nathan tells King David that no grand place is needed to house it, because God's promise is to be with his people for ever, and a great new king will be born of David's line.

Romans 16:25-27
CONTEXT: Personal greetings conclude a profoundly theological letter.
IDEAS: Divine wisdom now revealed; God for all nations.

Paul's letter to the Roman Christians ends with glory to God, because the mystery of salvation, secret for long ages past, is now disclosed. Jesus Christ is present with us, and this revelation is for all people everywhere.

Luke 1:26-38
CONTEXT: Luke's beautiful nativity story.
IDEAS: Davidic descent; names and titles; amazing news.

The angel Gabriel's visit to Mary announces the coming of Jesus. He is the one to whom will be given the throne of David, and his kingdom will be without end.

Year B: CWL Christmas Eve (morning)

2 Samuel 7:1-5, 8-11, 16
CONTEXT: King David has defeated all the warring neighbours, and set up the Ark in Jerusalem.
IDEAS: A worthy place for God (cf. the stable); the king will bring peace; God will secure David's dynasty.

King David is told that God is content to dwell in the humblest of places. God has always been present, leading and guiding, and can always be trusted to guide and bless. Much of Jewish hope rested on the promise of a king like David, to be born of his line.

Acts 13:16-26
CONTEXT: A synagogue sermon in Galatia.
IDEAS: God's chosen people; David and his succession; now the Saviour has come.

Paul was invited to speak at a synagogue in Galatia. His Jewish audience heard him briefly review their history under God, and the promise of a Davidic King. The way was prepared, he says; now – to us – Jesus our Saviour has come.

Luke 1:67-79
CONTEXT: Luke's stories and songs declaring two wondrous births.
IDEAS: Zechariah released from dumbness for praise; all God's promises come true; the Lord's herald.

Now the hope of centuries is satisfied, and there is nothing left but praise – the praise of old Zechariah whose own son John will usher into the world the one who is the light of the world.

Year B: Christmas Day

SET I

Isaiah 9:2-7
CONTEXT: Judah will suffer defeat by Assyria – but God will deliver.
IDEAS: Poetry of praise; visions of God's wonders; names of the child.

The Bible readings in Advent have prepared us to celebrate the coming of the Lord. His people longed for him, and we know the joy of living with him here and now. So, we understand Isaiah's prophecy as greeting the birth of a child whose new kingdom of righteousness will last for ever.

Titus 2:11-14
CONTEXT: Pastoral instruction to an established church leader in Crete.
IDEAS: God's grace; Christian 'discipline' (= training, learning); vision of a future more perfect age; Jesus (unusually for the Bible) is called God.

The new morning of the world has dawned, says this writer. As we learn how to live in this bright new light, in gratitude for the first coming of Jesus who has made us his own, we await the greater glory when Christ will come again.

Luke 2:1-14 [15-20]
CONTEXT: Luke intertwines the birth stories of Jesus and John.
IDEAS: Dating the birth; Bethlehem and its history; no welcome; another angelic sign.

Luke, the master story-teller, gives us pictures we shall never forget, of the humble birth at Bethlehem of the Saviour of the world, and the shining glory which brought shepherds to worship the Lamb of God.

SET II

Isaiah 62:6-12
CONTEXT: Third Isaiah (post-exile); promise of a new Jerusalem.
IDEAS: Jerusalem (and Israel) restored and protected; renewed by God to be holy people.

The prophet proclaims that the news of God's deliverance will reach every corner of the world, to call all his people back to himself. He will redeem them, and make them his holy ones.

Year B: Christmas Day, continued

Titus 3:4-7
CONTEXT: See Set I above.
IDEAS: Grace; generosity; saved by faith to eternal life.

Christ has come to bring a new dawn, says this writer. Now we know we are not saved by our good deeds, but by grace alone. The divine mercy makes us heirs of eternal life.

Luke 2:[1-7] 8-20
See Set I above for details.

SET III

Isaiah 52:7-10
CONTEXT: Songs of encouragement and the victory to come.
IDEAS: Good news of deliverance; return to the holy city.

In typical Hebrew style, the prophet sings of a glorious future as if it had already happened. For us, God has indeed visited and redeemed his people, glory to Israel and light for the Gentiles.

Hebrews 1:1-4 [5-12]
CONTEXT: The culmination of all God's self-revelation is in Jesus.
IDEAS: Christ present in creation; now revealed to us; his work of salvation.

In this anonymous essay, the writer contrasts the partial revelation given in times past with the outpouring of God's word in his glorious Son.

[*If 5-12 is read:* with whom even the angels bear no comparison.]

John 1:1-14
CONTEXT: The divine disclosure in the Word made flesh.
IDEAS: Christ as *Logos* – Word, present in creation; seen on earth, rejected by many but new life for all believers.

In so few but wonderful words, John captures the majesty and the mystery of God disclosing himself; his divine Word is made flesh. Christ was from the beginning, is now, and all who believe this are children of God.

Year B: The First Sunday of Christmas

Isaiah 61:10-62:3
CONTEXT: Third Isaiah – post-exilic. Poems of warning and promise to the restored community. An 'anointed one' proclaims salvation (61:1).
IDEAS: Time to rejoice; wedding imagery; news for all nations; all things new.

Readings from Isaiah helped us prepare for the Lord's coming, both in his birth and in glory at the end of time. Now, as we celebrate, these words sing a fitting hymn of joy and gladness. New life, new glory, new kingdom, and God's people known by a new name.

Galatians 4:4-7
CONTEXT: Contrast between Jewish Law as a temporary 'guardian' and our status as adopted children of God.
IDEAS: Jesus born a Jew; Abba, the intimate name; children and heirs.

Because Christ is born, writes Paul, we are made children of God, living in the freedom of receiving the divine promises.

RCL: *Luke 2:22-40*
CONTEXT: See Exodus 13:1-2 and Leviticus 12:6-8.
IDEAS: Religious duty; offering; holy waiting; visionaries.

As the Law requires, Jesus the first-born is brought to the Temple with a thank-offering. Two old and holy people, Simeon and Anna, perceive that this child is the fulfilment of ancient prophecies of redemption, but the glory will not be without pain and suffering.

CWL: *Luke 2:15-21*
CONTEXT: The Child is born and heaven cries glory.
IDEAS: What the shepherds saw; Christ born subject to the Law (Gal 4:4); the new name.

Shepherds came to see Jesus, and praised God for all they had heard and seen. Eight days later, in accordance with Jewish Law, the child is circumcised and given the name above all other names: Jesus.

Year B: The Second Sunday of Christmas

Jeremiah 31:7-14
CONTEXT: Babylonian exile: a sequence of promises of restoration of the kingdom and the monarchy.
IDEAS: The remnant preserved; gathering together for celebration; gladness; bountiful provision.

Jeremiah speaks God's words, from the perspective when all nations and peoples shall be restored. The passage has many images which only found their full meaning in Christian vocabulary – God as father to his redeemed people, saviour, gatherer, shepherd and deliverer, giver of joy and gladness.

OR *Ecclesiasticus 24:1-12*
CONTEXT: The Apocrypha; in praise of wisdom (a 'person' of God).
IDEAS: God's attributes personified before Jesus came; present in creation, makes his dwelling with humankind; wisdom = Word (v. 3).

Not long before Christ's birth, these writings were collected in books we call the Apocrypha. Wisdom is here described in feminine imagery, personified as one who existed before time began, sent forth as the word of the Lord to dwell with God's people and make her home in their midst. Our Gospel will say the same of Jesus.

Ephesians 1:3-14
CONTEXT: The letter opens with a section of praise for God's blessings.
IDEAS: God's eternal purposes and choices; his gifts to us in and through Christ.

This letter begins with a hymn of praise to God for what he has done for us. The phrase 'in Christ' comes again and again: as God was in Christ Jesus, so we are one in Christ. God has made us his children and calls us to glory.

John 1:[1-9] 10-18
CONTEXT: The divine disclosure in the Word made flesh.
IDEAS: Christ as *Logos* – Word, present in creation; seen on earth, rejected by many but new life for all believers.

In so few but wonderful words, John captures the majesty and the mystery of God disclosing himself; his divine Word is made flesh. Christ was from the beginning, is now, and all who believe this are children of God.

Year B: The Epiphany: 6 January

Isaiah 60:1-6
CONTEXT: Call to respond to the promise of new Jerusalem.
IDEAS: Come and worship; glory dawns; abundance.

In Isaiah's vision of God's light shining into the world's darkness, symbolic gifts are brought to God from East and West as tribute and praise. So our Gospel's Magi visitors to the stable are foreshadowed.

Ephesians 3:1-12
CONTEXT: The 'near' and 'far-off' united; Jew and Gentile now fellow-citizens.
IDEAS: God's secrets now revealed; Paul in prison but rejoicing; all are one in Christ.

Riches beyond imagining, says Paul, are found in Christ. Although Paul is in prison for his faith, his gospel cannot be confined – it is good news that God's purposes, once so obscure, are now made clear for Jew and Gentile alike.

Matthew 2:1-12
CONTEXT: Matthew's (unique) nativity story of gifts to Jesus.
IDEAS: The greatest king has come; journeying to him; wisdom honours him; our gifts to him.

Only Matthew tells us how representatives of other strange religions came from the East to offer their homage to the one and only true God, the child who is king for ever over all earthly powers.

Year B: The Baptism of Christ: Epiphany 1

Genesis 1:1-5
CONTEXT: The great story of the Creation.
IDEAS: Maker of everything, seen and unseen; light for the world.

Today's readings all speak of new beginnings. We begin with the first words of the first book of the Bible and their poetic account of the origin of all things in the will of the Creator.

Acts 19:1-7
CONTEXT: Paul's third (and final) missionary journey – Corinth, Ephesus, etc.
IDEAS: John's baptism incomplete; gifts of the Spirit; new life in Christ.

At Ephesus, Paul found people who had already heard and believed the Gospel, but not been baptised in the name of Jesus. There and then they made this new beginning, and received the gifts of the Holy Spirit.

Mark 1:4-11
CONTEXT: Mark's Gospel begins with John's baptism of repentance, and his declaration of a fuller gift to come.
IDEAS: Repent and begin again; water and Spirit; the divine witness.

Baptism is a new beginning for Our Lord himself, as he comes to the river Jordan to be baptised by John before his public mission begins. Mark, like all the Gospels, tells us how God's Holy Spirit came to rest upon his Son, for he came to renew the whole creation.

Year B: Epiphany 2

1 Samuel 3:1-10 [& 11-20]
CONTEXT: Samuel born to the barren Hannah and dedicated to service of the Temple (2:11).
IDEAS: Lord's word rarely heard; recognising God's directions; [the prophetic calling].

Samuel became an important priest and prophet to Israel, but God's call to him, as a child, was quite unexpected. Our Gospel will be another example of God's surprises.

RCL: *1 Corinthians 6:12-20*
CONTEXT: Disciplinary problems in the church.
IDEAS: Christian 'freedom'; human sexuality; holy bodies.

In these Sundays of the Epiphany season we shall hear some passages from this letter to Greek Christians. It is a reply from Paul to some questions they had asked, and here deals specifically with immorality. Remember, he says, your body is where God's Spirit lives, and is therefore holy.

CWL: *Revelation 5:1-10*
CONTEXT: The first of the visions of all heaven at worship.
IDEAS: The meaning of things 'sealed' from human understanding; Jesus the Lion and the Lamb; universal salvation through Christ.

These Sundays of Epiphany set before us some extraordinary mystical visions of heaven. In this passage, Jesus appears as both lion and lamb, strong in weakness. He is the only one who can reveal the mysteries of God to us.

John 1:43-51
CONTEXT: Jesus recruiting the Twelve as his mission begins.
IDEAS: The sceptic converted; God's surprises; Jesus's complete understanding of people.

Following his baptism, of which we heard last Sunday, Jesus began to choose men to share his work. Among them was Nathanael, who received an unexpected invitation from Philip to 'Come and see', and was even more surprised to discover that Jesus knew all about his past, present and future.

Year B: Epiphany 3
(RCL readings; see following page for CWL provision.)

Jonah 3:1-5, 10
CONTEXT: A powerful fable of a petulant prophet, God's compulsions and his compassion.
IDEAS: Visiting preachers; call to repent; God changes his mind (?)

The message today of this reading and the Gospel is the call to repent. In the story of Jonah, God called him to warn the people of Nineveh of imminent punishment for their sin, and when they repented they were forgiven.

1 Corinthians 7:29-31
CONTEXT: Replies to questions (7:1).
IDEAS: Everything in this life is provisional; detachment from some worldly matters.

We continue reading from this letter, having heard last Sunday Paul's teaching about our bodies, which are holy because they are God's. Now he recommends a degree of detachment from too much worldly care and responsibility, with the sense that the end of all things is near.

Mark 1:14-20
CONTEXT: John baptizing; Jesus comes to him then goes into the wilderness.
IDEAS: Gospel of repentance; calling disciples; instant response.

According to Mark, Jesus's public ministry began by echoing John the Baptist, calling everyone to repent and recognise the coming of the kingdom. Some men immediately answered his call.

Year B: Epiphany 3
(CWL readings; see preceding page for RCL provision.)

Genesis 14:17-20
CONTEXT: Abram and Lot go separate ways (13:11, 12); Abram goes to the rescue of Lot, defeating the four eastern kings.
IDEAS: Salem (v. 18) = Jerusalem; ceremonial bread and wine; the great priest-king.

Today's readings are linked by the idea of the great banquet of the Messiah's kingdom in heaven. Here, the legendary priest-king Melchizedek acts to seal God's covenant with Abram in an offering of bread and wine, accompanied by a blessing.

Revelation 19:6-10
CONTEXT: The final defeat of evil (Babylon/Rome), the rejoicing that follows.
IDEAS: The heavenly/Messianic banquet; bridal imagery.

This vision is of the joy in heaven when all evil shall be defeated. It picks up an ancient image of faithful people as God's bride, called now to join the vast crowd at the wedding banquet of celebration.

John 2:1-11
CONTEXT: For John, Jesus's work begins quietly but significantly.
IDEAS: 'Signs' in John's Gospel; wine (and vines, etc.) in Biblical imagery; superabundant provision of finest quality; hastening the normal process of wine-making!

In the Gospel of John, the miracles of Jesus are signs – of who he is and therefore what God is like. The first sign occurs at a wedding banquet, where among his family and friends Jesus made extravagant quantities of water into the finest wine. The ordinary becomes the extraordinary.

Year B: Epiphany 4

Deuteronomy 18:15-20
CONTEXT: The laws set forth by God through Moses: social and religious – seeking God's will.
IDEAS: God calls prophets; fear of God; mediators between God and man.

Moses understands that so long as people find God threatening, and fear to meet him, they will need someone as a mediator. He gives God's promise to raise up a prophet like Moses himself, who will speak with divine authority.

RCL: *1 Corinthians 8:1-13*
CONTEXT: Problems and questions raised by the Corinthian Christians.
IDEAS: Consecration; holy things and holy people; strive to give no offence.

Paul continues to answer questions from the Greek Christians, who were troubled about whether they should eat food known to have been offered to an idol. The answer is, harm is only done if a fellow-Christian is offended by what he sees you doing. Our guiding principle must be sensitivity to the feelings of others.

CWL: *Revelation 12:1-5a*
CONTEXT: The sealed truths disclosed, the trumpets have sounded for woe and the final conflict begins.
IDEAS: The mother and child; Satan sees the Incarnation; flight to safety.

The last of these Sunday word-pictures of visions revealed to John speaks of a mother bearing a holy child, the dragon of evil, and everything kept safe in the firm hand of God.

Mark 1:21-28
CONTEXT: Jesus returns from the wilderness and begins to gather followers.
IDEAS: Beginnings at Capernaum; teaching in synagogue; Jesus's authority.

Mark begins Jesus's public ministry in a synagogue. When a man troubled in mind and body finds Jesus threatening, he is stilled with a word of divine authority. Everyone is amazed, and the reputation of Jesus for teaching and healing becomes widespread.

Year B: The Presentation of Christ in the Temple: Candlemas

Malachi 3:1-5
CONTEXT: About 500 BC, return from exile but under Persian rule.
IDEAS: Restoration of nationhood and Temple worship; the fate of those who cannot face the Lord's coming.

In today's Gospel, Simeon will greet the infant Jesus in the Temple. Malachi speaks of the Lord coming suddenly; he knows, like Simeon, that to encounter the Lord is a mixed blessing because we have to face his testing and purifying.

Hebrews 2:14-18
CONTEXT: The theology of the humanity and divinity of Jesus.
IDEAS: Christ fully human; he is our help under all trials.

Christ became flesh and blood like us, says this writer, and we shall hear how his parents did the same as for every first-born child in Israel. Jesus fully shared our human condition, so that he could unite us all to God.

Luke 2:22-40
CONTEXT: See Exodus 13:1-2 and Leviticus 12:6-8.
IDEAS: Religious duty; offering; holy waiting; visionaries.

As the Law requires, Jesus the first-born is brought to the Temple with a thank-offering. Two old and holy people, Simeon and Anna, perceive that this child is the fulfilment of ancient prophecies of redemption, but the glory will not be without pain and suffering.

Year B: CWL Proper 1, RCL Epiphany 5
(3-9 February, if earlier than 2 before Lent.)

Isaiah 40:21-31
CONTEXT: Second Isaiah – exile in Babylon. God in his majesty orders all things.
IDEAS: God beyond compare – unknowable in his fullness; ever-active creator and renewer.

This passage is the beginning of the work of a different writer, in a later period than the first Isaiah, whose warnings have now come true and Israel is in exile in Babylon. The people's faith wavers, but this prophet assures them God never grows faint nor weary, but is always active to renew his people's strength.

1 Corinthians 9:16-23
CONTEXT: Answering various questions from Corinth – Paul's recommendation about sensitivity to others; his own undemanding, self-sacrificial life.
IDEAS: Christian freedom; apostolic credentials and rewards; self-giving.

Paul has been writing about Christians being sensitive to each other's feelings. Now he explains that he himself always tries to adapt his preaching to his audience, so as never to harm or give offence.

Mark 1:29-39
CONTEXT: A synagogue healing – four of the Twelve already recruited.
IDEAS: Healing strangers and friends alike; demanding crowds – retreats.

Mark's story of Jesus has barely begun, but hastens on to three incidents after Jesus has shown his authority at a synagogue. Peter's mother-in-law is healed, then a great number of sick people. And so Jesus tries to find a quiet space for prayer before widening his work beyond Capernaum.

Year B: CWL Proper 2, RCL Epiphany 6
(10-16 February, if earlier than 2 before Lent.)

2 Kings 5:1-14
CONTEXT: A collection of miracle-stories showing the power of Elijah.
IDEAS: Biblical and modern leprosy; where is healing found? Do the simple things that God requires.

This reading complements the Gospel, as a story of men with leprosy, and God's healing power. Both Naaman and the leper who met Jesus are told to do something very simple to complete their cure.

1 Corinthians 9:24-27
CONTEXT: Christian behaviour – what is acceptable; Paul's own self-sacrificing testimony.
IDEAS: Spiritual and physical discipline.

This short extract follows last Sunday's reading about sensitivity and self-control. Christian disciples need to observe a personal discipline, says Paul, like an athlete in training. The prize for us is imperishable.

Mark 1:40-45
CONTEXT: Jesus's early work in and around Capernaum.
IDEAS: Biblical and modern leprosy; ratifying a cure (Lev 14); Jesus's strong emotions.

Mark has summarised much of Jesus's early ministry in a single phrase about teaching and healing. Now he records a specific incident, when Jesus healed a leper with a touch. The man ignores a warning to tell no-one, and Mark introduces one of the major themes of his Gospel: who is this Jesus, and where does his power come from?

Year B: CWL Proper 3 RCL Epiphany 7
(17-23 February, if earlier than 2 before Lent.)

Isaiah 43:18-25
CONTEXT: The Lord's promise of deliverance from Babylon, and renewal, despite the people's unfaithfulness.
IDEAS: All things new; our sins weary God; God forgives.

Isaiah promises a new initiative by God. Despite the people's failure to serve God and honour him, he will forgive their sin as only God can, and as Jesus did.

2 Corinthians 1:18-22
CONTEXT: Paul had been unable to make a visit apparently promised in a severe letter which has not been preserved.
IDEAS: Circumstances alter cases; God's constant immutability.

In this letter Paul felt the need to explain why he had not fulfilled his promise to visit. This leads him to make a profound statement about the God who is ever constant, ever faithful, ever reliable, summed up in the one word 'Yes'.

Mark 2:1-12
CONTEXT: Jesus proclaiming the kingdom in Capernaum and Galilee.
IDEAS: Crowds around the Lord; persistence; who can forgive sin?

The friends of a paralysed man were determined to bring him to Jesus, who healed him and pronounced his sins forgiven. All three synoptic gospels tell us how this seemed like a blasphemy to the Jews, because only God can forgive sin. No wonder they were troubled by Jesus.

Year B: CWL Second Sunday before Lent, RCL Epiphany 8

RCL readings; see following page for CWL readings.

Hosea 2:14-20
CONTEXT: Israel compared to Hosea's own unfaithful wife.
IDEAS: Love that never runs out; church the Bride of Christ; renewed covenant.

Hosea drew from his own troubled marriage a parallel with God's relationship to Israel. He uses the language of courtship, betrothal and marriage to speak of God's continuing love for his unfaithful people.

2 Corinthians 3:1b-6
CONTEXT: Paul's defence of his apostolic credentials.
IDEAS: Uses of letters and words; Christ in our heart; no power of ourselves to help ourselves.

Paul has written other letters to these Christians, and in this one he says that the word of the Lord is now written in our hearts. For himself, he claims no power other than what God is doing from within his heart.

Mark 2:13-22
CONTEXT: Jesus's ministry in Galilee.
IDEAS: Bias to the despised; joy when Jesus is present; his presence always a challenge.

We continue from last Sunday our reading of this Gospel, in which Mark has shown how popular Jesus was. But very soon his unusual friendships and his unconventional behaviour began to provoke the criticism which he would face throughout his life.

Year B: CWL Second Sunday before Lent, RCL Epiphany 8

CWL readings; see preceding page for RCL readings.

Proverbs 8:1, 22-31
CONTEXT: A collection of traditional teachings from many centuries – and some non-Israelite sources. The 'Wisdom of God' speaks in her own voice.
IDEAS: God's wisdom personified – present in creation, when all was play and delight (vv. 30, 31).

John's Gospel says that in the beginning was the Word. In this collection of ancient proverbs, we hear that in the beginning God created Wisdom, to be his companion, his joy and delight, and to work with him in the creation of this world.

Colossians 1:15-20
CONTEXT: Emphasis on Christ as superior to all other real or imagined beings.
IDEAS: Christ in creation; other supernatural beings/powers.

To ancient thinkers, wisdom was a person of God, present in creation. Paul applies this to Jesus. All that is, seen and unseen, was created through Christ; and now his resurrection life reconciles everything to God.

John 1:1-14
CONTEXT: The divine disclosure in the Word made flesh.
IDEAS: Christ as *Logos* – Word, present in creation; seen on earth, rejected by many but new life for all believers.

As a prologue to his story of Jesus, John sets out for us its background in eternity. When God's Word came to his world it was to bring us light and life.

Year B: : CWL The Sunday next before Lent RCL Epiphany 9

CWL readings: optional in RCL; see next page for the RCL-only alternatives.

2 Kings 2:1-12
CONTEXT: A direct continuation of 1 Kings – Elisha succeeds Elijah, in the crises of the 9th century BC.
IDEAS: The loyal successor; visionary experiences; Elijah's 'departure' led to expectations of his return.

Today's readings all speak of the mystery of glory sometimes revealed when earth and heaven are united. When Elijah's great prophetic work was done, we are told he was taken up to heaven with wind and fire, and his powers were inherited by Elisha.

2 Corinthians 4:3-6
CONTEXT: Paul's apostolic commission and the ministry of creative speaking/writing.
IDEAS: Not everyone can see the Gospel clearly; light and glory.

This passage is chosen to harmonise with today's theme of glory. Christ is glorious, says Paul, with the glory of God himself, and the light he brings shines in our hearts.

Mark 9:2-9
CONTEXT: The darker side of what will happen to Jesus begins to be disclosed, even as his true nature is revealed.
IDEAS: Moses and Elijah symbolising Law and Prophets – completed and fulfilled in Jesus; God encountered on mountain-tops; the 'cloud' of God's presence; a few see what all may long for.

The Lord's closest friends see him transfigured upon a mountain-top, in a disclosure of his true identity. In the presence of the figures of Moses and Elijah, a cloud of glory comes upon him and the voice of the holy one is heard.

Year B: CWL The Sunday next before Lent, RCL Epiphany 9

RCL only; see preceding page for CWL readings, which are alternatives in RCL.

Deuteronomy 5:12-15
CONTEXT: A review of the Sinai covenant and the Law as given.
IDEAS: Sabbath rest.

One of the Ten Commandments is to keep the Sabbath holy. In today's Gospel, Jesus challenges people's idea of what that meant. Here is one of the Bible's two versions of the law of the Sabbath.

2 Corinthians 4:5-12
CONTEXT: Paul defending and justifying his apostleship.
IDEAS: God's power not ours; the hardships of vocation.

All the resources for Paul's ministry come from his inner life with Jesus, and all his ordinary daily hardships serve to emphasise the light which transforms his heart and can also lighten ours.

Mark 2:23-3:6
CONTEXT: Capernaum and Galilee teaching and healing.
IDEAS: Sabbath observance; using Scripture; opposition becomes serious.

Mark has been showing us that the popularity of Jesus around the Galilean towns and villages was always tempered by the radical challenges he presented. His unconventional approach to the law of Sabbath observance now begins the controversies which brought him to his cross.

Year B: Ash Wednesday

Joel 2:1-2, 12-17
CONTEXT: Visionary apocalyptic of the Day of the Lord.
IDEAS: God's coming will be fearsome – yet gracious to the penitent; come together and fast.

The powerful and dramatic words of Joel are a solemn call to public repentance, to realise the divine mercy and goodness. It helps set the tone of the Lenten season as a time for self-examination and spiritual renewal, in preparation for the gifts of Easter.

OR *Isaiah 58:1-12*
CONTEXT: The restored community are ignoring the ways of God.
IDEAS: Right motives for fasting; right ways of fasting.

The prophet denounces the hypocrisy of people who make gestures of fasting but practice injustice and deceit. Make your fast work for God: he will hear you when you ask what you should do.

2 Corinthians 5:20b-6:10
CONTEXT: An appeal to Christians not to let grace go for nothing, but sustain mutual reconciliation.
IDEAS: God's work of reconciliation; preaching without self-glorification.

Paul calls upon the Corinthian Christians to be reconciled and reconcilers. He offers his own way of life as an example of the way of a peace-maker – to bear suffering, avoid self-aggrandisement, speak the truth in love.

Matthew 6:1-6, 16-21
CONTEXT: Sermon on the Mount – teaching on prayer and fasting.
IDEAS: vv. 2, 5 & 16 reiterate 'when', not 'if'; public and private devotion.

Jesus contrasts those who do religious acts to gain admiration from others with those who are sincere. All our acts of piety, whether fasting or the symbolic use of ashes, are worthless unless they express the spirit of true penitence, embodied in a life of prayer and service.

Alternative Gospel overleaf.

OR *John 8:1-11*

CONTEXT: A Passover visit to Jerusalem. (Many scholars regard this as not correctly a part of 'John', but an isolated pericope in the synoptic tradition.)

IDEAS: God infinitely merciful: no punishment. But don't sin again!

In Lent we are reminded of the need for repentance, as we hear again how God in Christ comes to us in forgiving tenderness. Jesus will not allow a sinful woman to be punished; his love offers new life free from sin.

Year B: The First Sunday of Lent

Genesis 9:8-17
CONTEXT: The great Flood saga comes to an end.
IDEAS: New covenants; new beginnings; signs.

During Lent this year we hear from Israel's books of the Law those passages which tell of the covenants that bind God and his people together. After the great flood, Noah and his family set out on God's new beginning for humanity, under a covenant promising God's new blessing to all creation.

1 Peter 3:18-22
CONTEXT: Christians under suffering and abuse.
IDEAS: Christ suffered for us, now glorified; links Noah/water to baptism (in the Gospel).

The writer explains the symbolic meaning of Noah and the flood water. Through the water used in Christian baptism everyone is brought to God's safety, because Christ has died, Christ is risen, and the power of his resurrection is present for us.

Mark 1:9-15
CONTEXT: John baptising, proclaiming the coming one.
IDEAS: Jesus submits to John's baptism; divine declaration; desert retreat; Gospel proclamation of repentance.

This Sunday's readings all have the powerful image of salvation through water. We hear now Mark's account of the baptism of Jesus, then Our Lord's call to repent and believe his good news. So begins our Lenten preparation, for those to be baptised at Easter, and for us all to reaffirm our baptismal covenant promises.

Year B: The Second Sunday of Lent

Genesis 17:1-7, 15-16
CONTEXT: The Lord's covenants and promises to Abraham.
IDEAS: New names; families and descendants; covenants.

This Lent our Old Testament readings pick out those moments in Israel's history when God seemed to have made new promises to his people, which the Bible calls 'covenants'. Here, the faithful Abraham and Sarah are promised descendants who will become a great nation, and the Lord will be their God for ever.

Romans 4:13-25
CONTEXT: Law and sin, faith and righteousness – what about Abraham?
IDEAS: Abraham's descendants and the promise; sheer grace.

Paul reminds his readers of God's covenant promise to Abraham and Sarah. It was their faithfulness that was blessed by God. So too we receive blessing by our faith in Christ raised from the dead.

Mark 8:31-38
CONTEXT: End of the Galilean ministry – after the successes, the tone becomes more sombre.
IDEAS: Peter inspired (v. 29) and fallible; living for self.

As Jesus began to reveal his destiny, Peter could not bear it. But Jesus teaches that just as his way was one of suffering for others, so for us all selfishness must be renounced as we take up our own cross.

OR (RCL only) *Mark 9:2-9*
CONTEXT: The darker side of what will happen to Jesus begins to be disclosed, even as his true nature is revealed.
IDEAS: Moses and Elijah symbolising Law and Prophets – completed and fulfilled in Jesus; God encountered on mountain-tops; the 'cloud' of God's presence; a few see what all may long for.

The Lord's closest friends see him transfigured upon a mountain-top, in a disclosure of his true identity. In the presence of the figures of Moses and Elijah, a cloud of glory comes upon him and the voice of the holy one is heard.

Year B: The Third Sunday of Lent

Exodus 20:1-17
CONTEXT: Three months after leaving Egypt, the Israelites reach Sinai; God appears on the mountain.
IDEAS: Holy places; holy laws; Christian perspectives on Commandments.

Our weekly readings continue the theme of God's covenants with his people. He requires obedience to his commandments, the heart of the Jewish Law and a foundation of Christian moral principles.

1 Corinthians 1:18-25
CONTEXT: Paul's corrective to congregational disputes.
IDEAS: God's wisdom versus human folly; human wisdom versus revelation.

To proclaim Christ nailed to a cross seems offensively foolish, says Paul, yet in reality it displays God's loving wisdom and mysterious saving power.

John 2:13-22
CONTEXT: Jesus making an early Passover visit to Jerusalem – uniquely to John.
IDEAS: Uses of 'holy' buildings; temple/church 'taxes'; the violent Jesus.

As we near the time to remember again the fateful confrontation between Jesus and the Temple authorities, we hear John's account of Jesus driving out all those who perverted the Temple's purposes for personal gain. From his resurrection perspective, John reflects on what this event means.

Year B: The Fourth Sunday of Lent

See next page for CWL readings if this Sunday is kept as Mothering Sunday.

Numbers 21:4-9
CONTEXT: The Israelites on the last stage of their journey to Canaan, the land of the Lord's promise. Progress both by detour (20:21) and victory (21:3).
IDEAS: Yet again blame the leadership; snakes (serpents) in Scripture; simply look (?ask) and be healed (cf. Wisdom 16:7).

For the third time in the Bible, the Israelites on the pilgrimage to the Promised Land run out of food and water. This time there is no miraculous supply, only some relief from snake-bites when Moses made a serpent of bronze for healing. As Jesus reminded his hearers, whenever people raised their eyes to this sign, their illness was lifted from them.

Ephesians 2:1-10
CONTEXT: Praise and prayer to God, who has made Christ head of the church.
IDEAS: Gentiles too are saved; Christ is raised and so are we; grace alone, not works.

It is by God's grace that we are saved, not by any effort of our own. Christ has been raised up into God's presence, and draws us up with him from death to life.

John 3:14-21
CONTEXT: Jesus in Jerusalem for Passover (a visit not referred to by the other Gospels).
IDEAS: 'Lifting-up' = crucifixion and glorification; faith brings eternal life.

Three times John's Gospel has Jesus speaking of being 'lifted up'. In this passage, Jesus recalls Moses lifting up the serpent for the healing of the people. Just so, says Jesus, the Son of Man must be lifted up, so that those who look to him and believe in him may have eternal life.

Year B: CWL Mothering Sunday

See previous page if this Sunday is kept as the Fourth Sunday of Lent.

Exodus 2:1-10
CONTEXT: There are too many Israelites for Egypt's stability: forced labour, and death to all male babies.
IDEAS: Mother's care for child; the eventual hero left to die and rescued.

The mother of Moses worked a deception to preserve her son's life, when the Egyptians were controlling the population by killing every new-born Jewish boy.

OR *1 Samuel 1:20-28*
CONTEXT: Elkanah and his two wives: Peninnah has children but Hannah has none and is mocked for it.
IDEAS: Longing for motherhood; barren wives conceive; God-given child offered back to God's service.

Samuel, that great Old Testament figure, was born to a mother who for years had been unable to bear a son. In thankfulness for God's gift, his mother took him to the Lord's house to give him back to God.

2 Corinthians 1:3-7
CONTEXT: A letter mostly of joy that the crisis in the Corinthian church was now overcome.
IDEAS: God is ever-present in trouble.

Paul writes of the consoling strength of God, the one we can all turn to in trouble, and how this grace we receive enables us to sustain one another.

OR *Colossians 3:12-17*
CONTEXT: Instructions in Christian behaviour – avoid all hurtful ways.
IDEAS: The enduring virtues, all summed up in love.

Paul writes of the compassionate gifts, forgiveness and love. These, received and given always in the name of Jesus, are a vocation for us all.

Luke 2:33-35
CONTEXT: Purification, presentation of Christ in the Temple.
IDEAS: Joseph and Mary's bewilderment; mother's suffering foreshadowed.

Jesus is the son of a human mother, just like us. In the Gospel, his earthly father and mother fade into the shadows as the nature of his life is hinted at. Yet we never forget his home, the love and teaching he received.

OR *John 19:25-27*
CONTEXT: The crucifixion of Jesus.
IDEAS: Jesus's mother sees him die; his love and concern for her.

Mary, who gave birth to Jesus, is there to watch his ugly death. Every mother's heart can suffer with her. In his last agony, Jesus's love for his mother ensures that she is not left alone.

Year B: The Fifth Sunday of Lent
(Passiontide begins)

Jeremiah 31:31-34
CONTEXT: The proclamation that God will restore both Judah and Israel.
IDEAS: Covenants; God's work of replanting/rebuilding after catastrophe (= death & resurrection).

Our Lenten readings have illustrated God's historic covenants with his people. Now, we hear Jeremiah's prophecy of an entirely new covenant, not based on ancient Law so easy to break, but written deep in the hearts of everyone who longs to know and be known by God.

Hebrews 5:5-10
CONTEXT: Jesus, apostle of our faith and high priest who opens heaven to us.
IDEAS: Christ subject to, and wholly obedient to, God; he became perfect.

The task of the Jewish High Priest was to offer sacrifices to God on behalf of sinful people. This writer says that Christ, by offering himself to God through his life and death, has become the source of eternal salvation for all who obey him.

John 12:20-33
CONTEXT: Jesus in and around Jerusalem preparing for Passover.
IDEAS: Death and glory; losing and keeping; light and dark.

Jesus was human enough to be greatly disturbed at what he sensed lay before him. Yet he will glorify his Father's name, trusting in that power not only to lift him up but draw all people to himself.

Year B: Palm Sunday

Mark 11:1-11 OR *John 12:12-16*
Within the Liturgy of the Palms, this passage precedes the procession, which is itself a dramatic commentary. It is therefore best read without introduction.

Isaiah 50:4-9a
CONTEXT: A 'Servant Song' of mission and suffering.
IDEAS: Obedience to God; patient dignity and endurance.

Isaiah pictures a faithful servant of God who is deeply and unjustly humiliated, but remains dignified in suffering. As we contemplate the mystery of the cross, these words take on a profound meaning for us in the Passion of Jesus.

Philippians 2:5-11
CONTEXT: Paul in prison, writing to friends.
IDEAS: The humility of Christ and his exaltation.

It is our faith that 'Jesus Christ is Lord', because he came from God in total self-giving, and overcame the humiliation of death on a cross by rising and ascending. He is indeed worthy of our adoration and worship.

Mark 14:1-15:47 OR *Mark 15:1-39 [& 40-47]*
Traditionally, the Gospel narrative of the passion and death of Jesus has no introduction except formal words such as: 'The Passion of Our Lord Jesus Christ according to Mark'.

Year B: Monday of Holy Week

Isaiah 42:1-9
CONTEXT: The first 'Servant Song' – Israel is God's servant, but we may read these songs as prophecies of Jesus.
IDEAS: God acknowledges his Servant; quiet bringing-in of justice; light for all nations.

The Isaiah readings these next three days are appropriately called 'Servant Songs'. Whatever their original application, they speak to us of the Jesus who did not complain as he faithfully walked the way of the cross for the world's salvation.

Hebrews 9:11-15
CONTEXT: The old covenant and high-priestly sacrificial duties.
IDEAS: Christ the new and perfect high priest; his own blood; new covenant.

Christ's offering of himself in his perfect purity, says this writer, completes and transcends all the sacrificial offerings made by the priests. He has procured for us what no other could: our eternal redemption.

John 12:1-11
CONTEXT: Jesus in and near Jerusalem preparing for Passover.
IDEAS: The last week of Jesus's life; company of friends; anointing for burial.

Throughout this week we follow John's account of the way to the cross. The week begins for Jesus in the home of his friends, where Mary of Bethany anoints his feet. Some condemn what they regard as wasteful, but Jesus accepts her gift as foreshadowing his impending death and burial.

Year B: Tuesday of Holy Week

Isaiah 49:1-7

CONTEXT: Second 'Servant Song' – the restoration of Israel from Babylon.
IDEAS: Vocation; revelation; light for the world.

This week's readings are the 'Servant Songs' of Isaiah, each of which speaks of the suffering that accompanies faithful witness. The prophet may have meant that Israel was the Servant, but we read it as the vocation of Jesus who, though he was despised, was true to God's will and brings light to all the ends of the earth.

1 Corinthians 1:18-3

CONTEXT: Paul's corrective to congregational disputes.
IDEAS: God's wisdom versus human folly; human wisdom versus revelation.

The cross of Christ, says Paul, is an offensive folly to most people, yet in reality it displays God's loving wisdom. We must stop trusting in our own wisdom and skills if we are to discern how freedom, salvation and righteousness are found in this cross.

John 12:20-36

CONTEXT: Jesus in and around Jerusalem preparing for Passover.
IDEAS: Death and glory; losing and keeping; light and dark.

In the week before he died, Jesus often spoke of his own suffering as being his glorification, but most people did not understand him. Those who do walk the way of the cross with him will share his light and become children of the light.

Year B: Wednesday of Holy Week

Isaiah 50:4-9a
CONTEXT: Third 'Servant Song' – of mission and suffering.
IDEAS: Obedience to God; patient dignity and endurance.

In this third of Isaiah's Servant Songs we hear of the humiliation unjustly suffered by one who teaches and consoles others. As we contemplate the mystery of the cross, these words take on a profound meaning for us in the Passion of Jesus.

Hebrews 12:1-3
CONTEXT: The great faith shown in past ages.
IDEAS: All the witnesses; perseverance; Jesus changes a cross into glory.

This writer urges us to keep our eyes fixed on Jesus. He was not deflected from his task by the ordeal he faced, and we are surrounded by examples of faithfulness which should strengthen our own resolve.

John 13:21-32
CONTEXT: Jesus in and near Jerusalem; farewell discourses to disciples.
IDEAS: Jesus betrayed; why did Judas do it? Evil turns to good in God's hands.

We are following John's narrative of the week leading Jesus to Calvary. Now and tomorrow the scene is the Last Supper, where Jesus seems to know that Judas will betray him. It was the darkest of moments when, John says, 'Judas went out. It was night.' Yet this passage does not end in despair but in Jesus glorified.

Year B: Maundy Thursday

Exodus 12:1-4 [& 5-10], 11-14
CONTEXT: The Israelites' hurried escape from Egyptian slavery.
IDEAS: Archetypal salvation event; Passover remembered and celebrated ever since.

At his last supper with his friends, Jesus transformed a Passover meal into our constant remembrance of the salvation we have in him. Appropriately today, we recall the story of the first Passover, the great saving event in Jewish history.

1 Corinthians 11:23-26
CONTEXT: How a divided congregation is to observe the Lord's Supper.
IDEAS: Eucharistic tradition; remembrance and proclamation.

This is almost certainly the earliest account of the Lord's Supper as celebrated by the church. Paul reminds the Corinthians that it was from the Lord that he received this tradition, and handed it on.

John 13:1-17, 31b-35
CONTEXT: Jesus's final meal with his friends.
IDEAS: Humble service; the ultimate commandment is to love.

We remember now another event of that night. Jesus washed his disciples' feet, and gave them a new commandment – the word is 'mandate', or 'maundy' – to follow his example in loving service to one another.

Year B: Good Friday

Isaiah 52:13-53:12
CONTEXT: Fourth 'Servant Song' – leading the return from Babylon (52:11).
IDEAS: Humiliation without complaint; despised and rejected for our sake.

This poem of God's servant facing suffering picks up a theme from earlier readings this week. Although written centuries before Jesus, it has become for Christians one of the most profound meditations on the events and the deep meaning of Good Friday.

Hebrews 10:16-25
CONTEXT: The place of sacrifice in human approaches to God.
IDEAS: Sin forgiven; nothing separates us from God; Christ's perfect priesthood.

The writer of this letter helps our solemn reflection on what Jesus did for us this day. The Jewish sacrificial priesthood could only dare approach God's holiness with offerings and with fear. But in Christ all our sins are forgiven, and we are free to know the new, living, open way to God.

OR *Hebrews 4:14-16, 5:7-9*
CONTEXT: Scripture tells of many partial understandings of God – Jesus perfectly opens to us his intimate knowledge.
IDEAS: The sinless High Priesthood of Jesus; his suffering obedience; our access to God.

By what he did this day Jesus became a greater high priest than there has ever been, making it possible for us to approach God without fear. The work of Christ is the means of our salvation.

John 18:1-19:42
Announce as: The Passion of Our Lord Jesus Christ according to John.

Year B: Easter Eve
For use at services other than the Easter Vigil

Job 14:1-14
CONTEXT: A theology of innocent suffering; a poetic cycle of speeches.
IDEAS: Transience of human life; in nature, new life follows death.

Job contemplates the fact that every human life ends in death. Plants cut down may rise again, but he knows of no such resurrection when we die.

OR *Lamentations 3:1-9, 19-24*
CONTEXT: Poems of lament over the fall of Jerusalem to Babylonia (587 BC).
IDEAS: Affliction within God's purposes; patient suffering; new mornings.

This writer is filled with anguish for himself and for Israel, but the reading ends in a confident and patient waiting for an act of God's love that comes 'new every morning'.

1 Peter 4:1-8
CONTEXT: Letter to Gentile Christians, probably under (Nero? Domitian?) persecution.
IDEAS: Enduring suffering and abuse; Christ 'descended to the dead'; the End is nigh.

The readers of this letter were enduring Roman persecution. The encouraging reminder here is that it was through suffering that Christ put an end to sin. The writer also hints at the idea of Christ descending to a place of the dead in an act of rescue.

Matthew 27:57-66
CONTEXT: Jesus has died; the body to be decently interred.
IDEAS: Generous act of Joseph; women waiting and mourning; Jewish fears that the story does not end here.

On the evening Jesus died, his body was decently placed in a tomb before the Sabbath. But even in death his influence lives on, as the religious authorities become anxious about what might happen next.

OR *John 19:38-42*
CONTEXT: Jesus has died; the body to be decently interred.
IDEAS: Acts of Joseph and Nicodemus; burial before Sabbath.

Two friends of Jesus, of whom we know so little, take care that his body is reverently placed in a garden tomb, in good time before the Sabbath when such work could not be done.

Year B: Easter Vigil

No introductions are provided for the readings at the Easter Vigil. Churches will wish to make their own choices from the provision of the Lectionary, and may use the opportunity to create a devotional sequence of lessons with psalms or canticles. It may be felt that on this occasion any introductory material to the readings would be intrusive.

Year B: Easter Day

Acts 10:34-43
CONTEXT: Peter's teaching to a Roman centurion.
IDEAS: The life and work of Jesus; forgiveness effective for everyone.
[*If the readings from Acts will be used as the first lesson throughout the Easter season:*
During the Easter season, in place of the Hebrew Scriptures, we read the witness of the early church to the power of the Lord's resurrection.]
This is a small part of the story of Peter and a centurion of the Roman occupying army, when the Gospel first reached beyond the Jews. The teaching sums up Jesus's old and new life.
OR *Isaiah 25:6-9*
CONTEXT: Praise to God for the deliverance he will bring about.
IDEAS: The (Messianic) banquet; holy mountains; joy for all in salvation.
The prophet holds out God's promise of a joyful end to all human travail, when there will be feasting and rejoicing as death is destroyed for ever and God saves his people.

1 Corinthians 15:1-11
CONTEXT: A new topic in the letter – perhaps answering another question (see 7:1) about resurrection.
IDEAS: Ours is a resurrection faith and Gospel; Christ's appearances.
Paul writes here of the very heart of the gospel: the fact that Jesus was raised from death and seen by many people. Paul's own apostleship, he says, stems from the appearance to him of the risen Christ.
OR *Acts 10:34-43: See above.*

John 20:1-18
CONTEXT: Jesus has died and is buried; after the Sabbath, mourning can resume.
IDEAS: The empty tomb; Peter and (?) John rush in; Jesus unrecognised; Mary the apostle to the apostles; incredibly good news.

Mary Magdalene is sometimes called 'The Apostle to the Apostles', for she was the first to see the risen Lord and tell the others. But his appearance had changed, and only love speaking to love made him known to her.

OR *Mark 16:1-8*
CONTEXT: The body of Jesus buried by Joseph; women watch.
IDEAS: Angelic messengers; complete bewilderment; news of the resurrection.

After the Sabbath, the women came to anoint the body of Jesus, but were amazed to find the tomb empty. A strange figure tells them he has been raised, and they must prepare the other disciples to see him again.

Year B: The Second Sunday of Easter

CWL: If the Old Testament reading is used, the reading from Acts must be used as the second reading.

CWL: *Exodus 14:10-31, 15:20-21*
CONTEXT: The Israelites have just left Egypt, taking the long way round (13:18). Pharoah then regrets the absence of the slaves and sets out after them.
IDEAS: The past was better (vv. 11, 12); a mighty miracle – the Lord acts to save.

The Jews continue to this day to give thanks for their deliverance from slavery, just as Christians continually give thanks for our salvation in Jesus. At the time of the Exodus, the Lord worked a great saving miracle at the Red Sea.

Acts 4:32-35
CONTEXT: The church in Jerusalem preaching the risen Christ, and developing a common life.
IDEAS: Possessions; living in community; care for needy.

[*If the Old Testament reading is not used:* During the Easter season, instead of reading the Hebrew Scriptures, we hear the experiences of those who were witnesses to the resurrection.]
Despite continuing harassment by the Jewish authorities, the believers in Jerusalem began to develop a new style of community life under the apostles' leadership, sharing everything and meeting everyone's needs.

1 John 1:1-2:2
CONTEXT: Prologue and opening of this tract or homily, whose main theme is the incarnation – the Word made flesh.
IDEAS: God heard and seen; joy of eternal life here and now; light and darkness; sin and forgiveness.

These Sundays of Eastertide we shall hear a series of passages from this letter. The eternal life from God, writes John, has been seen and touched on earth in the person of his incarnate Word. Now we know God's pure light, and in it we are cleansed and forgiven.

John 20:19-31

CONTEXT: The evening of Resurrection Day – Mary Magdalene is the only witness thus far.
IDEAS: Disciples keep together for safety; the same Jesus, wounded; commissioning with Holy Spirit and 'sent'; seeing and believing.

On the first Easter evening, Jesus appears to his disciples with his habitual greeting of peace, and a gift of the Holy Spirit. Thomas must wait another week until he can see, believe, and adore.

Year B: The Third Sunday of Easter

CWL: If the Old Testament reading is used, the reading from Acts must be used as the second reading.

CWL Zephaniah 3:14-20
CONTEXT: Judah and her neighbours to be destroyed for disobedience – but a remnant will be preserved.
IDEAS: The Lord is here – his Spirit is with us; gathered together by God.

This prophet of the 7th century BC sees a time when all will be joy and peace, for God will have saved his people, renewed them in his love, and will dwell in their midst.

Acts 3:12-19
CONTEXT: Peter and John together heal a cripple.
IDEAS: Whose healing power? Resurrection witnesses; prophecies fulfilled.

[*If the Old Testament reading is not used:* During the Easter season, instead of reading the Hebrew Scriptures, we hear some of the inspired activities of the followers of Jesus.]
Peter and John discovered that the power of the risen Christ was at work through them, to heal as he had done. Peter explained this miracle, and called the people to repent and believe in the Messiah whom the Jews had rejected.

1 John 3:1-7
CONTEXT: A treatise on the reality of the incarnation, and our call to remain steadfast.
IDEAS: Children of our Father in heaven; Christlikeness; sinlessness.

We do not know what our life after death will be like. Our faith is that we shall see and know completely the Christ whom we follow here, and so we shall be like him. Therefore, we must here and now put away all sin.

Luke 24:36b-48
CONTEXT: The 'Emmaus Road Two' returned to Jerusalem where the company were sharing the resurrection news.
IDEAS: A truly risen body; suffering Messiah; searching Scripture.

The appearances of the risen Jesus were always unexpected. This is Luke's end of the first Easter Day, and shows us Jesus still teaching his friends how the Scriptures were fulfilled in what has happened.

Year B: The Fourth Sunday of Easter

CWL: If the Old Testament reading is used, the reading from Acts must be used as the second reading.

CWL: *Genesis 7:1-5, 11-18, 8:6-18, 9:8-13*
CONTEXT: The world progressively worse since Eden, humankind proliferates and wickedness increases.
IDEAS: Myths and sagas adopted and adapted; new beginnings; the Ark of salvation and covenant.

The story of Noah is abbreviated in this reading. We hear the beginning, part of the middle, and the ending. In the ancient flood story, God destroys the wicked world, but uses Noah's obedience to save humanity and all created things so that there may be a new beginning.

Acts 4:5-12
CONTEXT: Peter and John arrested for preaching resurrection in the Temple.
IDEAS: Powers of the Sanhedrin under Rome; power in Jesus's Name.
[*If the Old Testament reading is not used:* **During the Easter season, instead of reading the Hebrew Scriptures, we hear some of the activities of the new Christians.**]
The followers of Jesus soon antagonised the Jewish authorities by preaching his resurrection. Peter explained to them how the power of Jesus lives on because God raised him from the dead.

1 John 3:16-24
CONTEXT: Christians to love one another, though hated by 'the world'.
IDEAS: Emulate Christ in our actions; clear conscience; prayer.

We continue to read John's first letter of Christian love, and hear that this must result in loving action. A clear conscience opens our way to God.

John 10:11-18
CONTEXT: Jesus picking up O.T. shepherd metaphors and applying them to himself.
IDEAS: Dying for the sheep; divine knowledge of us; seek others to bring in.

The ancient idea of the leader as a good shepherd of his people has been fulfilled in Jesus. He knows us intimately, and loves us enough to die for us.

Year B: The Fifth Sunday of Easter

CWL: If the Apocryphal or Old Testament reading is used, the reading from Acts must be used as the second reading.

CWL: *Baruch 3:9-15, 32-4:4*
CONTEXT: A late (?150 BC) anthology of poems, songs and prayers, attached to the name of Jeremiah's secretary.
IDEAS: The praise of wisdom, personified; God is incomparable.

This Apocryphal book was written much later than the Baruch we know as Jeremiah's secretary, though it contains some references to that period. This passage is typical of Hebrew wisdom literature – many of the words used about wisdom are the same as we use of Jesus. Wisdom appeared on earth and lived among us.

OR CWL: *Genesis 22:1-18*
CONTEXT: The last important sign of Abraham's total trust and obedience.
IDEAS: God tests the strong; prepare to sacrifice what you most love; faith and certainties; [God's] son given to suffer and die.

In today's Gospel, both Jesus and Judas Iscariot come to a moment of decision. In this passage, Abraham's faith and obedience are tested to the uttermost. He must be prepared to let his only son suffer and die if God is to work out his plan of salvation.

Acts 8:26-40
CONTEXT: Persecution of the church has become serious – disciples begin to disperse throughout Judea and Samaria.
IDEAS: God's promptings to action; understanding the O.T.; Christianity reaches Africa; baptism as response to faith.

[*If the Old Testament reading is not used:* During the Easter season, instead of reading the Hebrew Scriptures, we hear some of the events that befell the first Christian witnesses.]
The church soon began to reach beyond Jerusalem. Before this event, Philip, a deacon, had made converts in Samaria. Now, by way of a roadside encounter with an Ethiopian official, he spreads the good news even further.

1 John 4:7-21
CONTEXT: There are false 'spirits' and false prophets – be wary.
IDEAS: God's love underpins all ours; mutual indwelling; no longer fear God's punishment.

John, the great apostle of love, implores us to recognise how great is God's love shown in Jesus, and to live as those who are united by that love both to God and to one another.

John 15:1-8
CONTEXT: The farewell discourses – many words of encouragement.
IDEAS: Mutual indwelling; Christians energised by Christ; love God and each other, whatever the consequences.

In his letter John wrote of how we dwell in God and he in us. In this Gospel reading Jesus uses the metaphor of the vine to describe the way his life works in us, and how this bears fruit in loving action.

Year B: The Sixth Sunday of Easter

CWL: If the Old Testament reading is used, the reading from Acts must be used as the second reading.

CWL *Isaiah 55:1-11*
CONTEXT: Conclusion of 'Second' Isaiah – the promises of return from exile.
IDEAS: The Lord's Table; all nations called; turn to God who forgives.

We can hear these ancient prophetic words as a summons for ourselves, to put God first, to seek him and listen to him. Isaiah assures us, like Jesus in today's Gospel, of God's constant grace, love and forgiveness.

Acts 10:44-48
CONTEXT: Peter at Caesarea – the first Gentile convert, Cornelius.
IDEAS: Good news for all the world; baptism the response to faith.

**[*If the Old Testament reading is not used:* During the Easter season, instead of reading the Hebrew Scriptures, we hear the way that the Gospel began to spread through the disciples.]
A Roman centurion, Cornelius, and his family, had invited Peter and his Christian friends to explain about Jesus. To everyone's amazement, God's Holy Spirit palpably came upon them, and they were baptised into the Christian faith.**

1 John 5:1-6
CONTEXT: God is love – his redemptive work in Christ demonstrates this.
IDEAS: Faith, love and obedience; water, blood and Spirit.

Another short section from this letter brings us this week to one of the consequences of our love for God. John says we must be obedient, as a child to a loving parent, and we shall not find it difficult.

John 15:9-17
CONTEXT: Last teaching – encouragement. The mutual indwelling of Christ and the believer – image of the vine.
IDEAS: Obedience in love; servants and friends; chosen to be fruitful.

We heard last Sunday Jesus's illustration of how a vine and its branches are like his life flowing through us. This passage follows on directly, and expands the idea of Christ living in us as we live in him, his beloved friends, chosen by him to be fruitful in his work.

Year B: Ascension Day

The reading from Acts must be used as either the first or second reading.

Acts 1:1-11
CONTEXT: Introduction to Volume 2 of Luke.
IDEAS: Resurrection appearances; waiting for God; final departure.

Luke's account of the divine plan of salvation is in two parts. He ended the earthly life of Jesus, as we shall hear in the Gospel, with the event of the Ascension. Part two is the life of Christ in the church, and it begins as the Gospel ended, with the Lord leaving the earth to his home in heaven.

OR CWL only: *Daniel 7:9-14*
CONTEXT: The second half of this book, a series of visions written in the terrible times of Antiochus Epiphanes (170 BC).
IDEAS: Tyrannical oppressor ultimately overthrown; sovereignty passes to a 'son of man'.

The visionary Daniel in the second century BC saw a human figure from heaven, with all the power and authority of God, becoming the sovereign over every people and nation.

Ephesians 1:15-23
CONTEXT: Probably a general letter to Gentile Christians – about faith and conduct in the church.
IDEAS: Rejoice in the signs of faith; rejoice that Jesus Christ is risen, ascended and now in glory.

The writer of this letter to the churches gives thanks, in one great long sentence of praise in the Greek, for the glory of the risen and ascended Christ – ascended to heaven and therefore empowering his people everywhere. This is the faith of the church.

OR *Acts 1:1-11. See above.*

Luke 24:44-53
CONTEXT: Conclusion of Luke's Volume 1.
IDEAS: The Old Testament has foreseen these things; Gospel for all the world; witnesses; final departure.

Luke ends his life of Jesus with a last blessing, and the commission to go into every nation as witnesses to his suffering, his death, and his resurrection.

Year B: The Seventh Sunday of Easter (Sunday after Ascension Day)

CWL: If the Old Testament reading is used, the reading from Acts must be used as the second reading.

CWL: *Ezekiel 36:24-28*
CONTEXT: The prophet, in the role of watchman for the Lord's coming, affirms that God will be merciful to Israel.
IDEAS: Gathering after dispersion; purifying by water; the indwelling Spirit.

We shall hear in the Gospel our Lord's prayer for those he must leave behind in this world. Ezekiel reflects the same tender care of God for his people. His images speak to Christians of Pentecost: cleansing in pure water, the giving of a new heart and an outpouring of the Spirit.

Acts 1:15-17, 21-26
CONTEXT: The Jerusalem church begins to take shape following the Lord's Ascension.
IDEAS: The betrayal and fate of Judas; guidance from Scripture; human choices and God's choices.

Jesus had commissioned twelve men to preach and heal, but many more had been his constant companions. The church in Jerusalem decided that one of these others should replace Judas Iscariot, to restore the number of leaders to twelve.

1 John 5:9-13
CONTEXT: Asserting the truth of the Gospel and what has been written here.
IDEAS: Jesus revealed as Saviour (Jn 19:34-35); believe with heart and head.

John sums up his reason for writing this letter, which we have read week by week since Easter Day. It has been to give us the assurance that the Gospel is true, and that this faith in our hearts brings us eternal life.

John 17:6-19
CONTEXT: Jesus's last prayer, after encouragement to his friends.
IDEAS: Crucifixion = glorification; Jesus prays for our joy; unity in him.

Jesus's last words of prayer before his arrest are for those who will remain in this world after he has gone, that they may remain faithful and true, consecrated to the Father as he has been.

Year B: Day of Pentecost (Whit Sunday)

The reading from Acts must be used as the first or second reading.

Acts 2:1-21

CONTEXT: A hundred or more meet together – the Eleven plus Matthias and women and others; festival of Pentecost 50 days after Passover.

IDEAS: Pentecost and harvest thanksgiving; strange manifestations; awesome power of the Spirit; Gospel in every language.

In Jerusalem, many pilgrims had come for the great Pentecost Harvest Festival. As Jesus had promised, the Holy Spirit of God came upon the gathered company of disciples with great power. They found themselves impelled to proclaim the resurrection Gospel to everyone who would listen.

OR *Ezekiel 37:1-14*

CONTEXT: Our book 'Ezekiel' is not in chronological order; all the visions and oracles relate to the Babylonian exile and hopes for restoration.

IDEAS: Desolation and death. Wind = breath = spirit (Heb. *Ruarch*). God will give new life.

At the time of Ezekiel, Jerusalem was derelict and the land laid waste. In a vision he sees nothing but dried-up bones, until the breath of God – the Spirit of God – fills the valley with life. It is a sign that God will give new life to his people Israel.

Romans 8:22-27

CONTEXT: Contrasting unspiritual life and the Spirit's transforming power.

IDEAS: Frustrations of physical life; divinely-implanted longings; our struggle to pray – the Spirit's help.

We live with all our hopes founded on God, longing for him, but it is hard for us to know how to pray. Paul's assurance is that the Holy Spirit continues to work in the church and the world, and he will make known to God everything we mean.

OR *Acts 2:1-21. See above.*

John 15:26-27, 16:4b-15

CONTEXT: Last encouraging words from Jesus before his arrest.

IDEAS: Spirit as advocate and witness to ultimate truth; sent by Jesus.

Jesus's teaching about the Holy Spirit describes him as one who represents Christ to us, revealing to us many truths about the world and about God, leading us into all truth.

Year B: Trinity Sunday

Isaiah 6:1-8
CONTEXT: After a collection of the prophet's speeches, the events of his life are introduced by an account of his call.
IDEAS: Visions; unworthiness; purifying.

Isaiah was called to his prophetic task by an overpowering vision of the magnificence and holiness of God, whose glory filled the Temple and the world.

Romans 8:12-17
CONTEXT: Paul's description of new life in Christ, as the Holy Spirit changes our outlook on everything.
IDEAS: Life and death – God's adopted children; the intimacy of 'Abba'; what the Spirit does in us.

Jesus in today's Gospel will tell of the new life which the Holy Spirit brings. Paul too can rejoice that we have become adopted children of God the Father, by the gift of the Spirit, in union with Christ.

John 3:1-17
CONTEXT: Jesus in Jerusalem for Passover (a visit not referred to by the other Gospels).
IDEAS: Spiritual re-birth; 'lifting-up' = crucifixion and glorification; faith brings eternal life.

Nicodemus had to learn that a new kind of birth is necessary to carry us into a new kind of life. God's only son unites heaven and earth, and his Spirit, moving unseen like the wind, brings us into eternal life.

Year B: Day of Thanksgiving for Holy Communion
(Thursday after Trinity Sunday: Corpus Christi)

Genesis 14:18-20
CONTEXT: Abram and Lot go separate ways (13:11, 12); Abram goes to the rescue of Lot, defeating the four eastern kings.
IDEAS: Salem (v. 18) = Jerusalem; ceremonial bread and wine; the great priest-king.

Melchizedek is a legendary name from the Israelite past. He was believed to have been a priest-king of Jerusalem long before King David made it his capital. In this reading, he acts to seal God's covenant with Abram in an offering of bread and wine, and a blessing.

1 Corinthians 11:23-26
CONTEXT: How a divided congregation is to observe the Lord's Supper.
IDEAS: Eucharistic tradition; remembrance and proclamation.

This is almost certainly the earliest account of the Lord's Supper as celebrated by the church. Paul reminds the Corinthians that it was from the Lord that he received this tradition, and handed it on.

John 6:51-58
CONTEXT: Five thousand fed, and teaching about 'true bread' from heaven.
IDEAS: The bread of life (vv. 34, 48); Jesus's body and blood; eternal life.

To receive the body and blood of Jesus, he says, is to take his eternal life into our very being. This is not an easy truth to understand, yet it is the most profound of all realities.

Year B: Proper 4 (29 May-4 June, if after Trinity Sunday. Week 9.)

Continuous Old Testament: 1 Samuel 3:1-10 [& 11-20]
CONTEXT: The birth of Samuel to the barren Hannah – serving in the Temple (2:11).
IDEAS: Lord's word rarely heard; recognising God's directions; [the prophetic calling].

Our readings for the next three months follow Israel's history when they had settled in their Promised Land. For a few years there was a united kingdom, under Saul, then David and Solomon. We begin with Samuel, whose prophetic insight would identify the one chosen to be Israel's first-ever king. Here he is still a child, but responds to the calling of the Lord.

Related Old Testament: Deuteronomy 5:12-15
CONTEXT: A review of the Sinai covenant and the Law as given.
IDEAS: Sabbath rest.

One of the Ten Commandments is to keep the Sabbath holy. In today's Gospel, Jesus challenges people's idea of what that meant. Here is one of the Bible's two versions of the law of the Sabbath.

2 Corinthians 4:5-12
CONTEXT: Paul defending and justifying his apostleship.
IDEAS: God's power not ours; the hardships of vocation.

All the resources for Paul's ministry come from his inner life with Jesus, and all his ordinary daily hardships serve to emphasise the light which transforms his heart and can also lighten ours.

Mark 2:23-3:6
CONTEXT: Capernaum and Galilee teaching and healing.
IDEAS: Sabbath observance; using Scripture; opposition becomes serious.

On most Sundays of this year we shall be reading consecutively through Mark's account of Jesus. Mark has shown how popular Jesus had become in the Galilean towns and villages, but now his unconventional approach to Sabbath observance leads to serious controversy. Such challenges to tradition will bring him to his cross.

Year B: Proper 5 (5-11 June, if after Trinity Sunday. Week 10.)

Continuous Old Testament: 1 Samuel 8:4-11 [& 12-15], 16-20 [& 11:14 -15]
CONTEXT: Samuel judge as well as prophet – Philistines defeated and peace ensues.
IDEAS: Concepts of monarchy and government; God and social systems; [Saul the first king].
Either (a) if this Sunday is Trinity 1:
This year our readings give us a picture of Israel in the Promised Land, before the nation became divided.
or (b) if Proper 4 readings were read on the previous Sunday:
Last Sunday we began to read the story of Israel as a kingdom, when Samuel was called to serve God.
then the following:
Now, for the first time in their history, the people of Israel demanded a king to replace their fragmented tribal systems of government. We hear how the prophet Samuel warned them of the disadvantages of being ruled by a king, and that it was not God's will.

Related Old Testament: Genesis 3:8-15
CONTEXT: The creation myth – Adam and Eve and Paradise.
IDEAS: Where does sin derive from? 'It's not my fault!'

Eve and Adam had eaten the forbidden fruit of the Paradise Garden, in this ancient story attempting to explain how human sin corrupts God's perfect creation. Our Gospel similarly speaks of the sin that is present in the world.

2 Corinthians 4:13-5:1
CONTEXT: The divine power sustaining Paul in his sufferings.
IDEAS: Resurrection hope for all; this life a transient preparation.

Paul has been contrasting the frailty of our bodies with the spiritual strength we are given. His letter continues with the thought that God constantly renews us, and the hope of eternal glory outweighs all our present troubles.

Mark 3:20-35
CONTEXT: Crowds make Jesus's Galilean work impossible on his own – Twelve chosen to be with him.
IDEAS: Jesus's family; Satan, demons and sin; theological controversy.

If this Sunday is Trinity 1: [For most Sundays of this year we read consecutively through Mark's Gospel.]
Two memorable references to Jesus's family bracket this moment of serious controversy in his teaching, when he is accused of representing evil rather than good.

Year B: Proper 6 (12-18 June, if after Trinity Sunday. Week 11.)

Continuous Old Testament: 1 Samuel 15:34-16:13
CONTEXT: Saul has failed as Israel's (first) king; Samuel regretfully forces his abdication.
IDEAS: Bethlehem, city of David and Jesus; who and how does God choose.
Either (a) if this Sunday is Trinity 1:
This year our readings give us a picture of Israel in the Promised Land, before the nation became divided.
or (b) if Proper 5 readings were read on the previous Sunday:
We continue to read the history of those few years when Israel was a united kingdom.
then the following:
King David's reign will dominate the story, and we now approach those events. Saul had been Israel's first-ever king, but failed to fulfil God's commands. The prophet Samuel is now sent by God to Bethlehem, to the family of Jesse, where the least likely of his sons is the chosen one.

Related Old Testament: Ezekiel 17:22-24
CONTEXT: A tirade against King Zedekiah for seeking Egypt's help in the war against Assyria – this was not the Lord's will.
IDEAS: Great oaks from little acorns – under God.

To a people in exile, Ezekiel promises that even from a small new beginning God can make great things grow. Our Gospel contains just the same idea in parables.

2 Corinthians 5:6-10 [& 11-13], 14-17
CONTEXT: The frailty of the human body compared with the immortal/eternal life revealed in us and for which we are destined.
IDEAS: Trust in the Lord – long to be with him; [the apostolic example;] the compulsion of God's love; all things new.
If last Sunday was Proper 5: [**As we heard last Sunday.**]
Paul has been writing of the frailty of our bodies compared with the strength of God's grace within us. He goes on to say that once we make our decision to live wholly for Christ, both our future destiny and our present nature have been changed.

Mark 4:26-34
CONTEXT: Teaching in parables.
IDEAS: Small beginnings and great outcomes; seeds and growth.
If this Sunday is Trinity 1: [**For most Sundays of this year we read consecutively through Mark's Gospel.**]
Mark collected together several of Jesus's parables into one section of his Gospel. Here are two of them, about how the kingdom seems scarcely visible yet is inevitably growing, as God gives life to the seed.

Year B: Proper 7 (19-25 June, if after Trinity Sunday. Week 12.)

Continuous Old Testament:
Note: These sentences apply to both Old Testament alternatives:
Either (a) if this Sunday is Trinity 1:
This year our readings give us a picture of Israel under the Kings Saul, David and Solomon.
or (b) if Proper 6 readings were read on the previous Sunday:
We continue the history of those few years when Israel was a united kingdom.
then the introduction below:

1 Samuel 17:[1a, 4-11, 19-23] 32-49
CONTEXT: Saul's fall from grace as King. (NB: Ch.16 recounts a quite different story from that in 17, as to how David entered Saul's court.)
IDEAS: [Legends of boastful giants;] David the shepherd-king; armour.

There are two different accounts in the Bible about how David came to be in the court of King Saul, whom he eventually succeeded. This is one of them – the legendary defeat of the Philistine Goliath.

OR *1 Samuel 17:57-18:5, 10-16*
CONTEXT: See above ... by these verses, David has defeated Goliath.
IDEAS: David and Jonathan; David's welcome to court, and his military reputation; the madness of the King.

Jonathan was King Saul's son and his natural successor, but David's military successes and popularity grew, and he became a threat to the old and sick King.

Related Old Testament: Job 38:1-11
CONTEXT: Elihu calls Job to marvel at the greatness of the Lord.
IDEAS: How can humans comprehend God's greatness? All nature within God's mysterious power.

This passage and today's Gospel remind us that wind and water are not under our control. God's power in the universe is set forth here in rhetorical questions. Only God creates and sustains the workings of all natural forces.

2 Corinthians 6:1-13

CONTEXT: God's work of reconciliation, through Christ and given to us.
IDEAS: Don't waste God's grace; give no offence; patience and kindness in all relationships.

This letter reaches a climax, as Paul appeals to the Christians at Corinth to understand how kind and gentle he is for Christ's sake, despite the strong rebuke he has had to give them.

Mark 4:35-41

CONTEXT: Jesus in and around Galilee, teaching both his disciples and the general crowd.
IDEAS: Escape from the crowd (cf. Mt 8:18); call to the Lord in distress; faith through miracles?

If this Sunday is Trinity 1: [For most Sundays of this year we read consecutively through Mark's Gospel.]

Mark has shown Jesus's power to heal the sick in mind and body. Now he reveals to us the divine authority which was enough to still the raging wind and turbulent sea.

Year B: Proper 8 (26 June-2 July. Week 13.)

Continuous Old Testament: 2 Samuel 1:1, 17-27
CONTEXT: Direct continuation from 1 Samuel. David's rise to power and his military conquests.
IDEAS: Saul, Israel's first (reluctant) king; biblical lyric poetry.

We have been hearing each week something of Israel becoming a kingdom under Saul, with the historian's knowledge that it would end tragically. David led the army very successfully, but in a battle King Saul and his three sons died. This lament portrays David's unwavering loyalty to his king.

Related Old Testament: Wisdom 1:13-15, 2:23-24
CONTEXT: A first century BC writing, appealing to Wisdom as a true philosophy of life.
IDEAS: Life and death; God's eternal image in humankind.

Not long before Jesus's time, some Jewish thinkers perceived that if death means a total end, it is wasteful. So they began to say that God created humanity for fullness of life, imperishable and eternal.

OR *Lamentations 3:23-33*
CONTEXT: In a collection of poems which are primarily dirges, this section is of positive hope in the Lord.
IDEAS: Affirmation of God's goodness and love; compassion.

It is not God's will that any should suffer, says this writer. The reading serves to introduce today's Gospel in which Jesus does the work of God in the relief of suffering.

2 Corinthians 8:7-15
CONTEXT: Apology and encouragement, church life flourishing.
IDEAS: Rich in God's gifts; see things through; sharing resources.

For several years, Paul organised financial support from the churches in Asia to help relieve poverty among the Christians of Jerusalem. This passage is part of his appeal to Corinth for generosity that corresponds to Christ's own self-giving for our sakes.

Mark 5:21-43
CONTEXT: Jesus has been across Lake Galilee into Gentile territory, where a (psychiatric?) healing caused a stir.
IDEAS: Some religious leaders respected Jesus; interrupted plans; healing and ministry consumes energy.

Here is a story within a story. Jesus responds to a father's desperate plea for his daughter, and on his way performs an almost accidental healing. But always this work took power from Jesus.

Year B: Proper 9 (3-9 July. Week 14.)

Continuous Old Testament: 2 Samuel 5:1-5, 9-10
CONTEXT: David King of Judah (2:4) – continuing enmity of those loyal to the (dead) Saul, as David seeks to gain the entire kingdom.
IDEAS: Judah and Israel become united under David; Jerusalem becomes his capital.

We have been following the story of David's rise to power. By this time he had already been king of Judah for some time, and now takes control of Israel too. For the first time, Jerusalem takes on the importance it has had ever since.

Related Old Testament: Ezekiel 2:1-5
CONTEXT: The last years of Judah – Elijah's response to a strange vision.
IDEAS: Listening to God; speaking for God; prophets usually not welcome.

To be an apostle means sent as a messenger. Ezekiel, like our Lord's apostles in today's Gospel, is sent to speak in the name of God to the people of Israel. Like them, he will sometimes be rejected.

2 Corinthians 12:2-10
CONTEXT: Paul needing to justify his apostolic work, offering as credentials the suffering it brought him.
IDEAS: 'Seeing things'; spiritual experiences; some bodily ills don't go away.

The is the last of our weekly readings from this letter, in which Paul has had to justify his mission and his message at some length. Although he writes here as if of someone else, it was probably he who had this vision of heaven. Alongside such moments he has had to bear persistent pain.

Mark 6:1-13
CONTEXT: Jesus performing various miracle cures in towns and villages.
IDEAS: The gifts of 'ordinary' people; family life; significance of Twelve; sent with authority.

Mark now moves the ministry of Jesus from Galilee to Nazareth, and shows the universal truth that it is hard to impress the people you grew up with. The sceptics hinder Jesus's work. But the time has come for him to choose Twelve followers to be apostles for him, sent out in pairs to teach and heal.

Year B: Proper 10 (10-16 July. Week 15.)

Continuous Old Testament: 2 Samuel 6:1-5, 12b-19
CONTEXT: David established as king, at Jerusalem. An alliance with Tyre; battle with Philistines.
IDEAS: Symbols of God's presence; religious celebrations; food blessed and shared.

We have heard how David became king, and now read how he established Jerusalem not only as his capital city but the centre for worship. The Ark of God symbolised God's presence, and David had it brought to Jerusalem from Judah and set in place with great ceremony.

Related Old Testament: Amos 7:7-15
CONTEXT: Israel prosperous, before the Assyrian conquest. To Amos the countryman, corruption and moral degradation in the city was unbearable.
IDEAS: Things need straightening out; God's imperative to speak.

When a prophet feels compelled to speak out against kings and priests, he cannot expect a sympathetic hearing. We shall hear how John the Baptist suffered under Herod; in this reading Amos is banished from Israel for his message of doom.

Ephesians 1:3-14
CONTEXT: The letter opens with a section of praise for God's blessings.
IDEAS: God's eternal purposes and choices; his gifts to us in and through Christ.

The main theme of this letter, from which we shall hear key passages these next Sundays, is the concept of the church as Christ's body on earth. The idea is familiar to us, but was new then. The letter begins with great praise for what God has done in Christ.

Mark 6:14-29
CONTEXT: Apostles sent out – the return is at v. 30: perhaps this interpolation is to denote time passing?
IDEAS: Herod interested in John; the fate of the prophet; rash (like fairy-story) promises.

Mark interrupts his story of Jesus to tell us how John the Baptist came to be executed, because his forthright criticism of Herod and Herodias was intolerable.

Year B: Proper 11 (17-23 July. Week 16.)

Continuous Old Testament: 2 Samuel 7:1-14a
CONTEXT: David's kingdom is secure; Jerusalem established.
IDEAS: 'House' and 'dynasty' wordplay; wise advisors; building (and beautifying) churches.

The Ark was the symbol of God's presence, and David had brought it to Jerusalem. He wanted to build a fine house for God, but the prophet Nathan told him that instead the Lord would build the house of David.

Related Old Testament: Jeremiah 23:1-6
CONTEXT: A series of warnings to kings and misleading prophets.
IDEAS: Sheep and shepherds; failures in leadership; God's own gathering.

The Lord's people are sheep without a shepherd, says Jeremiah, as Jesus also said much later. Jeremiah denounces kings for ineffective leadership, and promises a new and righteous king descended from the shepherd-king David.

Ephesians 2:11-22
CONTEXT: The nature of the church, the body of Christ.
IDEAS: The unity of all races as Christians; inclusive faith; where God dwells.

Jesus came to save both Jew and Gentile alike. This good news brings into God's household all those who once had neither hope nor knowledge of God. Christ has broken down all human barriers.

Mark 6:30-34, 53-56
CONTEXT: The Twelve sent out (vv. 7, 12) on a mission.
IDEAS: Need for quiet times and de-briefing; clamour surrounds charismatic figures; the power of touch.

The apostles returned from the mission on which Jesus had sent them, and looked for a time of rest. But people would not leave Jesus alone, and his heart went out to them as sheep without a shepherd. Always, the needy drew his compassion and healing.

Year B: Proper 12 (24-30 July. Week 17.)

Continuous Old Testament: 2 Samuel 11:1-15
CONTEXT: Stirring stories of David's conquests, but also his sinfulness.
IDEAS: Greatness and fallibility; sexuality; leadership and deceit.

Our weekly story of King David continues with the affair of Bathsheba. The Bible is often very honest about the failings of its heroes, and tells us here that Israel's greatest king was guilty of adultery and murder.

Related Old Testament: 2 Kings 4:42-44
CONTEXT: A collection of Elisha's miraculous works.
IDEAS: Bread; not enough for the crowd; miraculous provision.

This brief account of a miraculous meal makes us think of Jesus feeding the crowds. Elisha took a small quantity of bread and grain, and God made it more than enough for a hundred people.

Ephesians 3:14-21
CONTEXT: Gentiles are fellow-citizens of the new kingdom.
IDEAS: The family of God; prayer for the church; power at work.

Paul's theme in this letter is the unity of Jew and Gentile in the church, acting as Christ's body. He has expressed his joy that the Christians of Ephesus are fellow-citizens with all Jewish believers, and is now moved to prayer and praise.

John 6:1-21
CONTEXT: A profound section of John's Gospel on earthly and heavenly bread.
IDEAS: Miracles as signs; more than we desire or deserve; what sort of king?

For a few Sundays now, we interrupt the sequence from Mark, and hear John's teaching about bread – bread as necessary daily food and Jesus himself as bread from heaven, food of eternal life. It begins with the miraculous feeding of the five thousand.

Year B: Proper 13 (31 July-6 August. Week 18.)

Continuous Old Testament: 2 Samuel 11:26-12:13a
CONTEXT: David's adultery with Bathsheba and murder of her husband.
IDEAS: The voices of conscience; effect of grievous sin through generations.
Last Sunday we read of David's sin of adultery and murder. Now we hear the rebuke of the prophet Nathan. It introduces us to the family troubles which persisted through the rest of David's life.

Related Old Testament: Exodus 16:2-4, 9-15
CONTEXT: Continuing the salvation-history of the Israelite exodus from Egypt.
IDEAS: The good old days were better; blame the leadership; God's miraculous provision for those in need.
In their desert pilgrimage, the people of Israel missed what comforts there had been in Egypt. Yet they were miraculously fed. Today's Gospel will remind us that it was bread from heaven which the Lord gave them.

Ephesians 4:1-16
CONTEXT: The unity of everyone within the church, and the Christian's calling.
IDEAS: All are gifted in diverse ways; the range of skills the church needs – and has; maturity.
This letter is all about the nature of the church as Christ's body. This section calls us to our essential unity, despite our different gifts and personalities. We are to grow into a mature faith, bound together by truth and love.

John 6:24-35
CONTEXT: 5000 miraculously fed – now the teaching about true bread.
IDEAS: Satisfactions people look for; faith as 'work'; bread of life; physical/spiritual hunger; eucharist.
Jesus made a small amount of bread enough for several thousand people – and they want more of the same. He teaches them the deeper meaning of the sign of the bread he gives: that he is himself the satisfaction of all our deepest needs.

Year B: Proper 14 (7-13 August. Week 19.)

Continuous Old Testament: 2 Samuel 18:5-9, 15, 31-33
CONTEXT: Conflict within David's family – he has to flee from Jerusalem – factions forming.
IDEAS: Fathers and sons in conflict; family love survives crises.

King David's reign became less effective, and Absalom, his eldest son, led a rebellion against his father. The culmination was a battle between forces loyal to David and the rebel army, and to David's great sorrow his favourite son was killed.

Related Old Testament: 1 Kings 19:4-8
CONTEXT: Elijah's despair, despite defeating prophets of Baal (18:40); his life under threat from Ahab.
IDEAS: Run away when things get tough; encounter with God in bleakness; angelic appearances and provision.

Elijah had to flee for his life when King Ahab and his wife Jezebel tried to crush all worship of the Lord. In the desert, he found food and water miraculously supplied – 'bread from heaven', in the phrase today's Gospel uses.

Ephesians 4:2-5:2
CONTEXT: The church and the appropriate conduct for Christians both towards each other and outside their community.
IDEAS: Some of the world's ways and values have to be rejected; no spite or grudges; imitate Christ.

Life in the church will not always be smooth and joyful. But Christians should be marked as gentle people, loving and forgiving, just as Jesus himself was.

John 6:35, 41-51
CONTEXT: The teaching about Jesus as the true bread from heaven.
IDEAS: Spiritual hunger and thirst; bread of eucharist; life and death.

After the feeding of the five thousand, John records Jesus speaking at length about the mysterious real and true bread he proclaimed himself to be. The listening people found all this hard to understand.

Year B: Proper 15 (14-20 August. Week 20.)

Continuous Old Testament: 1 Kings 2:10-12, 3:3-14
CONTEXT: Jewish history after David – Solomon succeeds him.
IDEAS: Solomon's reputation for wisdom; 'wisdom' as a gift from God.

Our weekly extracts from the history of Israel's kings now tell of Solomon succeeding his father David to the throne. Solomon acquired a great reputation for showing God's wisdom in everything he did.

Related Old Testament: Proverbs 9:1-6
CONTEXT: Wisdom and foolishness personified and contrasted.
IDEAS: Wisdom (as God) welcomes all; biblical banquets.

To this writer, wisdom was one of God's personal attributes. Here, just as Jesus was to do, God invites all to come in and eat bread and wine at the Lord's table.

Ephesians 5:15-20
CONTEXT: Christian conduct is to be Christlike, living in his light.
IDEAS: Commonsense; to know God's will; thankfulness.

This letter has much to say about the details of Christian behaviour, and now encourages us to be sensible and moderate people, constant in worship and always thankful for all things.

John 6:51-58
CONTEXT: Five thousand fed, and teaching about 'true bread' from heaven.
IDEAS: The bread of life (vv. 34, 48); Jesus's body and blood; eternal life.

For several Sundays we have been following John's extended section of Jesus's teaching about spiritual food. To those who first heard Jesus talk about his body and blood, the words made little sense. But John and the church cherish the words as the meaning of every Communion.

Year B: Proper 16 (21-27 August. Week 21.)

Continuous Old Testament: 1 Kings 8 [1, 6, 10-11] 22-30, 41-43
CONTEXT: A time of political stability: Solomon's Temple completed.
IDEAS: God and buildings; Symbols of the presence; a Temple for all nations.

King David had planned the Temple in Jerusalem, and King Solomon completed the building. Now, with great and joyful ceremony, it is dedicated to the worship of God.

Related Old Testament: Joshua 24:1-2a, 14-18
CONTEXT: The Israelite tribes settled in the Promised Land; Joshua's last words and his death.
IDEAS: New covenant for a new generation; life-changing choices.

This reading and the Gospel are about the one great choice we must make – to serve God or not. Joshua's final appeal to the people is to convince them to serve the Lord their God.

Ephesians 6:10-20
CONTEXT: Injunctions on Christian behaviour, and the resources needed to stand firm in the faith.
IDEAS: Christian life as a battle; evil is superhuman; prayer as the great weapon.

These familiar words bring this letter to a close. We need to use all the armour God provides in the Christian fight against so much that is evil.

John 6:56-69
CONTEXT: The discourse and reflections on 'bread', continued.
IDEAS: Jesus's uncomfortable words; his divine perceptiveness; who else to choose to follow.

Jesus has been speaking of himself as the bread from heaven, of his body and blood for our eternal life. The spiritual truth of this teaching is baffling to many and offensive to some, but Peter voices the disciples' choice to continue with Jesus and accept what he gives.

Year B: Proper 17 (28 August-3 September. Week 22.)

Continuous Old Testament: Song of Solomon 2:8-13

CONTEXT: An anthology of love poems and songs, perhaps allegorical: a bride's song.
IDEAS: The coming of the beloved; he takes his bride with him; Christ and the church.

We begin now some readings from what we call the 'Wisdom literature' of Israel. This is from one of the Bible's rarest books, a collection of love songs sometimes attributed to Solomon, whose life we have briefly heard about in recent weeks. Although the poetry is never obviously religious, it can speak to us of the God who comes to us and in love draws us to himself.

Related Old Testament: Deuteronomy 4:1-2, 6-9

CONTEXT: Moses reviews the wilderness journeyings, and now re-states some of the Law before the move on into Canaan.
IDEAS: Some laws remain unchanging; nations measured by their ordering of society; when to bend the law?

The injunction from Moses to the Israelites was to obey every detailed commandment in God's Law. This would be good for them, and a good witness to other nations. But Jesus, we shall hear, had a rather different approach to the minutiae of legal systems.

James 1:17-27

CONTEXT: An unknown author, to all Christians – perhaps an encyclical letter, containing moral teaching rather than doctrine.
IDEAS: The unchanging God; new birth of Christians; listen and act; charity and purity.

We shall hear passages from this letter for several consecutive weeks. It is a kind of manual for Christian conduct. This section exhorts us to behaviour worthy of the truths we have received.

Mark 7:1-8, 14-15, 21-23

CONTEXT: (Picking up from the break at Proper 11) Successful mission in Galilee, and Jesus's notoriety, provokes an official enquiry from Jerusalem.
IDEAS: Petty criticism masking deeper unease; what 'defiles'? Bending details of law.

After a few Sundays listening to St John, we resume our reading of St Mark at a point where religious leaders begin to be troubled by what they hear of Jesus. The question they pose seems trivial, but to the Pharisee every detail in the Law was necessary for righteousness.

Year B: Proper 18 (4-10 September. Week 23.)

Continuous Old Testament: Proverbs 22:1-2, 8-9, 22-23
CONTEXT: A collection of wise sayings, some religious but mostly secular.
IDEAS: Reputation; generosity; compassion.

This is a very brief sample of many sayings and aphorisms said to have been collected and written by Solomon. They form part of Israel's wisdom literature, and are often quite worldly rather than religious. Good reputation, justice, mercy, are virtues to be valued.

Related Old Testament: Isaiah 35:4-7a
CONTEXT: Assurance that Yahweh will destroy Israel's enemies, and restore her.
IDEAS: God comes to save/heal; blind and deaf cured.

When the Lord comes, says the prophet, every ill and every pain will be healed. And when Jesus came these words came true wherever he went.

James 2:1-10 [& 11-13], 14-1
CONTEXT: A variety of topics concerning the necessary distinctiveness of Christian conduct.
IDEAS: Strangers in church; judging by appearances; faith and love in action.

This letter is characterised by exhortations about putting faith to work. This passage deals with how the church should welcome visitors, and the uselessness of faith without charitable action.

Mark 7:24-37
CONTEXT: Miracles, teachings and challenges amongst the Jews.
IDEAS: Jesus's reaction (v. 27); Aramaic words preserved; ministry concealed or revealed?

Jesus moved for a while away from Jewish people into Gentile territory. His compassion and his healing power still reached out to all who came with faith at their time of need.

Year B: Proper 19 (11-17 September. Week 24.)

Continuous Old Testament: Proverbs 1:20-33
CONTEXT: A collection from many ancient traditions of wise mottoes and aphorisms. Ignore the voice of folly, listen to that of wisdom.
IDEAS: Wisdom actively personified; similarities to prophetic calls.

This collection of sayings, religious and secular, is attributed to the proverbial wisdom of Solomon. Here wisdom is given a voice, and a divine quality, as she appeals to us not to be foolish, to listen to her and turn away from sin.

Related Old Testament: Isaiah 50:4-9a
CONTEXT: A 'Servant Song' of mission and suffering.
IDEAS: Obedience to God; patient dignity and endurance.

Isaiah pictures a faithful servant of God who is deeply and unjustly humiliated, but remains dignified in suffering. Whatever the original context of these words, the church has always seen them as foretelling the suffering of Jesus.

James 3:1-12
CONTEXT: Relationships towards neighbours – faith and action.
IDEAS: Watch your tongue! Listen to what you say; the power of words.

This general letter of instruction in Christian behaviour now tells us to take great care not only in what we may teach others but in everything we say. Our tongue can be greatly influential for good or for ill.

Mark 8:27-38
CONTEXT: Four thousand fed – teaching about signs of the kingdom.
IDEAS: The Suffering Servant; Jesus's foreknowledge; discipleship implies (some form of) suffering.

Mark has already shown that opposition to Jesus simmered beneath all the popularity. Now we come to a turning point in his Gospel. He introduces the darker themes of cross and rejection – which in some way every disciple must expect to face.

Year B: Proper 20 (18-24 September. Week 25.)

Continuous Old Testament: Proverbs 31:10-31
CONTEXT: An appendix (from 30:1) of riddles and poems.
IDEAS: Skilful word-power (the poem is an acrostic); wise wives and happy families.

We heard last Sunday the beginning of this book of collected wise sayings. This is how it ends, with a complete poem about the ideal wife.

Related Old Testament: Wisdom of Solomon 1:16-2:1, 12-22
CONTEXT: Wisdom and folly contrasted in this 1st century BC writing.
IDEAS: The pride and certainties of godless people; mockery of the godly; rewards of holiness.

Those who have rejected God are both foolish and wicked, says this writer. Although they mock the godly, and even kill them as they did to Jesus, they should learn that holiness has its own rewards.

OR *Jeremiah 11:18-20*
CONTEXT: Woe to Judah and Jerusalem for apostasy.
IDEAS: The wicked work to destroy the godly; sacrificial lamb.

Jeremiah in his time suffered greatly and, like Jesus, endured plots to kill him and destroy all he stood for. He was, he says, like a lamb being led to slaughter.

James 3:13-4:3, 7-8a
CONTEXT: Christian behaviour in detail — neighbourliness, speech, peace-making.
IDEAS: Pride, jealousy, ambition; holy wisdom and sincerity.

The writer asks his Christian readers always to consider their motives. So much harm is done when jealousy and envy determine our actions. The wise want only what God wants for them.

Mark 9:30-37
CONTEXT: Transfiguration, and indications of the imminent suffering.
IDEAS: What discipleship implies; children of the kingdom; humility.

Jesus tries to make his destiny clear to his disciples, but they are still thinking there is only glory ahead and arguing about greatness in the kingdom. They do not understand that a leader must always be a servant.

Year B: Proper 21 (25 September-1 October. Week 26.)

Continuous Old Testament: Esther 7:1-6, 9-10, 9:20-22
CONTEXT: Probably not real history: a story of the Jews in Persia and a young Jewish girl (see Apocrypha for expanded version). The Feast of Purim instituted to commemorate saving the nation.
IDEAS: Power of good stories; goodies and baddies; woman's influence; religious memories and ceremonies.

This reading gives us only a small glimpse into a lovely story. Esther is a Jewish girl who became queen in the Persian Empire. She was able to foil a plot by the evil Haman to execute all Jews. This work of saving her people is shown as the explanation for one of the great feasts in the Jewish calendar.

Related Old Testament: Numbers 11:4-6, 10-16, 24-29
CONTEXT: The Israelites journeying from Sinai on towards Canaan.
IDEAS: Complaints about leadership; spirit-giving (sharing); God at work in those not 'ordained'.
Moses laboured under the weight of leadership of the travelling Israelites. He chose some elders to share the work. It became clear, as in today's Gospel, that beside those who are obviously chosen and set apart, others too can be seen to serve God's purposes.

James 5:13-20
CONTEXT: Many practical instructions concerning Christian behaviour – lastly, about prayer.
IDEAS: Confession and absolution; the healing ministry; purposes of prayer.

Week by week we have heard James's letter of instruction. Finally he begs us always to turn to prayer in any sickness or distress. This passage is a familiar one to all engaged in the Christian ministry of healing.

Mark 9:38-50
CONTEXT: Some teaching about what discipleship implies.
IDEAS: Who does God's work; setting a good example; what holds us back from the kingdom.

There are many people, says Jesus, who do good work without acknowledging him as Lord, and we are not to despise them. The people to beware of are those who cause trouble, not those who do good.

Year B: Proper 22 (2 October-8 October. Week 27.)

Continuous Old Testament: Job 1:1, 2:1-10
CONTEXT: A theological explanation of why the good suffer.
IDEAS: God's Adversary; anthropomorphic representations; stories to explore and illustrate doctrines.

The book of Job is a kind of drama. We shall hear some of the long speeches over the coming weeks, as the writer explores the problem of human suffering within the will of a loving God. The scene opens in heaven, where permission is given for Job to be harmed, apparently to see how much he can take without cursing God.

Related Old Testament: Genesis 2:18-24
CONTEXT: The Creation stories – the Garden of Eden.
IDEAS: Man and animals; man and woman; marriage.

This passage ends with words we shall hear Jesus quote. God made the human race as male and female, and in his intention a man and woman become as one when they marry each other.

Hebrews 1:1-4, 2:5-12
CONTEXT: The culmination of all God's self-revelation is in Jesus.
IDEAS: Christ present in creation; now exalted over creation.

Readings from this long essay on Christ's saving work will now take us to the end of our year. Throughout the book, Christ is praised as supreme in all creation, the one who has been glorified through suffering and has opened for all of us the way to God and to glory.

Mark 10:2-16
CONTEXT: A section on the implications of being Christ's disciple.
IDEAS: Marriage and divorce; Christian simplicity.

Husbands, wives and children feature here in Jesus's teaching. He affirms marriage as intended by God to be lifelong, although the Jewish Law made provision for divorce. Children, and all who are childlike, are welcome in his kingdom.

Year B: Proper 23 (9 October-15 October. Week 28.)

Continuous Old Testament: Job 23:1-9, 16-17
CONTEXT: The third cycle of speeches – Job must surely have sinned greatly or he would not be so severely punished.
IDEAS: The distant God; God knows everything and will understand us.

We began this book last Sunday, as it explores the theology of suffering. Here Job protests that even in a court he would be found innocent; therefore his illness and the tragic events of his life cannot be regarded as God's punishment for any wrongdoing.

Related Old Testament: Amos 5:6 -7, 10-15
CONTEXT: Israel has denied her Lord by allowing injustice to flourish; punishment is threatened.
IDEAS: Go where God is; be prepared for judgement; seek justice.

The only good life is life with God. Therefore, says Amos, although worldly wealth and comforts seem desirable, they can bring harm both to yourself and to others.

Hebrews 4:12-16
CONTEXT: Scripture tells of many partial understandings of God – but the Jewish people failed to listen to it.
IDEAS: The power of Scripture to speak to us; God knows everything; our access to God.

This treatise often switches between doctrine and ethics. In this short passage we find both a statement of our way to God through the work of Christ and the motive for all our behaviour.

Mark 10:17-31
CONTEXT: The ways – and the costs – of being a disciple.
IDEAS: Hard to be good; keeping commandments; some need to reject all worldly ties; kingdom blessings.

It is not easy to be good, says Jesus. There are commandments to be kept; there is wealth to be handled wisely; there are many worldly attractions and ties which may distract us from receiving all the joys found in his kingdom.

Year B: Proper 24 (16 October-22 October. Week 29.)

Continuous Old Testament: Job 38:1-7 [& 3 -41]
CONTEXT: A speech of Elihu calling Job to marvel at the greatness of the Lord.
IDEAS: How can humans comprehend God's greatness? All nature within God's mysterious power.

This book explores why Job, or any other person, should suffer. Surely God could prevent it? In this answer the writer's imagination soars as he explains that none of us can possibly understand the immensity of God nor comprehend his ways.

Related Old Testament: Isaiah 53:4-12
CONTEXT: Fourth 'Servant Song' – leading the return from Babylon (52:11).
IDEAS: Humiliation without complaint; despised and rejected for our sake; bearing sin for others.

The prophet describes the suffering undergone by the Jews, and their time of exile, as being undergone on behalf of the sins of others. The familiar words are easily transferred to Jesus, who according to today's Gospel foresaw that he must undergo death and resurrection for our sake.

Hebrews 5:1-10
CONTEXT: Jesus, apostle of our faith and high priest who opens heaven to us.
IDEAS: Christ subject to, and wholly obedient to, God; he became perfect.

This author's great purpose is to interpret Christ's work in terms of the Jewish priesthood, whose task was to offer sacrifices to God for the sins of the people. Here, with many echoes of the Old Testament, he tells how Christ as the perfect and eternal High Priest offered himself once for all, for the world's salvation.

Mark 10:35-45
CONTEXT: The fateful journey to Jerusalem and its outcome.
IDEAS: Disciples still not understanding (cf. 9:34); rivalries within the Twelve; vocation to service.

Jesus has just shared with his friends his expectation that soon, in Jerusalem, he will be executed. But the Twelve still argue between themselves about the greatness and glory they believe is about to come, not understanding the kingdom life of self-giving and service.

Year B: Proper 25 (23 October-29 October. Week 30.)

Continuous Old Testament: Job 42:1-6, 10-17

CONTEXT: The happy ending – Job's fortitude rewarded, his penitence accepted; he acknowledges that suffering remains a mystery.

IDEAS: God beyond our knowledge; intercession for friends; life's blessings.

This last of our four extracts from a profound exploration of the mystery of suffering brings the book to an end. Job now submits totally to the unfathomable but gracious will of God, and is blessed as his fortunes are restored.

Related Old Testament: Jeremiah 31:7-9

CONTEXT: Babylonian exile: a sequence of promises of restoration of the kingdom and the monarchy.

IDEAS: The remnant preserved; gathering together for celebration; God with us.

The separated kingdom of Judah is promised by Jeremiah that God has not forgotten them. The blind – like Bartimeus in today's Gospel – will receive their sight and all in need of comfort will know the ways of joy and praise.

Hebrews 7:23-28

CONTEXT: Further elucidation of Christ as our High Priest.

IDEAS: Sacrificing priesthood; transient humanity and Christ's perfection in eternity; our salvation; Christ's intercession.

This treatise dwells at length on Christ as a greater priest than any in the Jewish religious system. His work is uniquely and completely redemptive, because as God's own sinless Son he offered himself for us.

Mark 10:46-52

CONTEXT: Jesus and disciples approaching Jerusalem for the last time.

IDEAS: The need to ask Jesus (God); secrecy and publicity; Bartimeus sees what the Sanhedrin failed to observe.

Mark is about to show us Our Lord's destiny. Significantly, one blind man sees Jesus as the Son of David he truly is, while the authorities still only see a dangerous heretic.

Year B: CWL Bible Sunday

Isaiah 55:1-11
CONTEXT: Conclusion of 'Second' Isaiah – the promises of return from exile.
IDEAS: The Lord's Table; God's word gives life; turn to God who forgives.

Listen to me, says the Lord through Isaiah. The word of God is life-giving power, for those who hear it and in repentance turn to God.

2 Timothy 3:14-4:5
CONTEXT: Continuing the charge to a church elder to keep to the Gospel truths.
IDEAS: Be steeped in scripture; constantly preach its message.

A Christian leader writing to another emphasises the place of scripture as the inspiration for teaching and our guide to holy living.

John 5:36b-47
CONTEXT: Jesus in Jerusalem, citing testimony which validates his life and work.
IDEAS: Recognising who/where Jesus is; scriptural testimony; uses of Torah.

Those Jews who opposed Jesus could not accept his interpretation of their Scriptures. He pleads with them to believe him and see how much the ancient writings point to him as the one sent from God.

Year B: CWL Dedication Festival
(First Sunday in October or Last after Trinity)

Genesis 28:11-18
CONTEXT: Time for Isaac to marry – return to homeland to find a wife from his own people.
IDEAS: Racial intermarriage; God is present even in pagan places.

Jacob, journeying from Canaan back to the land of his ancestors, had a vision of heaven and the presence of God. The place, once a shrine to Canaanite gods, became sacred to the worship of the Lord.

OR *Revelation 21:9-14*
CONTEXT: The new heaven and new earth which shall come to pass.
IDEAS: Visions of God's splendour; twelves = completeness; no need of church or temple (v. 22).

In this vision of God's eternal city, there is no need for a Temple because God's glory shines in everything. The new Jerusalem includes all twelve tribes of Israel, and all who have received the Gospel through the twelve Apostles.

1 Peter 2:1-10
CONTEXT: A letter of encouragement, probably to Christians under persecution. Concerning lifestyle, faithfulness and holiness.
IDEAS: Stones – foundation, and living; Gentiles now included as God's people.

The early church searched their scriptures for passages that seemed to foreshadow Jesus. Here, texts about stones and foundations are used to suggest that we are a living spiritual building of which Christ is the corner-stone.

John 10:22-29
CONTEXT: Jesus in Jerusalem; healings and teachings; controversies.
IDEAS: Dedication Festival; sheep and shepherd; gift of eternal life.

Jesus always joined in the worship of synagogues and the Jerusalem Temple. This passage is a conversation with some Jews who were gathering at the Temple for the annual Festival of its Dedication.

Year B: CWL: Fourth before Advent, RCL: Proper 26
(30 October-5 November. Week 31.)

RCL: *Ruth 1:1-18*
CONTEXT: A book impossible to date; most likely a 'parable' whose point is to counter any
exclusiveness in Judaism – a Moabitess recognised Israel's God and was David's ancestor.
IDEAS: Moabites latterly enemies of Israel; love, piety and faithfulness; women in the
genealogy of Jesus (Mt 1:5).

**Ruth, a Moabite woman, will become great-grandmother of King David
– and Jesus is 'Son of David'. Most of this story takes place in Bethlehem,
but these introductory verses give the background: following the death of
Naomi's husband and sons, she sets out to return to Israel, and Ruth
promises 'Where you go, I will go; your God shall be my God.'**

CWL: RCL alternative: *Deuteronomy 6:1-9*
CONTEXT: A discourse of Moses setting out the terms of the Sinai Covenant.
IDEAS: Fear and obey God; monotheism; committing to memory.

**The first commandment given by God to Moses was to love and honour
the one and only God. As Jesus was to repeat to an enquirer, love with
heart and soul and strength is required of us before all else.**

Hebrews 9:11-14
CONTEXT: The old covenant and high-priestly sacrificial duties.
IDEAS: Christ the new and perfect high priest; his own blood; new covenant.

**This writer continues to expound his concept of Christ entering heaven
in a way similar to the Jewish High Priest entering the holy place of the
Temple. Once and for all, he writes, Christ's sacrifice of himself cleanses
from every taint of sin.**

Mark 12:28-34
CONTEXT: Jesus in the Temple grounds, encountering serious questions and challenges.
IDEAS: Clever man acknowledges Jesus's debating skills; total love.

**Jesus quotes to a questioner the two greatest commandments – love of
God and of neighbour – and tells the man that to know these comes close
to knowing his kingdom.**

Year B: All Saints' Day
(Sunday between 30 October and 5 November, or 1 November.)

Wisdom 3:1-9
CONTEXT: Apocrypha; probably 1st century BC. Wisdom personified as the traditional spirit of the Lord.
IDEAS: 'Immortality' (a very late Jewish development) and life after death; God's infinite future for the good, with him.

Throughout Old Testament times, the Jewish religion had no expectation of life after death. But not long before Jesus came, the theologians had begun to think there ought to be rewards and punishments hereafter. This writer expresses his confidence in the blessings stored up for the just.

OR *Isaiah 25:6-9*
CONTEXT: Praise to God for the love he will show by ending foreign domination.
IDEAS: The (Messianic) banquet; holy mountains; joy for all in salvation.

The prophet holds out God's promise of a joyful end to all human travail, where there will be feasting and rejoicing as death is destroyed for ever and God saves his people.

Revelation 21:1-6a
CONTEXT: The final visions – the last judgement, all things made new.
IDEAS: Both earth and heaven renewed; eternal presence of God.

At the end of time, as John sees it, God will be seen and known by everyone, in a new world where all pain and sorrow have come to an end.

John 11:32-44
CONTEXT: The extended story/'sign' of the healing of Lazarus.
IDEAS: Jesus's human emotions; dramatic events; cave tombs, stones, really dead.

We hear just the end of the well-known story of the resurrection of Lazarus, whom Jesus restored to his sisters Martha and Mary. For John, this work of Jesus is a supreme sign of his power.

Year B: CWL November 1
(If the All Saints' Day material is used on the Sunday.)

Isaiah 56:3-8
CONTEXT: Warnings and promises to the restored community.
IDEAS: All people will be safely gathered in.

As early as 500 BC, some religious thinkers in Israel had begun to see that the God of their people must in fact be the only God, with the whole world in his hands. So the hope for a time of restoration and peace embraces every nation and race. In the Gospel Jesus will tell us who are blessed by God.

OR *2 Esdras 2:42-48*
CONTEXT: Part of the Christian prefix added later to some Jewish writings of around 100 AD, which are apocalyptic visions ascribed to the ancient priest Ezra.
IDEAS: Vast crowd of the saints surround the Son of God.

This reading comes from a book in our Apocrypha, a collection of Jewish symbolic visions to which were added some Christian passages like this, where all those who acknowledge Christ are gathered round him in his glory.

Hebrews 12:18-24
CONTEXT: The enduring history of faith; the new perspective in the revelation of God in Christ.
IDEAS: Face to face with God; the city of God; vast crowds come to worship.

In ancient times, to meet God was awesome, and Mount Zion a fearful holy place. By contrast, says this writer, we know Christ brings us the new covenant promises, and we can always come into God's presence without fear.

Matthew 5:1-12
CONTEXT: Jesus's popularity in and around Capernaum; his early ministry of teaching and healing.
IDEAS: The Blessed/Happy (translations vary) are made so by God; challenge to be unpopular; unexpected people enter the kingdom.

In these strange paradoxes we call the Beatitudes, Jesus teaches us who are the holy people in God's sight, the ones who will find his blessings as his kingdom comes.

Year B: CWL Third before Advent, RCL Proper 27
(6-12 November. Week 32.)

RCL readings. See following page for CWL readings.

Ruth 3:1-5, 4:13-17
CONTEXT: Widows from Moab go to Bethlehem; the kindness of Boaz to this poor foreign woman.
IDEAS: God's coincidences; inclusive religion; genealogy of Jesus (Mk 1:5).

The widowed Ruth had travelled from her native Moab to Bethlehem with Naomi her mother-in-law, and was devoted both to her and to Israel's God. The final words today are the climax of this lovely story, when we learn that this foreign woman was a direct ancestor of King David.

OR *1 Kings 17:8-16*
CONTEXT: Episodic accounts of Elijah's life and work.
IDEAS: God works with power through his servants; miraculous provision.

In this story of Elijah God changes something ordinary into the extraordinary, to meet human need. A widow's life is saved as her last drop of oil and flour become a supply that lasts throughout a drought.

Hebrews 9:24-28
CONTEXT: A long and profound exposition of Christ's work, sacrifice, and entry to heaven as High Priest.
IDEAS: God's presence; once for all; second coming.

By entering heaven, says this writer, Jesus has opened the way for us to follow. Like the Jewish High Priest who once a year entered the Temple sanctuary, Christ has once for all offered himself to bring salvation to all.

Mark 12:38-44
CONTEXT: Jesus in the Temple grounds, encountering serious questions and challenges.
IDEAS: Clever man acknowledges Jesus's debating skills; total love.

Jesus quotes to a questioner the two greatest commandments – love of God and of neighbour – and tells the man that to know these comes close to knowing his kingdom.

Year B: CWL Third before Advent, RCL Proper 27
(6-12 November. Week 32.)

CWL readings. See previous page for RCL readings.

Jonah 3:1-5, 10
CONTEXT: A powerful fable of a petulant prophet, God's compulsions and his compassion.
IDEAS: Visiting preachers; call to repent; God changes his mind (?)

The message today of this reading and the Gospel is the call to repent. In the story of Jonah, God called him to warn the people of Nineveh of imminent punishment for their sin, and when they repented they were forgiven.

Hebrews 9:24-28
CONTEXT: A long and profound exposition of Christ's work, sacrifice, and entry to heaven as High Priest.
IDEAS: God's presence; once for all; second coming.

By entering heaven, says this writer, Jesus has opened the way for us to follow. Like the Jewish High Priest who once a year entered the Temple sanctuary, Christ has once for all offered himself to bring salvation to all.

Mark 1:14-20
CONTEXT: John baptizing; Jesus comes to him then goes into the wilderness.
IDEAS: Gospel of repentance; calling disciples; instant response.

According to Mark, Jesus's public ministry began by echoing John the Baptist, calling everyone to repent and recognise the coming of the kingdom. Some men immediately answered his call.

Year B: CWL Second before Advent, RCL Proper 28
(13-19 November. Week 33.)

RCL: *1 Samuel 1:4-20*
CONTEXT: The beginning of the history of Samuel and the establishment of the Kingdom under Saul and his successors.
IDEAS: Birth stories; barren wives; prayers and promises to God.

As we come near to the Advent season, and its preparation for the Lord's birth, it is good to be reminded of a much earlier child of promise. Hannah, one of Elkinah's wives, was to give birth to Samuel whose deeds as prophet and judge would be honoured by Jews and Christians for all time.

CWL: RCL alternative: *Daniel 12:1-3*
CONTEXT: The severe oppression of Antiochus Epiphanes, an apocalyptic vision of wars and distresses, until God's end-time.
IDEAS: Angels and archangels; the end of history; good rewarded.

The book of Daniel is a late Hebrew writing. This reading and the Gospel illustrate the faith of Jews and Christians that in God's time human history will reach an end. That time will not come without much distress, but God and his angels will deliver the faithful.

Hebrews 10:11-14 [& 15-18], 19-25
CONTEXT: The place of sacrifice in human approaches to God.
IDEAS: Sin forgiven; nothing separates us from God; Christ's perfect priesthood.

We having been hearing over several weeks this extended teaching about Christ's work being similar to, but far greater than, a Jewish High Priest. The treatise ends with a call to be constant in our faith, because God's end of time is always near.

Mark 13:1-8
CONTEXT: The final days in Jerusalem – eager crowds but hostile leaders.
IDEAS: The fall of Jerusalem/the end of time; signs; new age.

Jesus warns against a false understanding of the signs of the times; we are not to be greatly alarmed by the distress which must happen while God is working his purpose out.

Year B: Christ the King (20-26 November.)

RCL: *2 Samuel 23:1-7*
CONTEXT: David's reign summarised; some of his songs/psalms.
IDEAS: Famous last words; anointing; house and lineage of David.

David was Israel's one great king, and we end the church year at the end of his life. David's last words are a poem of the faithfulness of the God who raised him to rule the kingdom, and made an everlasting covenant with his dynasty.

CWL: RCL alternative: *Daniel 7:9-10, 13-14*
CONTEXT: The second half of this book, a series of visions written in the terrible times of Antiochus Epiphanes (170 BC).
IDEAS: Tyrannical oppressor ultimately overthrown; sovereignty passes to a 'son of man'.

Our church year comes to an end with this vision of heaven, picturing God upon a throne. He sends to earth one who is both like himself and like us, to be sovereign over all the world for ever.

Revelation 1:4b-8
CONTEXT: Opening of this unique apocalyptic work, written in exile.
IDEAS: Christ has died, is risen, will come again; God from and through eternity.

John's witness to Jesus is of the one whose rule extends over all earthly kings, and includes us within his royal kingdom.

John 18:33-37
CONTEXT: The Jews take Jesus for trial by Pilate.
IDEAS: What do kings do? Kingdom come; not of this world.

The scene now is a total contrast to the splendour of our earlier readings. Jesus is on trial before Pilate. When challenged about his kingship, Jesus answers that he came to us to reveal it, but his kingdom is not a worldly one.

Year C: The First Sunday of Advent

Jeremiah 33:14-16
CONTEXT: A prose reminder of the poem at 23:5-6; earlier hopes have not come true, but they will in God's time.
IDEAS: Promised blessings; descendant of David; his Name

Parts of our book called 'Jeremiah' are from a later commentary on his work. Here, one such passage repeats the prophet's promise that a righteous king will be born of David's line. It is a fitting introduction to our preparation for the Saviour's birth.

1 Thessalonians 3:9-13
CONTEXT: Paul's thwarted attempt to re-visit – Timothy returns with good news.
IDEAS: The rewards of mission; care for churches; the imminent advent of the Lord.

Paul prays he may have the opportunity to see these friends again, who are faithful under great hardships; and that they will continue strong and loving until that time when the Lord Jesus comes again.

Luke 21:25-36
CONTEXT: A discourse of Jesus concerning 'The End'.
IDEAS: Signs of the times; Son of Man comes; the cloud of the presence; watchfulness.

In this new church year, the Gospel on most Sundays will be that of Luke. Jesus speaks in this passage of the future coming of the Son of Man. He expects a time of great distress before the end of the world, and the faithful must be alert and stand firm.

Year C: The Second Sunday of Advent

Baruch 5:1-9
CONTEXT: A late BC anthology of poems and prophecies, purporting to be during the Babylonian exile. A call to Jerusalem like Isaiah's.
IDEAS: Sorrow turns to joy when God acts; God's holy ones gathered.

Baruch was a companion to Jeremiah, and our Apocrypha has a collection of poetry under his name – though mostly written much later. This passage is similar to many songs of Isaiah, expressing the hope for the coming Messiah to restore the fortunes of Israel.

OR *Malachi 3:1-4*

CONTEXT: Not the 'latest' OT book though placed last. Concerns the 5th century BC return from exile.
IDEAS: 'Malachi' means 'my messenger'; God judges and separates.

This messenger expects the Lord to come suddenly, heralded by another messenger to prepare his way. Christians see this fulfilled in John the Baptist, who also warned people that to encounter the Lord is not an unmixed blessing – always there is a testing and a purifying we have to face.

Philippians 1:3-11

CONTEXT: An affectionate letter to friends in Europe, written from prison.
IDEAS: Love between Christians; growing to perfection; the 'day of Christ'.

Paul writes warmly to his dear friends in Philippi. In expectation of the day of Christ's coming again he prays they may increase in love and understanding.

Luke 3:1-6

CONTEXT: Jesus and John now adults – their mission and ministry begins.
IDEAS: Preparing for Jesus to come; historical context; the messenger/herald.

We read from Luke these coming months, but in all four Gospels John the Baptist appears as the messenger whom ancient Scripture had expected. He is the forerunner and herald of Jesus, preparing the way of the Lord by calling people to repent and be baptised.

Year C: The Third Sunday of Advent

Zephaniah 3:14-20
CONTEXT: Judah and her neighbours to be destroyed for disobedience – but a remnant will be preserved.
IDEAS: The Lord is here – his Spirit is with us; gathered together by God.

This prophet of the 7th century BC is mostly a voice of doom, but this passage ends his work on a note of hope. God will always preserve a remnant of the faithful through the worst of times, and come in his own person as king and saviour.

Philippians 4:4-7
CONTEXT: Final personal greetings to dear friends.
IDEAS: Christian friendships; love and mutual concern; 'The Lord is near' = the Parousia.

'The Lord is near', wrote Paul. He means that the coming in glory of the resurrected Jesus will happen soon. During the time of waiting, be joyful, be peaceable, be prayerful, be thankful.

Luke 3:7-18
CONTEXT: Luke intertwines not only the nativity stories of Jesus and John, but the beginnings of their public ministries.
IDEAS: John the last great prophet; he baptised; strong condemnations; preparing for Jesus.

As we heard last Sunday, Christians understand John the Baptist as the one to whom ancient Scripture had pointed as God's messenger preparing the way for Jesus. John's teaching provoked controversy, but his proclamation of repentance and baptism gained him many disciples.

Year C: The Fourth Sunday of Advent

Micah 5:2-5a
CONTEXT: The restoration of the dynasty of David is anticipated.
IDEAS: David's city (1 Sam 17:12, Ephratha = Bethlehem); a pregnancy and birth; exiles return.

Like so many of the prophets, Micah embraces both judgement and hope. In his poetic language, a new king will be born in David's birthplace, Bethlehem, and will lead his people in peace.

Hebrews 10:5-10
CONTEXT: Old sacrificial systems once and for all done away with, in the sacrificial coming-to-earth and death of Christ.
IDEAS: Ps 40:6-8; Jesus's self-offering; sacrifice(s).

This writer puts words from Psalm 40 into Jesus's mouth, to show that Jesus came in complete obedience to God's will, and he abolished the old sacrificial systems by which people had approached God. He has consecrated us all in his own person.

Luke 1:39-45 [& 46-55]
CONTEXT: Angelic disclosures to Elizabeth and Mary of their miraculous pregnancies.
IDEAS: Two expectant mothers; perception and discernment.

Luke weaves together the wonderful stories of the sons born to Elizabeth and Mary. The mother of Jesus visits the mother of John, and the two are joined in the joy of what God is doing. [*If verses 46-55 are read:* Mary's hymn of praise and revolution is like that of Hannah in the Old Testament, when she named her son Samuel meaning 'one who comes from God'.]

Year C: CWL Christmas Eve (morning)

2 Samuel 7:1-5, 8-11, 16
CONTEXT: King David has defeated all the warring neighbours, and set up the Ark in Jerusalem.
IDEAS: A worthy place for God (cf. the stable); the king will bring peace; God will secure David's dynasty.

King David was told that God is content to dwell in the humblest of places. God has always been present, leading and guiding, and can always be trusted to guide and bless. All Jewish hope rested on the promise of a king like this, born of David's line.

Acts 13:16-26
CONTEXT: A synagogue sermon in Galatia.
IDEAS: God's chosen people; David and his succession; now the Saviour has come.

Paul was invited to speak at a synagogue in Galatia. His Jewish audience heard him briefly review their history under God, and the promise of a Davidic King. The way was prepared, he says; now – to us – Jesus our Saviour has come.

Luke 1:67-79
CONTEXT: Luke's stories and songs declaring two wondrous births.
IDEAS: Zechariah released from dumbness for praise; all God's promises come true; the Lord's herald.

Now the hope of centuries is satisfied, and there is nothing left but praise – the praise of old Zechariah whose own son John will usher into the world the one who is the light of the world.

Year C: Christmas Day

SET I

Isaiah 9:2-7
CONTEXT: Judah will suffer defeat by Assyria – but God will deliver.
IDEAS: Poetry of praise; visions of God's wonders; names of the child.

The Bible readings in Advent have prepared us to celebrate the coming of the Lord. His people longed for him, and we know the joy of living with him here and now. So, we understand Isaiah's prophecy as greeting the birth of a child whose new kingdom of righteousness will last for ever.

Titus 2:11-14
CONTEXT: Pastoral instruction to an established church leader in Crete.
IDEAS: God's grace; Christian 'discipline' (= training, learning); vision of a future more perfect age; Jesus (unusually for the Bible) is called God.

The new morning of the world has dawned, says this writer. As we learn how to live in this bright new light, in gratitude for the first coming of Jesus who has made us his own, we await the greater glory when Christ will come again.

Luke 2:1-14 [15-20]
CONTEXT: Luke intertwines the birth stories of Jesus and John.
IDEAS: Dating the birth; Bethlehem and its history; no welcome; another angelic sign.

Luke, the master story-teller, gives us pictures we shall never forget, of the humble birth at Bethlehem of the Saviour of the world, and the shining glory which brought shepherds to worship the Lamb of God.

SET II

Isaiah 62:6-12
CONTEXT: Third Isaiah (post-exile); promise of a new Jerusalem.
IDEAS: Jerusalem (and Israel) restored and protected; renewed by God to be holy people.

The prophet proclaims that the news of God's deliverance will reach every corner of the world, to call all his people back to himself. He will redeem them, and make them his holy ones.

Christmas Day, continued

Titus 3:4-7
CONTEXT: See Set I above.
IDEAS: Grace; generosity; saved by faith to eternal life.

Christ has come to bring a new dawn, says this writer. Now we know we are not saved by our good deeds, but by grace alone. The divine mercy makes us heirs of eternal life.

Luke 2:[1-7] 8-20
See Set I above for details.

SET III

Isaiah 52:7-10
CONTEXT: Songs of encouragement and the victory to come.
IDEAS: Good news of deliverance; return to the holy city.

In typical Hebrew style, the prophet sings of a glorious future as if it had already happened. For us, God has indeed visited and redeemed his people, glory to Israel and light for the Gentiles.

Hebrews 1:1-4 [5-12]
CONTEXT: The culmination of all God's self-revelation is in Jesus.
IDEAS: Christ present in creation; now revealed to us; his work of salvation.

In this anonymous essay, the writer contrasts the partial revelation given in times past with the outpouring of God's word in his glorious Son [*if 5-12 read:* with whom even the angels bear no comparison.]

John 1:1-14
CONTEXT: The divine disclosure in the Word made flesh.
IDEAS: Christ as *Logos* – Word, present in creation; seen on earth, rejected by many but new life for all believers.

In so few but wonderful words, John captures the majesty and the mystery of God disclosing himself; his divine Word is made flesh. Christ was from the beginning, is now, and all who believe this are children of God.

Year C: The First Sunday of Christmas

1 Samuel 2:18-20, 26
CONTEXT: Hannah's longing for a son; her prayer answered so she keeps the vow (1:11) and Samuel is 'given back to the Lord' (1:28, 2:11) for Temple service.
IDEAS: Temple as primary worship centre; growing up to please God and people.

A thousand years before Christ, the birth of Samuel was in its own way miraculous. In her gratitude for a son, his mother Hannah gave him to the service of God in the Temple, and this reading ends with words very like those Luke wrote of Jesus – a child growing up in favour with God and people.

Colossians 3:12-17
CONTEXT: Instructions on Christian behaviour.
IDEAS: All virtues summed up in love; instruction in the Gospel, gaining wisdom.

Paul says we are to teach each other the richness of the Gospel of Christ as we live and worship together, in love and peace.

Luke 2:41-52
CONTEXT: Unique to Luke, the childhood visit to Jerusalem and Temple.
IDEAS: Duty of annual Passover visit; losing and finding; Jesus had to learn; growing up with good reputation.

This precious story is all the Gospels tell us about Jesus as a boy. He accompanied his parents on their annual Passover visit to Jerusalem, and was found in deep and absorbing conversation with the religious teachers. He grew up in favour with God and people.

Year C: The Second Sunday of Christmas

Jeremiah 31:7-14
CONTEXT: Babylonian exile: a sequence of promises of restoration of the kingdom and the monarchy.
IDEAS: The remnant preserved; gathering together for celebration; gladness; bountiful provision.

Jeremiah speaks God's words, from the perspective when all nations and peoples shall be restored. The passage has many images which only found their full meaning in Christian vocabulary – God as father to his redeemed people, saviour, gatherer, shepherd and deliverer, giver of joy and gladness.

OR *Ecclesiasticus 24:1-12*
CONTEXT: The Apocrypha; in praise of wisdom (a 'person' of God).
IDEAS: God's attributes personified before Jesus came; present in creation, makes his dwelling with humankind; wisdom = Word (v. 3).

Not long before Christ's birth, these writings were collected in books we call the Apocrypha. Wisdom is here described in feminine imagery, personified as one who existed before time began, sent forth as the word of the Lord to dwell with God's people and make her home in their midst.

Ephesians 1:3-14
CONTEXT: The letter opens with a section of praise for God's blessings.
IDEAS: God's eternal purposes and choices; his gifts to us in and through Christ.

This letter begins with a hymn of praise to God for what he has done for us. The phrase 'in Christ' comes again and again: as God was in Christ Jesus, so we are one in Christ. God has made us his children and calls us to glory.

John 1:[1-9] 10-18
CONTEXT: The divine disclosure in the Word made flesh.
IDEAS: Christ as *Logos* – Word, present in creation; seen on earth, rejected by many but new life for all believers.

In so few but wonderful words, John captures the majesty and the mystery of God disclosing himself; his divine Word is made flesh. Christ was from the beginning, is now, and all who believe this are children of God.

Year C: The Epiphany: 6 January

Isaiah 60: -6
CONTEXT: Call to respond to the promise of new Jerusalem.
IDEAS: Come and worship; glory dawns; abundance.

In Isaiah's vision of God's light shining into the world's darkness, symbolic gifts are brought to God from East and West as tribute and praise. So our Gospel's Magi visitors to the Bethlehem stable are foreshadowed.

Ephesians 3:1-12
CONTEXT: The 'near' and 'far-off' united; Jew and Gentile now fellow citizens.
IDEAS: God's secrets now revealed; Paul in prison but rejoicing; all are one in Christ.

Riches beyond imagining, says Paul, are found in Christ. Though he is in prison for his faith, his gospel cannot be confined – the good news that God's purposes, once so obscure, are now made clear for Jew and Gentile alike.

Matthew 2:1-12
CONTEXT: Matthew's (unique) nativity story of gifts to Jesus.
IDEAS: The greatest king has come; journeying to him; wisdom honours him; our gifts to him.

Only Matthew tells us how representatives of other strange religions came from the East to offer their homage to the one and only true God, the child who is king for ever over all earthly powers.

Year C: The Baptism of Christ: Epiphany 1

Isaiah 43:1-7
CONTEXT: Second Isaiah, seeing all Israel redeemed from captivity.
IDEAS: God knows our name, we bear his name; safekeeping.

Whatever adversity comes upon us, wrote the prophet, we are to have no fear. We may be reminded of baptism by his words about passing through water, and God knowing us by name. Every one of us is precious to God and loved by him.

Acts 8:14-17
CONTEXT: The Gospel begins to reach beyond Jerusalem – apostles forced out of Jerusalem. Philip gains converts in Samaria.
IDEAS: Jews and Samaritans; conversion processes; baptism and the Holy Spirit.

Jews hated Samaritans, who claimed God for themselves. So when the Gospel first spread beyond Jerusalem, it was significant that Philip's preaching was effective in Samaria. Peter and John were sent to confirm this was true, and lay hands on the converts.

Luke 3:15-17, 21-22
CONTEXT: The baptising ministry of John.
IDEAS: Water baptism/Spirit baptism; sorting out the chaff; Jesus himself baptised, divine confirmation of his calling.

John the Baptist points always to the greater one whose way he was preparing, and promises a different kind of baptism from his. Jesus submits himself to John, for baptism and prayer.

Year C: Epiphany 2

Isaiah 62:1-5
CONTEXT: Third Isaiah (post-exilic); songs of praise as if the new Jerusalem had already arrived.
IDEAS: A change of status for Israel – God's delight and his bride.

Today's Gospel tells us of Jesus at a wedding; ancient poems sang of God becoming a bridegroom to his people, and giving them a new name. Listen as Isaiah delights in what the Lord will do.

1 Corinthians 12:1-11
CONTEXT: Clarifications on appropriate Christian behaviour, written to an unruly church.
IDEAS: The gifts of the Spirit; all are gifted; all parts of one body.

We begin today a series of readings from this letter, in which Paul teaches the Corinthian Christians about the gifts bestowed on us by the Holy Spirit. They are so various that not one of us can say we have no holy gift.

John 2:1-11
CONTEXT: For John, Jesus's work begins quietly but significantly.
IDEAS: 'Signs' in John's Gospel; wine (and vines, etc.) in biblical imagery; superabundant provision of finest quality; hastening the normal process of wine-making!

In the Gospel of John, the miracles of Jesus are signs – of who he is and therefore what God is like. The first sign is almost unnoticed. At a village wedding among his family and friends Jesus made extravagant quantities of water into the finest wine. The ordinary becomes the extraordinary.

Year C: Epiphany 3

Nehemiah 8:1-3, 5-6, 8-10

CONTEXT: Return from exile in Babylon; rebuilding of Jerusalem and the Temple; Nehemiah the governor, Ezra the leading priest.

IDEAS: God's Word/Law highly prized; public reading of Scripture; explanation and instruction.

Lives can be changed by reading the Scriptures. So it was when Jesus read from Isaiah in the synagogue, and so it was in the 5th century BC when the holy books, once lost, were read aloud by Ezra to the Israelites returned from exile.

1 Corinthians 12:12-31a

CONTEXT: Paul presumably answering questions (7:1a) – here about gifts of the Spirit.

IDEAS: Church as one body – the body of Christ; many functions as there are many spiritual gifts.

This reading continues the letter from last Sunday. Paul has said the gifts of the Spirit are many and various, and now he shows that these do not divide us but unite us in the body of Christ on earth, all members together.

Luke 4:14-21

CONTEXT: For Luke, the beginning of Jesus's ministry, in Galilee.

IDEAS: Regular sabbath worship; use of the O.T.; fulfilment in Jesus.

When Jesus read from Isaiah in the Nazareth synagogue, he proclaimed that he was himself the expected anointed one, bringer of good news of freedom and healing.

Year C: Epiphany 4

RCL: *Jeremiah 1:4-10*
CONTEXT: Political/religious crisis – leading to the destruction of Jerusalem and depor-
tation of many people.
IDEAS: God's knowledge and choice; a vocation implies the gifts to fulfil it.

**Sometimes it happens, as with Jeremiah, that a man or woman feels directly
confronted by the God who challenges, calls and enables people to speak for
him wherever he may need them to go.**

CWL: *Ezekiel 43:27-44:4*
CONTEXT: Chapters 40-48 describe an ideal religious centre and community (which
were never fulfilled). These verses follow the rubrics for consecrating the altar.
IDEAS: Holy things and places – who may enter and touch?

**Luke's Gospel today will tell us of Jesus the Lord coming to the Temple.
500 years earlier, Ezekiel had a vision of perfect worship in a perfect
Temple, where God himself dwelt. This passage begins after seven days
of ceremonies to consecrate the altar.**

1 Corinthians 13:1-13
CONTEXT: Paul probably answering questions (see 7:1a), here about the gifts of the Spirit.
IDEAS: Love above everything else; a gift.

**This much-loved hymn to love has a profound meaning which must rest
deeply within us all.**

RCL: *Luke 4:21-30*
CONTEXT: Jesus's ministry began in Galilee and Nazareth.
IDEAS: Fulfilment of prophetic hope; God's surprises in those we know best; furious
worshippers.

**We heard last Sunday of Jesus at a synagogue on Nazareth, where he had
been brought up. He chose to read a prophecy of Isaiah, and claimed the
promised spirit of the Lord for himself. This is the sceptical and hostile
reaction of those who heard him.**

CWL overleaf.

CWL: *Luke 2:22-40*
CONTEXT: See Exodus 13:1-2 and Leviticus 12:6-8
IDEAS: Religious duty; offering; holy waiting; visionaries.

As the Law requires, Jesus the first-born is brought to the Temple with a thank-offering. Two old and holy people, Simeon and Anna, perceive that this child is the fulfilment of ancient prophecies of redemption, but the glory will not be without pain and suffering.

Year C: The Presentation of Christ in the Temple: Candlemas

Malachi 3:1-5

CONTEXT: About 500 BC, return from exile but under Persian rule.
IDEAS: Restoration of nationhood and Temple worship; the fate of those who cannot face the Lord's coming.

In today's Gospel, Simeon will greet the infant Jesus in the Temple. Malachi speaks of the Lord coming suddenly; he knows, like Simeon, that to encounter the Lord is a mixed blessing because we have to face his testing and purifying.

Hebrews 2:14-18

CONTEXT: The theology of the humanity and divinity of Jesus.
IDEAS: Christ fully human; he is our help under all trials.

Christ became flesh and blood like us, says this writer, and we shall hear how his parents did the same as for every first-born child in Israel. Jesus fully shared our human condition, so that he could unite us all to God.

Luke 2:22-40

CONTEXT: See Exodus 13:1-2 and Leviticus 12:6-8.
IDEAS: Religious duty; offering; holy waiting; visionaries.

As the Law requires, Jesus the first-born is brought to the Temple with a thank-offering. Two old and holy people, Simeon and Anna, perceive that this child is the fulfilment of ancient prophecies of redemption, but the glory will not be without pain and suffering.

Year C: CWL Proper 1, RCL Epiphany 5
(3-9 February, if earlier than 2 before Lent.)

Isaiah 6:1-8 [& 9-13]

CONTEXT: After a collection of the prophet's speeches, the events of his life are introduced by an account of his call.

IDEAS: Visions; unworthiness; purifying; (one sent).

This reading and the Gospel illustrate different ways God calls people to his service. Isaiah was at prayer in the Temple, and overcome by the awesome holiness of God. With the vision came the promise of sin taken away [*if 9-13 are read:* and his faithful response, 'Here am I. Send me'].

1 Corinthians 15:1-11

CONTEXT: A new topic in the letter – perhaps answering another question (see 7:1) about resurrection.

IDEAS: Ours is a resurrection faith and Gospel; Christ's appearances.

We have been hearing over several weeks Paul's efforts to clarify his teaching. He turns now to the very heart of the Gospel: the fact that Jesus was raised from death and seen by many people. Paul's own apostleship stems from the appearance to him of the risen Christ.

Luke 5:1-11

CONTEXT: Luke's account of the call of Simon Peter, James, and John.

IDEAS: These three are often with Jesus when others were not; called whilst at work, to a different work; instant obedience.

This year's Gospel readings are taken consecutively from St Luke. We take up his story very early in Jesus's public ministry, around Capernaum and Lake Galilee. His call to Peter, James and John came when they were doing their everyday work.

Year C: CWL Proper 2, RCL Epiphany 6
(10-16 February, if earlier than 2 before Lent)

Jeremiah 17:5-10
CONTEXT: Miscellaneous remarks and prayer; Judah under God's judgement because of their infidelity to the covenant (17:1-4).
IDEAS: Trust in men, or in God?

The prophet reminds us not to put all our trust in people, but find the blessedness of which our Gospel will speak by casting all our care and trust on the Lord who knows us through and through.

1 Corinthians 15:12-20
CONTEXT: Explaining the pivotal truth of Christ's resurrection.
IDEAS: No resurrection = no hope; the *fact* is, Christ *was* raised.

As we heard last Sunday from this letter, all Christian faith rests on the fact of Christ's resurrection. Paul now expands this truth. We would be the most foolish people to believe a lie, but it is certain that Christ was raised to life and we are therefore saved from the state of sin.

Luke 6:17-26
CONTEXT: A decisive night of prayer brings Jesus to select the Twelve; the demanding crowds want his teaching and healing.
IDEAS: Blessed/happy (translations vary) are – or will be – those who suffer now; the rich and happy now will come to grief.

Our readings continue week by week Luke's account of the Gospel events. Very many people demanded the healing touch of Jesus. The troubled and the poor heard his promise of blessing in his kingdom.

Year C: CWL Proper 3, RCL Epiphany 7
(17-23 February, if earlier than 2 before Lent.)

Genesis 45:3-11, 15
CONTEXT: Culmination of the Joseph story – in Egypt.
IDEAS: God's history works through people; the ancestors of the 12 tribes are preserved.

Jesus teaches love, generosity and compassion. In ancient times, Joseph who had been so harshly treated by his brothers, was by the end of the story able to forgive, to love them, and provide for their need.

1 Corinthians 15:35-38, 42-50
CONTEXT: Teaching on the nature/mechanics of our 'resurrection'.
IDEAS: Seeds produce plants; physical and spiritual bodies.

This reading has a quite different theme from the other readings. It continues Paul's teaching about the fact of Christ's resurrection and our hope to be raised to life with him. He tries to explain how that can be, and what it will be like.

Luke 6:27-38
CONTEXT: Jesus's radical teaching: the Beatitudes are followed by more surprising injunctions to go beyond norms.
IDEAS: No limit to love, generosity, compassion; 'rewards'; Jesus lived what he taught.

Jesus teaches that his disciples have obligations to every neighbour that go far beyond conventionally nice behaviour. Never hit back, love your enemies, do good to everyone, always give and forgive.

Year C: : CWL Second Sunday before Lent, RCL Epiphany 8

RCL readings. See following page for CWL readings.

Ecclesiasticus 27:4-7
CONTEXT: Some proverbial sayings about honesty and character.
IDEAS: What reveals true nature.

One of Jesus's parables, as we shall hear, likens us to a tree whose fruit may be good or bad. The writer here uses similar language to speak of the things which show up a person's real qualities.

OR *Isaiah 55:10-13*
CONTEXT: The end of Second Isaiah – various instructions, and reiteration of God's faithfulness.
IDEAS: All God's actions purposeful; power of his word; rejoicing in nature.

Nothing the Lord does is wasted, writes this prophet. Even the exile of Israel in Babylon, now ending, has been an experience through which people may learn of God's purposes and the new joy and peace in his mind for them.

1 Corinthians 15:51-58
CONTEXT: Teaching on the nature and process of our 'resurrection'.
IDEAS: Kingdom not of this world; new nature; death defeated.

As on past Sundays, this reading is from Paul's profound explanation of the resurrection of Jesus, and what it means for Christians to speak of our resurrection. This was a difficult concept for the Corinthians, brought up on the Greek idea of the immortality of the human soul.

Luke 6:39-49
CONTEXT: Teaching disciples in Galilee – parables about behaviour.
IDEAS: Self-awareness; the source of our motives; foundation for life.

Four short parables of Jesus are offered by Luke, about criticising others, about the signs of faith and the foundations of faith. Each of the four has its own powerful meaning.

Year C: CWL Second Sunday before Lent, RCL Epiphany 8

CWL readings. See preceding page for RCL readings.

Genesis 2:4b-9, 15-25

CONTEXT: The theological explanation of creation.

IDEAS: Humankind last work of God; responsibility; 'green' issues and animal welfare.

Today's readings all illuminate our understanding of God as Creator. In the ancient saga of the world's creation, human beings are the last and greatest thing God made, and he gave to men and women responsibility to care for all other living things and the earth itself.

Revelation 4

CONTEXT: The first vision of this document; heaven is filled with the worship of God the creator.

IDEAS: Pictures of heaven; symbols in numbers, and creatures; God the Creator.

God is the one who created and sustains all things, says this song of praise in John's vision of the holy sovereign Lord enthroned and worshipped in heaven.

Luke 8:22-25

CONTEXT: The teaching/healing work around Capernaum and Galilee, with the Twelve and the women disciples.

IDEAS: Jesus needing sleep (see Mk 4:35 – 'evening'); sudden storms of life; divine power over nature.

The Gospels tell us that Jesus had power to calm the winds and waves, and the disciples wondered whether he was himself the creator God who alone controls the way the universe works.

Year C: CWL The Sunday next before Lent, RCL Epiphany 9

CWL readings: optional in RCL; see next page for the RCL-only alternatives.

Exodus 34:29-35

CONTEXT: Israel journeying from Egypt to Canaan; camp at Mount Sinai; the commandments and covenant renewed.

IDEAS: Transforming encounters with God – the visible effect.

This reading prepares us for the Gospel of the Transfiguration, when Our Lord's appearance became glorious. Moses, we are told, was so changed by his experiences of meeting God directly that his face shone with the reflected glory and he had to wear a veil.

2 Corinthians 3:12-4:2

CONTEXT: Paul the spokesman for God in Christ, with a ministry in the Spirit's power, of greater glory than the Moses covenant (v. 7).

IDEAS: Veiled minds; perceiving the truth and proclaiming it.

When Moses was transformed by meeting God, he veiled his face until the glory faded. Paul argues that the minds of the Jews are still veiled from a true vision and understanding, while Christians see the unfading glory of God fully revealed to us in Christ.

Luke 9:28-36 [37-43]

CONTEXT: The mission of the Twelve – further experiences for the closest three of his miraculous power and true identity.

IDEAS: Revelations on hilltops; 'departure' (v. 31) = 'exodus', implying death; Law and Prophets – completed and fulfilled in Jesus; (down to earth with a bang).

The Lord's closest friends see him transfigured upon a mountain-top, in a disclosure of his true identity. In the presence of the figures of Moses and Elijah, a cloud of glory comes upon him and the voice of the holy one is heard. [*If 37-43 are read:* But they cannot stay away from the demanding crowds.]

Year C: : CWL The Sunday next before Lent, RCL Epiphany 9

RCL only; see preceding page for CWL readings, which are alternatives in RCL.

1 Kings 8:22-23, 41-43

CONTEXT: A time of political stability: the presence of the Lord (the Ark) can be established in a permanent dwelling – Solomon's Temple.

IDEAS: God and buildings; a Temple for all nations.

At their best, the Jews remembered that God chose them not for their own sakes but to reach every nation. When Solomon dedicated the Temple he had built, his prayer included a blessing for every foreigner who might come there.

Galatians 1:1-12

CONTEXT: The letter's purpose is to counter some who would have Christians keep the Jewish Laws.

IDEAS: Paul's divine commission; only one true Gospel.

Paul's letter to the Galatian Christians begins with a conventional greeting, then quickly turns to his reason for writing. He wants to assert his independence from the Jerusalem church and its Jewish influence, for he works under a divine commission.

Luke 7:1b-10

CONTEXT: Jesus's early ministry in Galilee, based on Capernaum.

IDEAS: Approaches to Jesus; Roman soldier respected; 'remote' healing.

St Luke's Gospel is distinctive in highlighting Jesus's mission to Gentiles as well as to Jews. Here, a Roman centurion is the first foreigner to whose household Jesus brings his healing power.

Year C: Ash Wednesday

Joel 2:1-2, 12-17
CONTEXT: Visionary apocalyptic of the Day of the Lord.
IDEAS: God's coming will be fearsome – yet gracious to the penitent; come together and fast.

The powerful and dramatic words of Joel are a solemn call to public repentance, to realise the divine mercy and goodness. It helps set the tone of the Lenten season as a time for self-examination and spiritual renewal, in preparation for the gifts of Easter.

OR *Isaiah 58:1-12*
CONTEXT: The restored community are ignoring the ways of God.
IDEAS: Right motives for fasting; right ways of fasting.

The prophet denounces the hypocrisy of people who make gestures of fasting but practice injustice and deceit. Make your fast work for God: he will hear you when you ask what you should do.

2 Corinthians 5:20b-6:10
CONTEXT: An appeal to Christians not to let grace go for nothing, but sustain mutual reconciliation.
IDEAS: God's work of reconciliation; preaching without self-glorification.

Paul calls upon the Corinthian Christians to be reconciled and reconcilers. He offers his own way of life as an example of the way of a peace-maker – to bear suffering, avoid self-aggrandisement, speak the truth in love.

Matthew 6:1-6, 16-21
CONTEXT: Sermon on the Mount – teaching on prayer and fasting.
IDEAS: vv. 2, 5 & 16 reiterate 'when', not 'if'; public and private devotion.

Jesus contrasts those who do religious acts to gain admiration from others with those who are sincere. All our acts of piety, whether fasting or the symbolic use of ashes which gives this day its name, are empty or even hypocritical unless they express the spirit of true penitence, embodied in a life of prayer and service.

Alternative reading overleaf.

OR *John 8:1-11*

CONTEXT: A Passover in Jerusalem. (Many scholars regard this as not correctly a part of 'John', but an isolated pericope in the synoptic tradition.)

IDEAS: God infinitely merciful: no punishment. But don't sin again!

In Lent we are reminded of the need for repentance, as we hear again how God in Christ comes to us in forgiving tenderness. Jesus will not allow a sinful woman to be punished; his love offers new life free from sin.

Year C: The First Sunday of Lent

Deuteronomy 26:1-11
CONTEXT: Prescriptions for social and ritual behaviour in the land of Canaan.
IDEAS: Harvest thanksgiving; firstfruits; thankfulness for God's work in (exodus) salvation; religious laws.

The people of God are to have constantly in mind God's powerful wonders in history. In worship, they are to recite his great deeds and bring him offerings.

Romans 10:8b-13
CONTEXT: Righteousness sought by keeping law – now only faith in Christ.
IDEAS: The first creed, 'Jesus is Lord'; Jew and Greek both have salvation by faith.

This short passage acts as a bridge between the Old Testament and Gospel readings. Paul has been contrasting the historic Jewish faith with our faith in Christ. They looked to God for miraculous works, and mistakenly relied on doing good deeds to win salvation, whereas we know we are saved simply by our faith.

Luke 4:1-13
CONTEXT: Jesus's private retreat after his baptism by John.
IDEAS: Time to reflect; tempting prospects of easy success; revelation not by fantastic phenomena.

Jesus has to face the temptation to reveal the power of God within him by a show of mighty supernatural force. He rejects that for the ways of gentleness and compassion.

Year C: The Second Sunday of Lent

Genesis 15:1-12, 17-18
CONTEXT: Abram's journeyings, wealth, and victory in battle.
IDEAS: The Abrahamic covenant; his descendants; the Promised Land.

God's ancient covenant promise to Abram, sealed with a sacrificial offering, was that he would have more descendants than could be counted, and a vast country to call their homeland.

Philippians 3:17-4:1
CONTEXT: Paul's own example, of his past subsumed by present faith and future hope.
IDEAS: Examine your life-style; heavenly citizenship.

Paul's tone here is rather sharp, telling his Philippian converts to examine their way of life in the light of the cross, and remain faithful to their heavenly hope.

Luke 13:31-35
CONTEXT: Jesus and his disciples on the final journey to Jerusalem.
IDEAS: Good Pharisees (!); the purposeful Jesus; Jerusalem still has no peace; holy places.

God promised Abraham long ago a peaceful and fruitful land for his descendants. In due time, Jerusalem became its centre, and the Temple God's dwelling-place. Jesus laments the way his people have treated this holy gift.

Year C: The Third Sunday of Lent

Isaiah 55:1-9
CONTEXT: Conclusion of 'Second' Isaiah – the promises of return from exile.
IDEAS: The Lord's Table; all nations called; turn to God who forgives.

We can hear these ancient prophetic words as a summons for ourselves, to put God first, to seek him and listen to him. Like Jesus in today's Gospel, Isaiah calls us to repentance, for God is great and freely forgiving.

1 Corinthians 10:1-13
CONTEXT: Paul's own experience, authority and example.
IDEAS: History shows God sometimes punishes; don't try his patience!

This passage is a reminder of the fate of people who were determined to rebel against God. We, says Paul, should be strong to resist anything tempting us away from the life to which Christ calls us.

Luke 13:1-9
CONTEXT: Journeying to Jerusalem: events and encounters.
IDEAS: Sin and punishment; time for repentance.

Jesus refers to some recent events in warning of the need for repentance. A parable suggests that God always allows us second and third chances to turn to a truly fruitful life.

Year C: The Fourth Sunday of Lent

See next page for CWL readings if this Sunday is kept as Mothering Sunday.

Joshua 5:9-12

CONTEXT: The Exodus people approaching Jericho; the ancient practice of circumcision (a covenant sign) restored.

IDEAS: New beginnings, covenant renewal.

This reading has a play on words in the Hebrew. The place-name 'Gilgal' means circle, like a wheel – and as with a cartwheel God 'rolls away' the past. The Israelites are given a new start, symbolised by eating for the first time the produce of the fruitful land to which God has led them.

2 Corinthians 5:16-21

CONTEXT: Living for others, with openness, because of Christ's reconciling work.

IDEAS: New beginnings; reconciliation with God and others.

Paul tells his readers that everything is made new by Christ. There is a new order in our relationships, because in Christ the world has been reconciled to God and us to each other. We are to carry this message of reconciliation.

Luke 15:1-3, 11b-32

CONTEXT: Various teachings and encounters on the way to Jerusalem.

IDEAS: Lost and found; repentance and reconciliation; Father's welcome.

We call this parable 'The Prodigal Son', but its true meaning is The Loving Father. However far we may stray from God, or squander his gifts, his arms are always stretched out in welcome when we repent and turn back to him.

Year C: CWL Mothering Sunday

See previous page if this Sunday is kept as the Fourth Sunday of Lent.

Exodus 2:1-10
CONTEXT: There are too many Israelites for Egypt's stability: forced labour, and death to all male babies.
IDEAS: Mother's care for child; the eventual hero left to die and rescued.

The mother of Moses worked a deception to preserve her son's life, when the Egyptians were controlling the population by killing every new-born Jewish boy.

OR *1 Samuel 1:20-28*
CONTEXT: Elkanah and his two wives: Peninnah has children but Hannah has none and is mocked for it.
IDEAS: Longing for motherhood; barren wives conceive; God-given child offered back to God's service.

Samuel, that great Old Testament figure, was born to a mother who for years had been unable to bear a son. In thankfulness for God's gift, his mother took him to the Lord's house to give him back to God.

2 Corinthians 1:3-7
CONTEXT: A letter mostly of joy that the crisis in the Corinthian church was now overcome.
IDEAS: God is ever-present in trouble.

Paul writes of the consoling strength of God, the one we can all turn to in trouble, and how this grace we receive enables us to sustain one another.

OR *Colossians 3:12-17*
CONTEXT: Instructions in Christian behaviour – avoid all hurtful ways.
IDEAS: The enduring virtues, all summed up in love.

Paul writes of the compassionate gifts, forgiveness and love. These, received and given always in the name of Jesus, are a vocation for us all.

Luke 2:33-35
CONTEXT: Purification, presentation of Christ in the Temple.
IDEAS: Joseph and Mary's bewilderment; mother's suffering foreshadowed.

Jesus is the son of a human mother, just like us. In the Gospel, his earthly father and mother fade into the shadows as the nature of his life is hinted at. Yet we never forget his home, the love and teaching he received.

OR *John 19:25-27*
CONTEXT: The crucifixion of Jesus.
IDEAS: Jesus's mother sees him die; his love and concern for her.

Mary, who gave birth to Jesus, is there to watch his ugly death. Every mother's heart can suffer with her. In his last agony, Jesus's love for his mother ensures that she is not left alone.

Year C: The Fifth Sunday of Lent
(Passiontide begins)

Isaiah 43:16-21
CONTEXT: Second Isaiah – the hope of deliverance from Babylon and affirmations of God's continuing love (see 43:1-4).
IDEAS: Don't brood on past tribulations; God's ever-new ways with his people.

The prophet speaks of hope in God: for Israel, the hope of past sorrows forgotten and restoration to a land of plenty. We Christians find in this poetry a foretaste of Jesus in his holy work of making all things new by death and triumph.

Philippians 3:4b-14
CONTEXT: Paul in prison, making plans and pondering over our destiny.
IDEAS: His respectable background no longer important; yearning for greater knowledge and spiritual perfection.

Isaiah urged people not to dwell on the past, but take heart in the promise of God's radical new activity. In similar vein, Paul counts all his past as trivial compared with the marvellous knowledge of the resurrection and the hope of full union with Christ hereafter.

John 12:1-8
CONTEXT: Jesus in and near Jerusalem preparing for Passover.
IDEAS: The last week of Jesus's life; company of friends; anointing for burial.

As Jesus prepared for what would be his last Passover, he stayed with friends in Bethany. We hear the only indication in all the Gospels that Judas Iscariot, the one of the chosen Twelve who would betray him, had not always been a good and honest friend.

Year C: Palm Sunday

Luke 19:28-40:
Within the Liturgy of the Palms, this passage precedes the procession, which is itself a dramatic commentary. It is therefore best read without introduction.

Isaiah 50:4-9a
CONTEXT: A 'Servant Song' of mission and suffering.
IDEAS: Obedience to God; patient dignity and endurance.

Isaiah pictures a faithful servant of God who is deeply and unjustly humiliated, but remains dignified in suffering. As we contemplate the mystery of the cross, these words take on a profound meaning for us in the Passion of Jesus.

Philippians 2:5-11
CONTEXT: Paul in prison, writing to friends.
IDEAS: The humility of Christ and his exaltation.

It is our faith that 'Jesus Christ is Lord', because he came from God in total self-giving, and overcame the humiliation of death on a cross by rising and ascending. He is indeed worthy of our adoration and worship.

Luke 22:14-23:56 OR *Luke 23:1-49*
Traditionally, the Gospel narrative of the passion and death of Jesus has no introduction except formal words such as: 'The Passion of Our Lord Jesus Christ according to Luke'.

Year C: Monday of Holy Week

Isaiah 42:1-9
CONTEXT: The first 'Servant Song' – Israel is God's servant, but we may read these songs as prophecies of Jesus.
IDEAS: God acknowledges his Servant; quiet bringing-in of justice; light for all nations.

The Isaiah readings these next three days are appropriately called 'Servant Songs'. Whatever their original application, they speak to us of the Jesus who did not complain as he faithfully walked the way of the cross for the world's salvation.

Hebrews 9:11-15
CONTEXT: The old covenant and high-priestly sacrificial duties.
IDEAS: Christ the new and perfect high priest; his own blood; new covenant.

Christ's offering of himself in his perfect purity, says this writer, completes and transcends all the sacrificial offerings made by the priests. He has procured for us what no other could: our eternal redemption.

John 12:1-11
CONTEXT: Jesus in and near Jerusalem preparing for Passover.
IDEAS: The last week of Jesus's life; company of friends; anointing for burial.

Throughout this week we follow John's account of the way to the cross. The week begins for Jesus in the home of his friends, where Mary of Bethany anoints his feet. Some condemn what they regard as wasteful, but Jesus accepts her gift as foreshadowing his impending death and burial.

Year C: Tuesday of Holy Week

Isaiah 49:1-7

CONTEXT: Second 'Servant Song' – the restoration of Israel from Babylon.
IDEAS: Vocation; revelation; light for the world.

This week's readings are the 'Servant Songs' of Isaiah, each of which speaks of the suffering that accompanies faithful witness. The prophet may have meant Israel as the Servant, but we read it as the vocation of Jesus who, though he was despised, is true to God's will and brings light to all the ends of the earth.

1 Corinthians 1:18-31

CONTEXT: Paul's corrective to congregational disputes.
IDEAS: God's wisdom versus human folly; human wisdom versus revelation.

The cross of Christ, says Paul, is an offensive folly to most people, yet in reality it displays God's loving wisdom. We must stop trusting in our own wisdom and skills if we are to discern how freedom, salvation and righteousness are found in this cross.

John 12:20-36

CONTEXT: Jesus in and around Jerusalem preparing for Passover.
IDEAS: Death and glory; losing and keeping; light and dark.

In the week before he died, Jesus often spoke of his own suffering as being his glorification, but most people did not understand him. Those who do walk the way of the cross with him will share his light and become children of the light.

Year C: Wednesday of Holy Week

Isaiah 50:4-9a
CONTEXT: Third 'Servant Song' – of mission and suffering.
IDEAS: Obedience to God; patient dignity and endurance.

In this third of Isaiah's Servant Songs we hear of the humiliation unjustly suffered by one who teaches and consoles others. As we contemplate the mystery of the cross, these words take on a profound meaning for us in the Passion of Jesus.

Hebrews 12:1-3
CONTEXT: The great faith shown in past ages.
IDEAS: All the witnesses; perseverance; Jesus changes a cross into glory.

This writer urges us to keep our eyes fixed on Jesus. He was not deflected from his task by the ordeal he faced, and we are surrounded by examples of faithfulness which should strengthen our own resolve.

John 13:21-32
CONTEXT: Jesus in and near Jerusalem; farewell discourses to disciples.
IDEAS: Jesus betrayed; why did Judas do it? Evil turns to good in God's hands.

We are following John's narrative of the week leading Jesus to Calvary. Now and tomorrow the scene is the Last Supper, where Jesus seems to know that Judas will betray him. It was the darkest of moments when, John says, 'Judas went out. It was night.' Yet this passage does not end in despair but in Jesus glorified.

Year C: Maundy Thursday

Exodus 12:1-4 [& 5-10], 11-14
CONTEXT: The Israelites' hurried escape from Egyptian slavery.
IDEAS: Archetypal salvation event; Passover remembered and celebrated ever since.

At his last supper with his friends, Jesus transformed a Passover meal into our constant remembrance of the salvation we have in him. Appropriately today, we recall the story of the first Passover, the great saving event in Jewish history.

1 Corinthians 11:23-26
CONTEXT: How a divided congregation is to observe the Lord's Supper.
IDEAS: Eucharistic tradition; remembrance and proclamation.

This is almost certainly the earliest account of the Lord's Supper as celebrated by the church. Paul reminds the Corinthians that it was from the Lord that he received this tradition, and handed it on.

John 13:1-17, 31b-35
CONTEXT: Jesus's final meal with his friends.
IDEAS: Humble service; the ultimate commandment is to love.

We remember now another event of that night. Jesus washed his disciples' feet, and gave them a new commandment – the word is 'mandate', or 'maundy' – to follow his example in loving service to one another.

Year C: Good Friday

Isaiah 52:13-53:12
CONTEXT: Fourth 'Servant Song' – leading the return from Babylon (52:11).
IDEAS: Humiliation without complaint; despised and rejected for our sake.

This poem of God's Servant facing suffering picks up a theme from earlier readings this week. Although written centuries before Jesus, it has become for Christians one of the most profound meditations on the events and the deep meaning of Good Friday.

Hebrews 10:16-25
CONTEXT: The place of sacrifice in human approaches to God.
IDEAS: Sin forgiven; nothing separates us from God; Christ's perfect priesthood.

The writer of this letter helps our solemn reflection on what Jesus did for us this day. The Jewish sacrificial priesthood could only dare approach God's holiness with offerings and with fear. But in Christ all our sins are forgiven, and we are free to know the new, living, open way to God.

OR *Hebrews 4:14-16, 5:7-9*
CONTEXT: Scripture tells of many partial understandings of God – Jesus perfectly opens to us his intimate knowledge.
IDEAS: The sinless High Priesthood of Jesus; his suffering obedience; our access to God.

By what he did this day Jesus became a greater high priest than there has ever been, making it possible for us to approach God without fear. The work of Christ is the means of our salvation.

John 18:1-19:42
Announce as: The Passion of Our Lord Jesus Christ according to John.

Year C: Easter Eve
For use at services other than the Easter Vigil.

Job 14:1-14
CONTEXT: A theology of innocent suffering; a poetic cycle of speeches.
IDEAS: Transience of human life; in nature, new life follows death.

Job contemplates the fact that every human life ends in death. Plants cut down may rise again, but he knows of no such resurrection when we die.

OR *Lamentations 3:1-9, 19-24*
CONTEXT: Poems of lament over the fall of Jerusalem to Babylonia (587 BC).
IDEAS: Affliction within God's purposes; patient suffering; new mornings.

This writer is filled with anguish for himself and for Israel, but the reading ends in a confident and patient waiting for an act of God's love that comes 'new every morning'. (v. 23)

1 Peter 4:1-8
CONTEXT: Letter to Gentile Christians, probably under (Nero? Domitian?) persecution.
IDEAS: Enduring suffering and abuse; Christ 'descended to the dead'; the End is nigh.

The readers of this letter were enduring Roman persecution. The encouraging reminder here is that it was through suffering that Christ put an end to sin. The writer also hints at the idea of Christ descending to a place of the dead in an act of rescue.

Matthew 27:57-66
CONTEXT: Jesus has died; the body to be decently interred.
IDEAS: Generous act of Joseph; women waiting and mourning; Jewish fears that the story does not end here.

On the evening Jesus died, his body was decently placed in a tomb before the Sabbath. But even in death his influence lives on, as the religious authorities become anxious about what might happen next.

OR *John 19:38-42*
CONTEXT: Jesus has died; the body to be decently interred..
IDEAS: Acts of Joseph and Nicodemus; burial before Sabbath.

Two friends of Jesus, of whom we know so little, take care that his body is reverently placed in a garden tomb, in good time before the Sabbath when such work could not be done.

Year C: Easter Vigil

No introductions are provided for the readings at the Easter Vigil. Churches will wish to make their own choices from the provision of the Lectionary, and may use the opportunity to create a devotional sequence of lessons with psalms or canticles. It may be felt that on this occasion any other introductory material to the readings would be intrusive.

Year C: Easter Day

Acts 10:34-43
CONTEXT: Peter's teaching to a Roman centurion.
IDEAS: The life and work of Jesus; forgiveness effective for everyone.
[*If the readings from Acts will be used as the first lesson throughout the Easter season:*
During the Easter season, in place of the Hebrew Scriptures, we read the witness of the early church to the power of the Lord's resurrection.]
This is a small part of the story of Peter and a centurion of the Roman occupying army, when the Gospel first reached beyond the Jews. The teaching sums up Jesus's old and new life.
OR *Isaiah 65:17-25*
CONTEXT: 'Third' Isaiah – post-exile, but the return to the Promised Land has not brought peace and joy.
IDEAS: God still has a wonderful future for the faithful; new starts; unity in all nature.
The prophet tells of a day of delight and rejoicing, in a new order of creation when God will put away all past sins and sorrows, bringing in the age of lasting peace to his people.

1 Corinthians 15:19-26
CONTEXT: Explaining the pivotal truth of Christ's resurrection.
IDEAS: Christ the first of a new order; all will be raised; death overcome.
All Christian faith rests on the fact of Christ's resurrection, says Paul. It brings in the new hope of the resurrection age, for all Christians.
OR *Acts 10:34-43: See above.*

Year C: Easter Day, continued

John 20:1-18
CONTEXT: Jesus has died and is buried; after the Sabbath, mourning can resume.
IDEAS: The empty tomb; Peter and (?) John rush in; Jesus unrecognised; Mary the apostle to the apostles; incredibly good news.

Mary Magdalene is sometimes called 'The Apostle to the Apostles', for she was the first to see the risen Lord and tell the others. But his appearance had changed, and only love speaking to love made him known to her.

OR *Luke 24:1-12*
CONTEXT: The body of Jesus buried by Joseph; women watch.
IDEAS: Angelic messengers; complete bewilderment; news of the resurrection.

After the Sabbath, the women came to anoint the body of Jesus, but were amazed to find the tomb empty. Two strange figures reminded them he had said he would rise on the third day.

Year C: The Second Sunday of Easter

If the Old Testament reading is used, the reading from Acts must be used as the second reading.

Exodus 14:10-31, 15:20-21
CONTEXT: The Israelites have just left Egypt, taking the long way round (13:18). Pharoah then regrets the absence of the slaves and sets out after them.
IDEAS: The past was better (vv. 11, 12); a mighty miracle – the Lord acts to save.

The Jews continue to this day to give thanks for their deliverance from slavery, just as Christians continually give thanks for our salvation in Jesus. At the time of the Exodus, the Lord worked a great saving miracle at the Red Sea.

Acts 5:2 -32
CONTEXT: The church in Jerusalem, meeting regularly; preaching and healing; opposition from Sanhedrin, and arrests.
IDEAS: The Gospel cannot be silenced; Jesus raised and exalted.

[*If the Old Testament reading is not used:* During the Easter season, instead of reading the Hebrew Scriptures, we hear the effects of Christians preaching the truth of the resurrection.]
The apostles were put in prison by the Jewish authorities for preaching the resurrection. This is Peter's defence of their action before the Sanhedrin. God's witnesses cannot keep silent.

Revelation 1:4-8
CONTEXT: Opening of this unique apocalyptic work, written in exile.
IDEAS: Christ has died, is risen, will come again; God from and through eternity.

This Easter season we shall hear each week from the often difficult Revelation of John. This opening greeting is more than a conventional letter: it extols the glory of Jesus, first-born from the dead, and the God who was in the beginning, is now, and shall be for ever.

John 20:19-31
CONTEXT: The evening of Resurrection Day – Mary Magdalene is the only witness thus far.
IDEAS: Disciples keep together for safety; the same Jesus, wounded; commissioning with
Holy Spirit and 'sent'; seeing and believing.

**On the first Easter evening, Jesus appears to his disciples with his habitual
greeting of peace, and a gift of the Holy Spirit. Thomas must wait another
week until he can see, believe, and adore.**

Year C: The Third Sunday of Easter

If the Old Testament reading is used, the reading from Acts must be used as the second reading.

Zephaniah 3:14-20
CONTEXT: Judah and her neighbours to be destroyed for disobedience – but a remnant will be preserved.
IDEAS: The Lord is here – his Spirit is with us; gathered together by God.

This prophet of the 7th century BC sees a time when all will be joy and peace, for God will have saved his people, renewed them in his love, and will dwell in their midst.

Acts 9:1-6 [7-20]
CONTEXT: Persecution of the Jerusalem church (8:1b) and dispersion carrying the Gospel into the countryside; Paul a foremost antagonist (8:1a).
IDEAS: Sudden divine encounters and epiphanies; Jesus's last appearance; [Ananias's reluctance, and courage].

[*If the Old Testament reading is not used:* During this Easter season, instead of reading the Hebrew Scriptures, we read of the events which followed Christ's resurrection.]
Saul, whom we know as Paul, was one of the strongest opponents of the apostles' teaching. In what he came to describe as a sudden and abnormal birth, a life-changing encounter with the risen Christ transformed him into a great apostle and missionary.

Revelation 5:11-14
CONTEXT: Specific messages to seven churches are completed; now John's visions of heaven.
IDEAS: Ideas of symbolic/poetic language; uncountable numbers; constant praise.

Week by week we hear John's mystical visions of the glories of heaven. As he perceives it, everything God has ever created comes together to proclaim the glory of the Lord.

John 21:1-19

CONTEXT: An epilogue – perhaps by a later hand? – to John's account of the resurrection appearances.

IDEAS: Disciples back at their old working lives; Jesus breaks bread again; threefold challenge to Peter echoes his threefold denial.

Jesus, in his risen body, appeared many times to many people. Here, he joins some of his disciples for breakfast on the shore of the lake where it all began. Peter is challenged about his commitment to a life of love and service.

Year C: The Fourth Sunday of Easter

If the Old Testament reading is used, the reading from Acts must be used as the second reading.

Genesis 7:1-5, 11-18, 8:6-18, 9:8-13
CONTEXT: The world progressively worse since Eden, humankind proliferates and wickedness increases.
IDEAS: Myths and sagas adopted and adapted; new beginnings; the Ark of salvation and covenant.

The story of Noah is abbreviated in this reading. We hear the beginning, part of the middle, and the ending. In the ancient flood story, God destroys the wicked world, but uses Noah's obedience to save humanity and all created things so that there may be a new beginning.

Acts 9:36-43
CONTEXT: Paul converted, briefly joins the Jerusalem church. Numbers increase – Peter tours the region, healing.
IDEAS: Apostles perform miracles like Jesus; prayer for healing; the signs attract believers.

[*If the Old Testament reading is not used:* During this Easter season, in place of the Old Testament, we hear something of the life and witness of the first Christians.]
After the resurrection, the disciples found themselves filled with the same teaching and healing power of Jesus himself. Peter's gifts were such that, like his Master, he miraculously brought the dead back to life.

Revelation 7:9-17
CONTEXT: The faithful seen as gathered in heaven after 'The Day of the Lord'.
IDEAS: From all nations; glory through suffering; no more needs.

In John's vision of heaven, God has gathered people from all over the world. They are free of all pain and sorrow, brought into the presence of God through the work of Jesus.

John 10:22-30

CONTEXT: Jesus in Jerusalem; healings and teachings; controversies.
IDEAS: Jesus the Messiah; sheep and shepherd; gift of eternal life.

During Jesus's human lifetime, most people did not perceive him to be the expected Messiah. In this reading, as so often, Jesus points to the things he does as signs of who he is. To those who see, and follow, there is his promise of eternal life.

Year C: The Fifth Sunday of Easter

If the Old Testament reading is used, the reading from Acts must be used as the second reading.

Baruch 3:9-15, 32-4:4
CONTEXT: A late (?150 BC) anthology of poems, songs and prayers, attached to the name of Jeremiah's secretary.
IDEAS: The praise of wisdom, personified; God is incomparable.

This Apocryphal book was written much later than the Baruch we know as Jeremiah's secretary, though it contains some references to that period. This passage is typical of Hebrew wisdom literature – many of the words used about wisdom are the same as we use of Jesus. Wisdom appeared on earth and lived among men.

OR *Genesis 22:1-18*
CONTEXT: The last important sign of Abraham's total trust and obedience.
IDEAS: God tests the strong; prepare to sacrifice what you most love; faith and certainties; God's son given to suffer and die.

In today's Gospel, both Jesus and Judas Iscariot come to a moment of decision. In this passage, Abraham's faith and obedience are tested to the uttermost. He must be prepared to let his only son suffer and die if God is to work out his plan of salvation.

Acts 11:1-18
CONTEXT: Peter and Cornelius in Caesarea – the first reaching out of the Gospel to Gentiles.
IDEAS: Authority in the church; new ideas; radical reforms; old divisions swept away.

[*If the Old Testament reading is not used:* During this Easter season, we are reading about the teaching mission of the apostles.]
These Acts are those of the risen Christ in and with his church. The Jerusalem church here calls on Peter to justify his eating and preaching among Gentiles, and they realise that the new life in Christ is not restricted to a privileged few.

Revelation 21:1-6

CONTEXT: The final visions – the last judgement, all things made new.
IDEAS: Both earth and heaven renewed; eternal presence of God.

Our weekly readings are giving us some of John's visions of the glory of the risen and ascended Christ, worshipped in heaven by all the faithful. At the end of this age, John believes, there will be a new heaven and a renewed world, and God's presence will fill them both.

John 13:31-35

CONTEXT: The Last Supper – Judas has left to betray Jesus.
IDEAS: Jesus's destiny as glory.

The Gospel takes us back to the night of the Last Supper. Judas has gone out to betray Jesus, who now speaks of his own destiny not as failure but as glory, fulfilling to the uttermost God's way of love.

Year C: The Sixth Sunday of Easter

If the Old Testament reading is used, the reading from Acts must be used as the second reading.

Ezekiel 37:1-14
CONTEXT: Our book 'Ezekiel' is not in chronological order; all the visions and oracles relate to the Babylonian exile and hopes for restoration.
IDEAS: Desolation and death. Wind = breath = spirit (Heb. *Ruach*). God will give new life.

At the time of Ezekiel's vision, Jerusalem was derelict and the land laid waste. He sees nothing but dried-up bones, until the breath of God – the Spirit of God – fills the valley with life. It is a sign that God will give new life to his people Israel.

Acts 16:9-15
CONTEXT: Paul's second missionary journey – moving further westward in Asia Minor, as far as Greece.
IDEAS: God's guidance; Philippi – the great warmth of his later letter to them; 'they' becomes 'we' in this narrative – Luke himself?

[*If the Old Testament reading is not used:* During this Easter season, instead of reading the Hebrew Scriptures, we hear the work of the risen Christ in and through the apostles.]
Paul's missionary work took him into northern Greece, as he and his companions felt themselves directed by the Holy Spirit. We know that Paul made many friends, as well as converts, in Philippi.

Revelation 21:10, 22-22:5
CONTEXT: Final vision of Jerusalem (symbolic of the entire world) renewed at the end of time.
IDEAS: Holy cities; open to all; perfection.

These weekly readings now move from John's pictures of heaven back down to earth. His new Jerusalem symbolises a new kind of paradise; all humanity is redeemed, and everything is blessed by the perpetual presence of the Lord God.

John 14:23-29
CONTEXT: Jesus's farewell discourses – promise of his presence here and hereafter.
IDEAS: Love and obedience; Spirit as advocate; Jesus will return.

Jesus promised his Apostles that even when he had left them, his peace would remain, and the Holy Spirit would be sent in his name to be their teacher and guide.

OR *John 5:1-9*
CONTEXT: Jesus's second 'sign' (a healing at a distance) in Galilee; now his second visit to Jerusalem.
IDEAS: Keeping religious festivals; the helpless (contrast with rich/powerful of preceding story); genuine desire for healing.

As John tells his Gospel, Jesus's public work began with a great deal of teaching before any miraculous work. But now he shows us that the power to heal is strong enough to overcome a lifetime of disability, when Jesus comes face to face with suffering.

Year C: Ascension Day

The reading from Acts must be used as either the first or second reading.

Acts 1:1-11
CONTEXT: Introduction to Volume 2 of Luke.
IDEAS: Resurrection appearances; waiting for God; final departure.

Luke's account of the divine plan of salvation is in two parts. He ended the earthly life of Jesus, as we shall hear in the Gospel, with the event of the Ascension. Part two is the life of Christ in the church, and it begins as the Gospel ended, with the Lord leaving the earth to his home in heaven.

OR *Daniel 7:9-14*
CONTEXT: The second half of this book, a series of visions written in the terrible times of Antiochus Epiphanes (170 BC).
IDEAS: Tyrannical oppressor ultimately overthrown; sovereignty passes to a 'son of man'.

The visionary Daniel in the second century BC sees a human figure from heaven, with all the power and authority of God, becoming the sovereign over every people and nation.

Ephesians 1:15-23
CONTEXT: Probably a general letter to Gentile Christians – about faith and conduct in the church.
IDEAS: Rejoice in the signs of faith; rejoice that Jesus Christ is risen, ascended and now in glory.

The writer of this letter to the churches gives thanks, in one great long sentence of praise in the Greek, for the glory of the risen and ascended Christ – ascended to heaven and therefore empowering his people everywhere. This is the faith of the church.

OR *Acts 1:1-11. See above.*

Luke 24:44-53
CONTEXT: Conclusion of Luke's Volume 1.
IDEAS: The Old Testament has foreseen these things; Gospel for all the world; witnesses; final departure.

Luke ends his life of Jesus with a last blessing, and the commission to go into every nation as witnesses to his suffering, his death, and his resurrection.

Year C: The Seventh Sunday of Easter (Sunday after Ascension Day)

If the Old Testament reading is used, the reading from Acts must be used as the second reading.

Ezekiel 36:24-28
CONTEXT: The prophet, in the role of watchman for the Lord's coming, affirms that God will be merciful to Israel.
IDEAS: Gathering after dispersion; purifying by water; the indwelling Spirit.

We shall hear in the Gospel our Lord's prayer for those he must leave behind in this world. Ezekiel reflects the same tender care of God for his people. His images speak to Christians of Pentecost: cleansing in pure water, the giving of a new heart and an outpouring of the Spirit.

Acts 16:16-34
CONTEXT: Paul's second missionary journey – into Greece.
IDEAS: Regular prayer; Christians and secular authority; divine interventions.

[*If the Old Testament reading is not used:*** During the Easter season, instead of reading the Hebrew Scriptures, we hear how the resurrection Gospel was carried far beyond Israel.]**
Paul now is travelling with Silas, Timothy and Luke. They have reached Philippi, and we know from his letter that he made many good friends there as well as some enemies. A mob riot ended with a prison sentence for Paul and a miraculous escape.

Revelation 22:12-14, 16-17, 20-21
CONTEXT: The end of the Bible! (but not of inspired Christian writing). John concludes in joyful hope.
IDEAS: The reciprocal invitations to 'come'; God from and to eternity.

This is the glorious conclusion to the Bible. John's visions end with the assurance that God is all, in all; that Christ comes to us as we invite his presence, and he calls us to come to him.

John 17:20-26
CONTEXT: Jesus's farewell discourse ends in prayer, as he sees the end of his earthly task and the glory of it all.
IDEAS: Jesus interceding for us; unity in Christ; the divine love.

Jesus's final prayer before his arrest embraced all who, then and ever since, put their faith in him. May we be one in him, that the world may believe.

Year C: Day of Pentecost (Whit Sunday)

The reading from Acts must be used as the first or second reading

Acts 2:1-21
CONTEXT: A hundred or more meet together – the Eleven plus Matthias and women and others; festival of Pentecost 50 days after Passover.
IDEAS: Pentecost and harvest thanksgiving; strange manifestations; awesome power of the Spirit; Gospel in every language; Babel reversed.

In Jerusalem, many pilgrims had come for the great Pentecost Harvest Festival. As Jesus had promised, the Holy Spirit of God came upon the gathered company of disciples with great power. They found themselves impelled to proclaim the resurrection Gospel to everyone who would listen.

OR *Genesis 11:1-9*
CONTEXT: The world's new start after the Flood. This ancient story of the diversity of human language is used by the editors of Genesis to preface the unifying work of God through Abraham.
IDEAS: Babel = babble; man's aspiration to be as God.

The ancient legend of the Tower of Babel is the last of the symbolic passages in Genesis that try to explain how God's good creation came to be spoiled. Humankind always aspires too high, and God keeps us in our place by making our language a babble, so we do not understand one another.

Romans 8:14-17
CONTEXT: Christian life is filled with the Holy Spirit, who changes our outlook upon everything.
IDEAS: Spirit of freedom; Abba, Father, all God's children.

Paul has been contrasting law and freedom, right and wrong. The logic leads him to a favourite phrase: God's Spirit makes us God's adopted children. It is the work of the Holy Spirit to bring us into that intimate relationship with God our Father in Heaven.

OR *Acts 2:1-21. See above.*

John 14:8-17 [25-27]

CONTEXT: The farewell discourses: to know Jesus is to know God our Father.

IDEAS: Jesus the agent of the Father but one with him; prayer 'in his name'; promise of the Spirit (as advocate and teacher).

Jesus tells his disciples that because of his intimate relationship with God the Father, we who have faith in him will receive the Holy Spirit's power to continue his work in the world.

Year C: Trinity Sunday

Proverbs 8:1-4, 22-31
CONTEXT: A collection of traditional teachings from many centuries – and some non-Israelite sources. The 'Wisdom of God' speaks in her own voice.
IDEAS: God's wisdom personified – present in creation, when all was play and delight (vv. 30, 31).

Ancient writers called wisdom a 'Person' of God, who was with him when all things were created. Wisdom comes forth from God, and her voice is to be listened to.

Romans 5:1-5
CONTEXT: Faith alone can set us free for life in Christ.
IDEAS: Joy and hope; the astounding work of Christ.

The love of God the Father, shown in Jesus Christ his Son, is brought to us by the Holy Spirit. So we can have peace and hope by our faith in the Holy Trinity.

John 16:12-15
CONTEXT: Jesus's farewell discourses to his disciples; the necessity of his departure from them.
IDEAS: The promise and work of the Spirit; what Jesus is, the Father is.

In his final teaching to his disciples, Jesus tells the deep truth of God as a trinity in unity. Whatever belongs to Jesus also belongs to God the Father, and this is revealed to us by the Holy Spirit.

Year C: Day of Thanksgiving for Holy Communion
Thursday after Trinity Sunday (Corpus Christi)

Genesis 14:18-20
CONTEXT: Abram and Lot go separate ways (13:11, 12); Abram goes to the rescue of Lot, defeating the four eastern kings.
IDEAS: Salem (v. 18) = Jerusalem; ceremonial bread and wine; the great priest-king.

Melchizedek is a legendary name from the Israelite past. He was believed to be a priest-king of Jerusalem long before King David made it his capital. In this reading, he acts to seal God's covenant with Abram in an offering of bread and wine, and a blessing.

1 Corinthians 11:23-26
CONTEXT: How a divided congregation is to observe the Lord's Supper.
IDEAS: Eucharistic tradition; remembrance and proclamation.

This is almost certainly the earliest account of the Lord's Supper as celebrated by the church. Paul reminds the Corinthians that it was from the Lord that he received this tradition, and handed it on.

John 6:51-58
CONTEXT: Five thousand fed, and teaching about 'true bread' from heaven.
IDEAS: The bread of life (vv. 34, 48); Jesus's body and blood; eternal life.

To receive the body and blood of Jesus, he says, is to take his eternal life into our very being. This is not an easy truth to understand, yet it is the most profound of all realities.

Year C: Proper 4 (29 May-4 June, if after Trinity Sunday. Week 9.)

Continuous Old Testament: 1 Kings 18:20-21 [& 22-29], 30-39
CONTEXT: Chapters 17-19 are a collection of stories (legends?) told of the miraculous power of God through Elijah. Ahab had introduced Baal-worship.
IDEAS: Sacrifices and fire (cf. 1 Chron 21:26); worship other gods; proving God's power.

We begin today a series of weekly readings that introduce us to the great prophetic tradition of Israel. This is the account of Elijah's dramatic victory over the followers of the false god Baal, by invoking the power of the Lord.

Related Old Testament: 1 Kings 8:22-23, 41-43
CONTEXT: A time of political stability: the presence of the Lord (the Ark) can be established in a permanent dwelling – Solomon's Temple.
IDEAS: God and buildings; a Temple for all nations.

At their best, the Jews remembered that God chose them not for their own sakes but to reach every nation. When Solomon dedicated the Temple he had built, his prayer included a blessing for every foreigner who might come there.

Galatians 1:1-12
CONTEXT: The letter's purpose is to counter some who would have Christians keep the Jewish Laws.
IDEAS: Paul's divine commission; only one true Gospel.

Paul's letter to the Galatian Christians begins with a conventional greeting, then quickly turns to his reason for writing. He wants to assert his independance from the Jerusalem church and its Jewish influence, for he works under a divine commission. We shall hear more of this in the coming weeks.

Luke 7:1-10
CONTEXT: Jesus's early ministry in Galilee, based on Capernaum.
IDEAS: Approaches to Jesus; Roman soldier respected; 'remote' healing.

Our Sunday Gospels are now read consecutively from St Luke, whose style is distinctive in highlighting Jesus's mission to Gentile as well as Jew. Here, a Roman centurion is the first foreigner to whose household Jesus brings his healing power.

Year C: Proper 5 (5-11 June, if after Trinity Sunday. Week 10.)

Continuous Old Testament: 1 Kings 17:8-16 [& 17-24]
CONTEXT: Episodic accounts of Elijah's life and work.
IDEAS: God works with power through his servants; miraculous provision.
Either (a) if this Sunday is Trinity 1:
For the rest of this year, we read Old Testament lessons about Israel's great prophets, beginning with Elijah.
or (b) if Proper 4 readings were read on the previous Sunday:
Our weekly accounts of Israel's prophets tell us more of Elijah.
then the following:
The miraculous supply of food for the hungry is a recurrent theme of the Bible [*if 17-24 are read:* as is the power to heal given to holy people].

Related Old Testament: 1 Kings 17:17-24
CONTEXT: Stories about Elijah, in his striving to hold Israel to the true God against the worship of Baal.
IDEAS: Raising the dead to life; the prophet blamed then praised.

Today's Gospel tells us that Jesus raised to life the dead son of a widow. No wonder some thought him to be Elijah come again, for they all knew this story of Elijah and the widow's son.

Galatians 1:11-24
CONTEXT: Paul justifying his independance from the Jerusalem church and its teaching which was still not free from Jewish observances.
IDEAS: True conversions; missionary styles; church structures and authority.

Readings from this letter continue independently of the other lessons. Paul is here strongly defending the authentic nature of his conversion. His teaching does not depend on the church developments in Jerusalem.

Luke 7:11-17
CONTEXT: A miracle story unique to Luke; neither the geography (see e.g. 7:1 & 8:1) nor the occasion are perhaps wholly reliable.
IDEAS: Jesus (at least as) powerful as Elijah; his growing reputation.
[*If this Sunday is Trinity 1:* Each Sunday we now read consecutively through Luke's Gospel.]
Luke has already told us of Jesus's power to heal the sick, and now he reveals greater divine power still. It is an extraordinary moment when Jesus, just like Elijah of old, restores life to the dead son of a widow.

Year C: Proper 6 (12-18 June, if after Trinity Sunday. Week 11.)

Continuous Old Testament: 1 Kings 21:1-10 [& 11-14], 15-21a
CONTEXT: Elijah's confrontations with King Ahab, who encouraged Baal-worship.
IDEAS: The abuses of power; Lady Macbeth?; confronting the king.
Either (a) if this Sunday is Trinity 1:
For the rest of this year, we read Old Testament lessons about Israel's great prophets, beginning with Elijah.
or (b) if Proper 5 readings were read on the previous Sunday:
This story adds to our week-by-week picture of Elijah.
then the following:
Naboth owned a vineyard, and King Ahab's wife Jezebel contrived both murder and theft. Elijah confronted royal authority with a pronouncement of God's condemnation of these crimes.

Related Old Testament: 2 Samuel 11:26-12:10, 13-15
CONTEXT: David – the heroic, ideal king – shown in a very bad light, a selfish murdering intriguer.
IDEAS: Dangers of sexual desires; deceit and discovery; David the fallible hero.

In this reading and the Gospel, women are prominent. Bathsheba was greatly wronged by King David. He had her husband killed to try and keep his adultery secret. In contrast to Jesus, who forgave an adulterous woman, the prophet Nathan severely condemned David, and it seems God punished him too.

Galatians 2:15-21
CONTEXT: Paul's apostolic authority and the irrelevance of Jewish principles to Christians.
IDEAS: Law and faith; life changed from the inside.

This is the key passage in this letter. Paul attacks any kind of religious legalism. The Christian life means quite simply we are accepted by God because of our faith in Christ, just as we are, yet absorbed into a new life because Christ is alive within us.

Luke 7:36-8:3
CONTEXT: Jesus's teaching and work around Galilee.
IDEAS: Not all Pharisees shunned Jesus; sincere repentance; love and forgiveness; saving and healing.

[*If this Sunday is Trinity 1:* **Each Sunday we now read consecutively through Luke's Gospel.**]

Anyone who comes to Jesus in penitence will know God's forgiveness, wrote Luke, however great their sin. So we hear that one woman with a background of immorality is saved, and many other women whom Jesus healed now gave their lives to his work.

Year C: Proper 7 (19-25 June, if after Trinity Sunday. Week 12.)

Continuous Old Testament: 1 Kings 19:1-4 [& 5-7], 8-15a
CONTEXT: Elijah's despair, despite defeating prophets of Baal (18:40); his life under threat from Ahab.
IDEAS: Run away when things get tough; encounter with God in bleakness; the still small voice.

Either (a) if this Sunday is Trinity 1:
For the rest of this year, we read Old Testament lessons about Israel's great prophets, beginning with Elijah.
or (b) if Proper 6 readings were read on the previous Sunday:
As we heard last Sunday, King Ahab and his wife Jezebel promoted the worship of Baal.
then the following:
When Elijah killed many of the prophets of Baal his own life became threatened. He ran away, but in his solitude the Lord called quietly to him, recalling him to the part he must play in the overthrow of Ahab.

Related Old Testament: Isaiah 65:1-9
CONTEXT: 'Third' Isaiah – the post-exilic community no more faithful than their ancestors.
IDEAS: God's judgements on behaviour – but always the promise of salvation.

This reading very specifically explains why Jesus's actions in today's Gospel caused such outrage. Isaiah rails against those who provoke God, he says, by frequenting such unholy places as graveyards and eating forbidden food such a pork. To the Jew a cemetery is the home of demons, all death is defiling, and pigs are taboo.

Galatians 3:23-29
CONTEXT: Jewish Law does not apply within Christian freedom.
IDEAS: The Law did have its value; the intimate union of all faithful with God and each other.

The Jewish Law was good and necessary, says Paul, but only until the time when Jesus Christ came to unite us to God and make all of us his children. Faith alone now justifies us.

Luke 8:26-39

CONTEXT: Jesus's teaching ministry in towns and villages around Lake Galilee – an excursion into Gentile territory.

IDEAS: Taboos and superstitions; demonic possession; Jesus (always!) causes a stir.

[*If this Sunday is Trinity 1:* **Each Sunday we now read consecutively through Luke's Gospel.**]

Luke shows us Jesus's power at work not just for Jews, but in Gentile territory too, where a graveyard and the pigs represent all that is most unholy. A demented and violent man is brought to wholeness.

Year C: Proper 8 (26 June-2 July. Week 13.)

Continuous Old Testament: 2 Kings 2:1-2, 6-14

CONTEXT: Direct continuation of 1 Kings – Elisha succeeds Elijah. (NB v. 15a is important, though this lection stops before it.)
IDEAS: Jordan divided again; 'the spirit' passes to a successor.

Sunday by Sunday we read stories of Israel's great prophets. This is the time when Elisha succeeded the great Elijah. It is said Elisha assumed the mantle of Elijah, and he soon demonstrated that God's power was equally at work in him.

Related Old Testament: 1 Kings 19:15-16, 19-21

CONTEXT: Elijah's despair and isolation, and his new commission from the Lord.
IDEAS: Prophetic succession; time to prepare for discipleship.

When Elijah called Elisha to follow him, he allowed time for him first to put his affairs in order, whereas Jesus – as we shall hear – required an immediate and urgent decision by those he called to be his disciples.

Galatians 5:1, 13-25

CONTEXT: Christians must not revert to the legalistic behaviour of Jews.
IDEAS: Our freedom is not free licence; life directed by love, Spirit-guided.

Paul has destroyed the arguments of those who wanted Christians to keep all the Jewish Law. He now warns that this freedom does not mean giving free rein to our desires, but a life of love for every neighbour with every action guided by the Spirit.

Luke 9:51-62

CONTEXT: Luke ends the Galilean work: the remainder is journeying to Jerusalem (though both timing and geography are confused!)
IDEAS: Journey through (hostile) Samaria; commitments or excuses prevent discipleship.

Luke's Gospel now sets Jesus on his way to his destiny in Jerusalem, though we shall hear of many encounters on the way. He, and the men and women with him, are not always welcomed; some who are at first attracted are not prepared to leave everything for his sake.

Year C: Proper 9 (3-9 July. Week 14.)

Continuous Old Testament: 2 Kings 5:1-14
CONTEXT: In this series on the prophets, the only Elisha story. One of several miraculous healings, raising the dead, feeding a crowd, purifying poisoned food and water.
IDEAS: Politics and diplomacy; some leprosy not crippling (v. 1a); God requiring only the simple thing.

Elisha is said to have received the healing power and authority of his teacher Elijah. In this well-known story, Naaman expected to pay a great price to be healed of leprosy, but Elisha's message is that for Naaman the simplest way is God's way.

Related Old Testament: Isaiah 66:10-14
CONTEXT: A collection of speeches of 'Third' Isaiah – resettlement after exile does not match the expectations.
IDEAS: Hopes for God's future of peace and prosperity.

It is the end of this short reading that relates to the Gospel. In the time of God's final act of salvation, says the writer, those who are his servants will know his power at work in them, So it was when Jesus sent out disciples with his power and authority.

Galatians 6:[1-6] 7-16
CONTEXT: Christian conduct under the Spirit's guidance; reminder (v. 13ff) of his main theme – Christian freedom from Jewish Law (see 2: 3ff).
IDEAS: [Mutual care; humility] always look to do good; beware those who make rules!

Paul brings to an end this letter, which we have read over several weeks. He continues to describe Christian life under the guidance of the Holy Spirit, then a postscript in his own handwriting sums up an earlier point of controversy.

Luke 10:1-11, 16-20
CONTEXT: Unique to Luke – see Ch 9: Mt. and Mk. both have parallels to sending Twelve. 70 (or 72 in some texts) lead the way.
IDEAS: 12 symbolise Israel, 70 equal Gentiles; mission is urgent, to prepare, bring peace, heal, proclaim the kingdom.

As we read through this Gospel we have already heard of a time when Jesus sent the Twelve on a mission. Now, Luke tells us of a different and larger group, sent by Jesus to do his work in his name, wherever he would soon follow.

Year C: Proper 10 (10-16 July. Week 15.)

Continuous Old Testament: Amos 7:7-17
CONTEXT: Israel prosperous, before the Assyrian conquest. To Amos the countryman, corruption and moral degradation in the city was unbearable.
IDEAS: Things need straightening out; God's imperative to speak.

This weekly series of brief snapshots from the prophets brings us to Amos. In his time, Israel was prosperous, but also greatly corrupt. Amos' upbringing was not typical of great men of God, and his voice is the fiercest to be found in the Old Testament.

Related Old Testament: Deuteronomy 30:9-14
CONTEXT: The end of Moses' great discourse before leadership passes to Joshua.
IDEAS: The one great life choice: God, or not God.

Moses set God's Law before the people not as a burden, but as a way to be followed with all their heart and soul. It was for them to choose this as a way of life.

Colossians 1:1-14
CONTEXT: A corrective to serious doctrinal errors; Christ unique and supreme.
IDEAS: Thankfulness for news of Christians; other early missionaries besides Paul; prayer for the church.

The Gospel was preached in Colossae by Epaphras, and we have no record of Paul going there. But he writes to assure them of his prayers, and to call them to a true doctrine of Christ alone as Saviour.

Luke 10:25-37
CONTEXT: An incident on the journey to Jerusalem.
IDEAS: Love sums up the law; response of the respectable to need; the world is my neighbour; what I can do is nearest to me.

A lawyer's encounter with Jesus gives us the familiar parable of the good Samaritan – an unexpected lesson in neighbourliness.

Year C: Proper 11 (17-23 July. Week 16.)

Continuous Old Testament: Amos 8:1-12

CONTEXT: (See Proper 10) Amos, from Judah, in Israel.

IDEAS: Hebrew wordplay on 'ripe' (v. 2); the strength of Amos's denunciation (9:8b ff becomes optimistic).

Last Sunday we heard how Amos, a country shepherd, found himself compelled by God to confront the moral decay of Israel. Here, a play on words in Hebrew links summer-time to an end of time, and Amos's fierce condemnation sees God's punishment as bringing cosmic destruction.

Related Old Testament: Genesis 18:1-10a

CONTEXT: The covenant with Abraham sealed by circumcision – promise of a son for Sarah.

IDEAS: Hospitality; 'angels unawares'; God's extraordinary promises.

Hospitality is the theme of this reading and the Gospel. Three strangers, whom we guess to be angels, are given a warm welcome by Abraham, and they tell him God's promise of exactly what he wanted to hear.

Colossians 1:15-28

CONTEXT: Emphasis on Christ as superior to all other real or imagined beings.

IDEAS: Christ in creation; other supernatural beings/powers; Gospel of reconciliation; God's secrets revealed.

Paul's hymn to the sovereignty of Christ is rich in images of his work in creation and salvation. The church, Paul says, is caught up into the very presence of God.

Luke 10:38-42

CONTEXT: Luke has Jesus now in Bethany, very near to Jerusalem, though later (e.g. 13:32) the journey is still much further away.

IDEAS: Christian hospitality and friendship; different gifts of discipleship.

This brief incident contrasts Martha and Mary, sisters in Bethany. The way of welcoming Jesus can be active, or contemplative, and both are good.

Year C: Proper 12 (24-30 July. Week 17.)

Continuous Old Testament: Hosea 1:2-10
CONTEXT: Probably a contemporary of Amos – the threat from Assyria. God's judgement and destruction tempered by love even for the faithless.
IDEAS: Lessons from unhappy marriage; names as powerful symbols; God's undying love.

The message of Hosea to a people soon to be overrun by Assyria is a mixture of God's judgement and his love. Hosea's prophetic witness is drawn from the sweet and bitter experience of his own marriage.

Related Old Testament: Genesis 18:20-32
CONTEXT: God's promises to Abraham – he and his descendants to be God's people, but the wicked destroyed.
IDEAS: The power of intercession; the bad spared because of the few good.

We learn today some lessons about prayer in this reading and the Gospel. Abraham's prayer is for God to spare a community for the sake of the innocent. We know that God listens to prayer and always answers.

Colossians 2:6-15 [16-19]
CONTEXT: Continuing the corrective to mistaken arguments and teachings.
IDEAS: Reject speculation; profound significance of baptism; [eschew extreme religious practices].

The purpose of this letter is to hold together the Colossian church in the face of a growing diversity of teaching. Avoid all pointless speculation, remain centred on Christ alone, says Paul. [If 16-19 are read: In particular, ignore those who go to extremes in living out their faith.]

Luke 11:1-13
CONTEXT: A miscellany of incidents and teachings.
IDEAS: The pattern prayer; persistence in prayer; God will hear and answer.

When Jesus taught his disciples about prayer, the words in one form or another became central for every Christian. His lesson is that God our Father never refuses to listen or respond to his children.

Year C: Proper 13 (31 July-6 August. Week 18.)

Continuous Old Testament: Hosea 11:1-11

CONTEXT: Israel has spurned God's love, worshipped other gods, and will be punished.

IDEAS: God nurturing his people; his love never lets go.

Hosea wrote from his own experience of an unfaithful wife. His poetry sings of the tender unfailing love of God for his people despite all their unfaithfulness.

Related Old Testament: Ecclesiastes 1:2, 12-14, 2:18-23

CONTEXT: A pessimistic book – all endeavour is futile, and God cannot be comprehended by mankind.

IDEAS: God is not comprehensible; worldly values are pointless; the Bible is not always encouraging!

This reading has a gloomy theme, as the writer describes all human endeavour as futile, ending in death for everyone. It undergirds Jesus's teaching about the futility of concentrating on worldly success and acquiring material things.

Colossians 3:1-11

CONTEXT: Continuing the teaching about true purposes and conduct.

IDEAS: New life in Christ changes everything; purity in behaviour; union.

As we have heard these past three Sundays, this letter uses rich language to teach the unique riches of life in Christ, as Paul strives to recall this church from its dangerous fragmentation. Their conduct as Christians, he now says, must be quite different from that of their previous lives.

Luke 12:13-21

CONTEXT: Luke's collected incidents and teachings: on ultimate things.

IDEAS: More does not mean better; the futility of acquisitiveness; God's riches.

In a parable, Jesus illustrates the folly of spending all our energies piling up wealth and success. God takes no account of the things we acquire, but only the spiritual riches we invest.

Year C: Proper 14 (7-13 August. Week 19.)

Continuous Old Testament: Isaiah 1:1, 10-20
CONTEXT: Isaiah of Jerusalem – the beginning of his 40-year prophetic work.
IDEAS: What God requires of us – action not ritual; sin can be forgiven.

Elijah, Elisha, Amos, Hosea – now Isaiah, as our weekly readings give a brief survey of Israel's great prophetic voices. Isaiah's first recorded speech contrasts religious ceremonial with the true service of God which is care for the poor and oppressed.

Related Old Testament: Genesis 15:1-6
CONTEXT: Abram's journeyings, wealth, and victory in battle.
IDEAS: Conversations with God; yearning for children; utter faith and commitment.

The end of this short reading is the link to the Gospel, because it speaks of the complete faith and trust in God characteristic of Abram.

Hebrews 11:1-3, 8-16
CONTEXT: After the deep theology of this document, a section on historic faith.
IDEAS: Scriptural examples of faith and its outcomes.

Late in the first century AD [CE], someone unknown wrote this profound theological document. This extract explores the nature of faith as seen in the Old Testament saints, and over the next few Sundays we shall hear of the faith of Christians.

Luke 12:32-40
CONTEXT: Sundry teachings on preparedness for a coming crisis, and giving God priority.
IDEAS: Lives dedicated to the kingdom; expectancy of Christ coming again.

Our hearts must be centred on God, says Jesus, as the only truly important thing in our life. Then we shall always be ready and expectant when Christ comes to us.

Year C: Proper 15 (14-20 August. Week 20.)

Continuous Old Testament: Isaiah 5:1-7
CONTEXT: The early Isaiah's prophecies of Judah's downfall because of disobedience.
IDEAS: Vineyards; good and bad fruit; dereliction is sometimes God's way.

Isaiah tells the parable of a vineyard, and then explains it. God's people are the Lord's vineyard, planted and nourished by him. Isaiah is here warning that because of the people's unfaithfulness and bad leadership, Jerusalem and Judah are about to be over-run by Assyria: it is sometimes the will of God to allow his vineyard to be ruined.

Related Old Testament: Jeremiah 23:23-29
CONTEXT: A harangue against godless prophets.
IDEAS: Contrast dreams with divine visions; the true power of God's word.

Do not expect the word of the Lord always to be comfortable, says Jeremiah. False prophets tell only their dreams and their lies, and comfortable messages; a true voice brings God's challenge, burning and breaking our stubborn hearts.

Hebrews 11:29-12:2
CONTEXT: Praise of examples of faith from the Scriptures.
IDEAS: Ancient faith and the evidence of its outcome; witnesses of our prayers.

This writer praises the faith of men and women of Israel in past times, as lessons for us who have received the far greater revelation of God in Jesus. We have inherited what they could only hope for.

Luke 12:49-56
CONTEXT: A section of Luke's collected teachings concerned with predictions of the Coming One.
IDEAS: Christ divides a household; signs of the times.

Jeremiah said God's coming would be like fire, separating out all impurity. Jesus says this is what he has come to do; he will be the cause of unhappy divisions, because of those who fail to recognise the signs of his presence and his kingdom.

Year C: Proper 16 (21-27 August. Week 21.)

Continuous Old Testament: Jeremiah 1:4-10
CONTEXT: Political/religious crisis – leading to destruction of Jerusalem and deportation of many people.
IDEAS: God's knowledge and choice; a vocation implies the gifts to fulfil it.

Our weekly brief survey of Israel's prophets now introduces Jeremiah, called to speak God's word to people who in his lifetime would be deported, their land devastated by the Babylonians.

Related Old Testament: Isaiah 58:9b-14
CONTEXT: The restored community of Israel still ignoring the demands of social justice.
IDEAS: God favours the generous and kind-hearted; sabbath observance.

Justice, and generosity, says Isaiah, are what God requires of us. And just as we find so often in the teachings of Jesus, there is here a challenge to the proper keeping of the Lord's Sabbath day.

Hebrews 12:18-29
CONTEXT: The enduring history of faith; the new perspective in the revelation of God in Christ.
IDEAS: Approaching God in his holiness – face to face with him.

On recent Sundays we have heard this writer praising the saints of ancient times, while drawing a contrast between their faith and ours. Unlike them, he says, we come to God through Jesus without fear, in reverence and awe and thanksgiving.

Luke 13:10-17
CONTEXT: Jesus has been speaking of the impending crisis – the kingdom of God has broken in.
IDEAS: Sabbath/Sunday observance; opposition to Jesus – and people's enthusiasm.

Jesus's ministry was to teach and to heal. On a Sabbath day, he was permitted to teach, but the synagogue President objected to him healing a crippled woman. Jesus responds with a sharp lesson about priorities.

Year C: Proper 17 (28 August-3 September. Week 22.)

Continuous Old Testament: Jeremiah 2:4-13
CONTEXT: Jeremiah's first recorded speech: reminding the people of their past apostasy.
IDEAS: God's greatness in times past; why reject him?

Jeremiah's early mission to Israel and Judah was to plead in God's name for them to reject false Canaanite gods, and recall the tender care of the Lord.

Related Old Testament: Ecclesiasticus 10:12-18
CONTEXT: Wisdom in government and neighbourliness.
IDEAS: The sin of pride; blessed are the meek.

This Apocryphal reading, and today's Gospel, contrast pride and humility. Those who are wise, says this writer, will realise that pride is a sin, contrary to the way God intends us to be.

OR *Proverbs 25:6-7*
CONTEXT: A collection of proverbial wisdom.
IDEAS: Pride and humility.

This very short reading must surely have been known by Jesus, for he also taught about taking the humblest place rather than pushing yourself forward.

Hebrews 13:1-8, 15-16
CONTEXT: The conclusion of this very theological document – some brief miscellaneous injunctions.
IDEAS: Love, hospitality, marriage, wealth, Christian leadership.

This essay, complex in many ways, ends simply with some specific instructions about the Christian way of life, which gives praise to God in both word and deed.

Luke 14:1, 7-14
CONTEXT: Encounters and teachings – the continuing debate with Pharisees.
IDEAS: Ambiguity in hospitality (v. 1); securing your position; exercises in humility.

Jesus's parable is a stern lesson not to think too highly of ourselves but to copy his humility – and also, like him, give our greatest concern to those in greatest need.

Year C: Proper 18 (4-10 September. Week 23.)

Continuous Old Testament: Jeremiah 18:1-11
CONTEXT: The threatened invasion – calls to repentance.
IDEAS: God gives the messages; teaching using familiar scenes; God's second thoughts(?).

Before the fall of Jerusalem to the Babylonians, Jeremiah's message was that the disaster could still be averted. If only the people would turn back faithfully to the Lord, he would act to save them.

Related Old Testament: Deuteronomy 30:15-20
CONTEXT: The end of Moses' great discourse before leadership passes to Joshua.
IDEAS: The one great life choice: God, or not God.

Everyone has one big choice to make, says Moses. Either you acknowledge God, obey his will, and find true life; or you can choose to reject God's ways and go your own way. It is literally a life or death choice.

Philemon 1-21
CONTEXT: A very personal letter, probably from Rome (?AD 60). Paul sends back a (now Christian) runaway slave to his erstwhile (also Christian) master.
IDEAS: Good friendships; love should temper punishment.

This reading gives us almost all the short and moving letter from Paul to a friend in Colossae whose house was the church meeting-place. Philemon's slave had run away; Paul pleads as one Christian to another that Onesimus now be received back as a dear brother.

Luke 14:25-33
CONTEXT: The journey to Jerusalem: teachings on the radical nature of the new kingdom and those who enter it.
IDEAS: Cost of commitment; reflecting on what discipleship means.

Jesus often makes it clear that to choose his way, bringing joy and life, also has a cost. In this passage he uses exaggerated language to speak about the radical nature of his demands.

Year C: Proper 19 (11-17 September. Week 24.)

Continuous Old Testament: Jeremiah 4:11-12, 22-28
CONTEXT: God appeals through Jeremiah for the people to reject false gods, because Assyria threatens apostate Judah and Jerusalem.
IDEAS: Consequences of unfaithfulness; wars never cease.

This is a typical lament of Jeremiah, as our weekly readings show us the great prophets declaring the ways of the Lord. The coming destruction of Judah is seen to represent divine judgement on the unfaithful people.

Related Old Testament: Exodus 32:7-14
CONTEXT: Camp at Sinai; Moses spending long times with God, and the people become impatient.
IDEAS: Absent leadership; people creating own gods; prayer for mercy.

In Moses's long absence, the Israelites made a golden calf to worship instead of God. Moses prays God to forgive them, and is shown the same mercy and grace which Jesus says is available to every penitent sinner.

1 Timothy 1:12-17
(Note: The introductions for Proper 19 to 25 inclusive, readings from 'Timothy', take the premise of most scholars that the letters are not the work of Paul, but later pastoral advice and instruction from a senior church figure to a local elder. I therefore deliberately avoid Pauline attribution, while also avoiding making explicit the case either way.)
CONTEXT: A 'pastoral charge' to an elder who has responsibility for a church.
IDEAS: Grace to equip for ministry; God's mercy; salvation in Christ.

The letters addressed to Timothy, which we now read over several weeks, concern pastoral matters in a young church, and the responsibilities of oversight. A familiar doctrine is quoted here, as a reminder that all can be forgiven, and Christian leaders receive grace sufficient for their task.

Luke 15:1-10
CONTEXT: Luke's loosely connected teachings and encounters; the first two of three parables about losing and finding.
IDEAS: God seeks the lost; Jesus's understanding of heaven; joy.

Two parables about recovering lost things demonstrate God's persistence and initiative in seeking to restore all who are lost, and the joy in heaven over penitent sinners.

Year C: Proper 20 (18-24 September. Week 25.)

Continuous Old Testament: Jeremiah 8:18-9:1
CONTEXT: Imminent war – political instability – Jeremiah laments judgement on Judah.
IDEAS: God calls but people don't respond; pain at the heart of God.

The very name of Jeremiah has become synonymous with gloom. In this short passage we hear him at his most despairing, for the distress that is about to overtake the nation.

Related Old Testament: Amos 8:4-7
CONTEXT: Amos proclaiming God's truth against the priest Amaziah.
IDEAS: God requires honest dealings; God remembers all we do.

The prophet rails against all who fail to show the virtues of honesty and compassion. What appear to be our best interests may well be only selfish sins.

1 Timothy 2:1-7
(See note at Proper 19 above.)
CONTEXT: Pastoral charge concerning church oversight.
IDEAS: Pray for God's world; Christ our mediator.

In phrases that were probably part of an early Christian liturgy, the church is called to prayer for the peace of the world and its leaders, because God's will is salvation for all.

Luke 16:1-13
CONTEXT: A section of teaching with the theme of wealth.
IDEAS: Difficult parables! the uses of ingenuity; self-interest and higher good.

This parable seems to praise dishonesty, but we must hear it as a challenge to perceive where our best interests lie, and to pursue the truest good.

Year C: Proper 21 (25 September-1 October. Week 26.)

Continuous Old Testament: Jeremiah 32:1-3a, 6-15
CONTEXT: A renewed covenant promise to Israel and Judah – but first, Jerusalem must fall to Babylon.
IDEAS: Faith demonstrated by action; hearing God's (unlikely) guidance.

Just a year before Jerusalem fell to Babylon, Jeremiah gave a practical demonstration of his confidence that within his lifetime God would restore the people and their land.

Related Old Testament: Amos 6:1a, 4-7
CONTEXT: Amos the countryman appalled at the corruption of city life.
IDEAS: The uncaring rich and comfortable; irresponsibility has its nemesis.

This prophetic condemnation of those who live in luxury without a care for others prepares us for our Lord's familiar parable of the rich man ignoring a beggar at his gate.

1 Timothy 6:6-19
(See note at Proper 19 above.)
CONTEXT: Some final instructions to a church elder, following many detailed sections on church discipline.
IDEAS: Material/spiritual needs; life's direction and goal; Christian authority.

This letter to a Christian pastor concludes with some advice about handling wealth, and a powerful plea for faithfulness in leading the church.

Luke 16:19-31
CONTEXT: Parables and teaching about money and responsibility (16:1-15).
IDEAS: Poor always with us; Jesus's images of heaven and hell; signs of God in the world.

This parable of Jesus is one of his severest warnings to those who go carelessly about their own selfish and sinful ways.

Year C: Proper 22 (2 October-8 October. Week 27.)

Continuous Old Testament: Lamentations 1:1-6
CONTEXT: A collection of dirge-like poems on the fall of Jerusalem and the Temple, used for centuries (and still today) in synagogue liturgy.
IDEAS: Sorrows of a defeated people; holy places deserted.

Our weekly survey of Israel's great prophets has brought us to Jeremiah. This reading is from a poetry collection ascribed to him, lamenting over a city captured by enemies and a Temple destroyed.

Related Old Testament: Habakkuk 1:1-4, 2:1-4
CONTEXT: Babylon has conquered Assyria, but this brought no release to Judah. Habakkuk pleads for God's justice and a renewal of the people's trust.
IDEAS: God permitting devastation and havoc; watch for the Lord; do not ever despair.

This short reading prepares us for the Gospel call to faithfulness. The prophet's appeal to God for justice is coupled with a call to the people to hold their loyalty to their God.

2 Timothy 1:1-14
(See note at Proper 19 above.)
CONTEXT: Pastoral concern for, and instruction to, a church elder.
IDEAS: Timothy's background (Acts 16:1 & 1 Cor 4:17); grace through laying on of hands; leadership tasks.

This letter begins with some personal touches, then quickly moves to the main theme which is the supreme gift of the Gospel, and the awesome task of those commissioned to serve in church leadership.

Luke 17:5-10
CONTEXT: A section of teaching on discipleship.
IDEAS: Use of hyperbole in teaching; constancy in Christian duty.

Jesus often exaggerates – here about what faith can do. Then he tells a parable calling us to a steady faithfulness in service to God.

Year C: Proper 23 (9 October-15 October. Week 28.)

Continuous Old Testament: Jeremiah 29:1, 4-7
CONTEXT: In Jerusalem, after many have been exiled to Babylon, Jeremiah has a confrontation with a false prophet, and writes to the exiles.
IDEAS: Don't despair; sometimes God's action is not immediate! pray and work for good wherever you are.

Jeremiah realised that those who had been taken into exile would not be released speedily. So, still in Jerusalem himself, he wrote believing it was God's will for them to settle as best they could and seek for the good of that place.

Related Old Testament: 2 Kings 5:1-3, 7-15b
CONTEXT: Elisha has taken up the teaching and healing work of Elijah.
IDEAS: Ancient and modern leprosy; do the simple things for God.

In this well-known story of Naaman, we see that Elisha had the power to heal leprosy, and Jesus did centuries later.

2 Timothy 2:8-15
(See note at Proper 19 above.)
CONTEXT: Teaching about leadership in the church.
IDEAS: Hardships of mission-preaching; faithful endurance.

Church leadership is not an easy vocation, says this letter. But in the words of a Christian hymn, the enduring hope of the Gospel is affirmed.

Luke 17:11-19
CONTEXT: Luke reminds us of his context for this middle section of his story – Jesus's progress towards Jerusalem.
IDEAS: Dealing with contagious disease; ritual uncleanness; thanks to God; ministries of healing.

To suffer leprosy in Jesus's time meant not only pain and disfigurement, but social exclusion. Jesus breaks taboos and heals even this severe ailment, but only one in ten says thank you – and he was a foreigner.

Year C: Proper 24 (16 October-22 October. Week 29.)

Continuous Old Testament: Jeremiah 31:27-34
CONTEXT: The proclamation that God will restore both Judah and Israel.
IDEAS: Inherited guilt; covenants; God's work of replanting/rebuilding after catastrophe (= death & resurrection).

Although Jeremiah's name has become proverbial for dismal tidings, he was able to offer hope to the exiled people. The Lord in his love would restore them and the devastated land.

Related Old Testament: Genesis 32:22-31
CONTEXT: Jacob returning to Canaan after many years, unsure of the reception he will get.
IDEAS: Angels (v. 1); names and identities; face to face with God.

Jacob has been away for many years, now returning with his new wives and children and not sure of a welcome. This story tells of his wrestling with an angel, the blessing and the new name he was given.

2 Timothy 3:14-4:5
(See note at Proper 19 above.)
CONTEXT: Continuing the charge to a church elder to keep to the Gospel truths.
IDEAS: Be steeped in scripture; constantly preach its message.

In the scriptures, old and new, we can find truths and instruction. The task of the Christian minister is to teach these truths at all times.

Luke 18:1-8
CONTEXT: Signs of the coming of the kingdom.
IDEAS: Don't give up praying; God is righteous and always hears us.

Jesus encourages us to keep wrestling in the hard work of prayer, for ourselves and for others, because God surely always hears us.

Year C: Proper 25 (23 October-29 October. Week 30.)

Continuous Old Testament: Joel 2:23-32
CONTEXT: A late work in the stylised manner of earlier prophets; greatly dramatic, but exact historical circumstances not known.
IDEAS: Harvest bounty; presence of the Lord; universal spirit gift and salvation.

Our long season with Israel's prophets nears its end with the voice of Joel, whose language is energetic and visionary. When God acts once again to restore his people, the harvests will be abundant, and the spirit that once inspired only a few will then be given to many.

Related Old Testament: Ecclesiasticus 35:12-17
CONTEXT: A section of sayings concerning true and false sacrifices and offerings to God.
IDEAS: God sees all alike – but favours the poor while punishing evil.

God has no favourites, says this writer, but as today's Gospel parable illustrates powerfully, the prayer of the humble and persistent is always answered.

OR *Jeremiah 14:7-10, 19-22*
CONTEXT: Plea for relief from drought.
IDEAS: Corporate confession and corporate petition.

This passage links two expressions of public prayer, which are echoed in the Gospel. Both are pleas for God's forgiveness; the first prays for his restoring presence and the second expresses total trust.

2 Timothy 4:6-8, 16-18
(See note at Proper 19 above.)
CONTEXT: The solemn charge laid on Christian ministers.
IDEAS: Preparing for death; a life God has used.

Our short series of readings from the two letters addressed to Timothy now concludes as the writer feels near to death, and gives his testimony to the Lord's work through him, and his hope of heaven.

Luke 18:9-14
CONTEXT: Teaching the disciples – the imminence of the kingdom.
IDEAS: Places of prayer; approaches to prayer; what more could God require? Invidious comparisons.

The familiar parable of the righteous Pharisee and the humble man are a lesson in our approach to our heavenly Father.

Year C: CWL Bible Sunday

Isaiah 45:22-25
CONTEXT: Isaiah of the Exile. Israel will be restored.
IDEAS: God alone the agent and deliverer of redemption.

All scripture points us to the one and only God who, says this prophet to Israel in exile, will restore and deliver all nations and all peoples when they turn to him.

Romans 15:1-6
CONTEXT: A section of the letter that deals with relationships.
IDEAS: Concede to the weaker, as Jesus did; search the scriptures for encouragement.

As Paul urges the Roman Christians to mutual respect and unity, he directs them to give close attention to the scriptures where instruction and encouragement will be found.

Luke 4:16-24
CONTEXT: Luke places the beginnings of Jesus's ministry in Nazareth.
IDEAS: Jesus in synagogues; all Old Testament scripture fulfilled; the preacher criticised!

Jesus was often given opportunities to teach in synagogues, but this is the only time when the Gospels record the scripture reading from which he preached.

Year C: CWL Dedication Festival
(First Sunday in October or Last after Trinity)

1 Chronicles 29:6-19
CONTEXT: Solomon succeeding David as king – provision for building the first Jerusalem Temple.
IDEAS: Giving; all comes from God; buildings for worship.

King David had planned the Temple; now Solomon could build it. The great wealth from the royal treasury starts the fund, for which the people contribute most generously, knowing that all things come from God and it is of his own that we give to him.

Ephesians 2:19-22
CONTEXT: The nature of the church, the body of Christ.
IDEAS: Unity of Christians; apostolic witness; where God dwells.

Paul likens the whole Christian community to a building, founded on apostles and prophets, with Christ himself the corner stone. We are becoming a holy temple in which God is pleased to dwell.

John 2:13-22
CONTEXT: Jesus making an early Passover visit to Jerusalem – uniquely to John.
IDEAS: Uses of 'holy' buildings; temple/church 'taxes'; the violent Jesus.

Jesus will not allow the Temple, the house of the Lord, to be used for any corrupt or dishonest purpose; it is to be a holy place of prayer.

Year C: CWL Fourth before Advent, RCL Proper 26
(30 October-5 November. Week 31.)

RCL only: *Habakkuk 1:1-4, 2:1-4*
CONTEXT: Babylon has conquered Assyria, but this brought no release to Judah. Habakkuk pleads for God's justice and a renewal of the people's trust.
IDEAS: God permitting devastation and havoc; watch for the Lord; do not ever despair.

Our year with Israel prophets is concluding with brief readings from those called 'Minor', of whose work we have only a little in the Bible. This prophet's appeal to God for justice is coupled with a call to the people to hold their loyalty to their God.

CWL: RCL alternative: *Isaiah 1:10-18*
CONTEXT: First Isaiah (of Jerusalem) – the beginning of his 40-year prophetic work.
IDEAS: What God requires; actions not ritual; purification and forgiveness.

Isaiah understands that God is not honoured by sacrificing to him the very things he gives to feed us, but by lives given to justice and care for the needy. Then our sins will be forgiven.

2 Thessalonians 1:1-4 [& 5-10], 1-12; CWL 1-12
CONTEXT: A letter concerned with expectations of the Parousia – the coming of Christ in final glory.
IDEAS: Steadfast faith; coming judgement; the glory to come.

We hear over three Sundays now this short letter, full of anticipation about the return of the Lord in glory. At that time, those who persevere in the faith will find their sufferings turned to joy.

Luke 19:1-10
CONTEXT: Jesus's momentous journey to Jerusalem (which for Luke began at 9:51).
IDEAS: Jesus's reputation; determination to meet him; repentance and recompense.

Jesus's mission, he said, was to seek and to save. Zaccheus is himself a seeker, and his encounter with Jesus proved to be his salvation – and with his conversion came restitution to all those he had wronged.

Year C: All Saints' Day
(Sunday between 30 October and 5 November, or 1 November.)

Daniel 7:1-3, 15-18
CONTEXT: The second half of this book, a series of visions written in the terrible times of Antiochus Epiphanes (170 BC).
IDEAS: The tyranny of some worldly kingdoms; inheritance of the saints.

In this strange vision of a world in chaos, the assurance comes that God's holy ones will be saved, and will share the life of their true king eternally.

Ephesians 1:11-23
CONTEXT: A general letter to Gentile Christians about the life of faith and proper conduct between Christians.
IDEAS: Inheritance of the saints; 'sealed' for eternity; Christ risen, ascended, and in the glory we hope for.

Paul, like Daniel, writes of the powers of heaven. Now, he says, the risen and ascended Christ is enthroned above all things, and we his holy ones have both the knowledge of his sustaining power here and the hope of glory with him hereafter.

Luke 6:20-31
CONTEXT: Jesus in Galilee, teaching his disciples.
IDEAS: Blessedness and happiness; unexpected people enter the kingdom.

Jesus reverses many of the world's standards. God does not bless those who are satisfied with themselves, but those who know their need of him and show his love to everyone.

Year C: CWL November 1
(If the All Saints' Day material is used on the Sunday.)

Isaiah 56:3-8
CONTEXT: Warnings and promises to the restored community.
IDEAS: All people will be safely gathered in.

As early as 500 BC, some religious thinkers in Israel had begun to see that the God of their people must in fact be the only God, with the whole world in his hands. So the hope for a time of restoration and peace embraces every nation and race. In the Gospel Jesus will tell us who are blessed by God.

OR *2 Esdras 2:42-48*
CONTEXT: Part of the Christian prefix added later to some Jewish writings of around 100 AD, which are apocalyptic visions ascribed to the ancient priest Ezra.
IDEAS: Vast crowd of the saints surround the Son of God.

This reading comes from a book in our Apocrypha, a collection of Jewish symbolic visions to which were added some Christian passages like this, where all those who acknowledge Christ are gathered round him in his glory.

Hebrews 12:18-24
CONTEXT: The enduring history of faith; the new perspective in the revelation of God in Christ.
IDEAS: Face to face with God; the city of God; vast crowds come to worship.

In ancient times, to meet God was awesome, and Mount Zion a fearful holy place. By contrast, says this writer, we know Christ brings us the new covenant promises, and we can always come into God's presence without fear.

Matthew 5:1-12
CONTEXT: Jesus's popularity in and around Capernaum; his early ministry of teaching and healing.
IDEAS: The Blessed/Happy (translations vary) are made so by God; challenge to be unpopular; unexpected people enter the kingdom.

In these strange paradoxes we call the Beatitudes, Jesus teaches us who are the holy people in God's sight, the ones who will find his blessings as his kingdom comes.

Year C: CWL Third before Advent, RCL Proper 27
(6-12 November. Week 32.)

RCL only: *Haggai 1:15b-2:9*
CONTEXT: After return from Babylon, call to restore worship by rebuilding the Temple.
IDEAS: Faith and prosperity; need for buildings for worship.

This last of our readings from Israel's prophets concerns the time when the Jews had just returned to Jerusalem from exile. Haggai calls the people to restore the devastated Temple, so that the foundation of their new community life would be their worship of their Lord.

CWL: RCL alternative: *Job 19:23-27a*
CONTEXT: The second cycle of this book's speeches; God has wronged Job, yet is also his vindicator.
IDEAS: Trust during suffering; God the advocate; seeing God.

Job asks that his words be written down as evidence, because he is confident that when he comes before God he will prove innocent of any great offence.

2 Thessalonians 2:1-5, 13-17
CONTEXT: Expectations of Christ's return in glory, and its delay.
IDEAS: Ancient eastern concepts of good and evil powers; biblical certainty of a 'last day'; God's choices.

Paul says that Christ's return will be preceded by evil in human form. His readers are however to remain calm, pursuing their own good deeds, because God has called and consecrated them.

Luke 20:27-38
CONTEXT: Jesus in Jerusalem – direct challenges to religious leaders.
IDEAS: Understanding resurrection life; place for those judged worthy.

Jesus reveals one aspect of how things will be for us hereafter, in answer to what seems a mocking question about husbands and wives in heaven. The promise of Jesus is of a new kind of existence in the presence of God.

Year C: CWL Second before Advent, RCL Proper 28
(13-19 November. Week 33.)

RCL only: *Isaiah 65:17-25*
CONTEXT: 'Third' Isaiah – post-exile, but the return to the Promised Land has not brought peace and joy.
IDEAS: God still has a wonderful future for the faithful; new starts; unity in all nature.

The prophet tells of a day of delight and rejoicing, in a new order of creation when God will put away all past sins and sorrows, bringing in the age of lasting peace to his people.

CWL: RCL alternative: *Malachi 4:1-2a*
CONTEXT: After the return from exile, the re-establishment of civil and religious law was difficult. The Lord's messenger offers hope.
IDEAS: 'The day of the Lord'; divine judgement and punishment; the righteous saved.

In a time when religious and moral values seemed to have been lost, this writer encourages the hope of a day when the Lord will come, to destroy evil and heal the righteous.

2 Thessalonians 3:6-13
CONTEXT: Right and wrong attitudes to the Second Coming of Christ.
IDEAS: A work ethic; gossips and busybodies; conscientiousness.

This reading concludes the three Sundays' excerpts from Paul's letter to those who expected the Lord's return at any moment. He urges them not to wait for it in idleness.

Luke 21:5-19
CONTEXT: Jesus in Jerusalem – a discourse on the end of the age.
IDEAS: Signs of the times; Christians persecuted; faith and life.

Luke, like Matthew and Mark, merges various sayings of Jesus about the destruction of Jerusalem with those about the end of time. The theme is of warning, and of God's judgement. We may well take this passage as a call for trust in God when the world seems to be collapsing into chaos.

Year C: Christ the King
(20-26 November)

Jeremiah 23:1-6
CONTEXT: A series of warnings to kings and misleading prophets.
IDEAS: Sheep and shepherds; failures in leadership; God's own gathering.

In Jeremiah's prophetic imagination, all those who have suffered from misguided or evil leadership will be gathered into a renewed kingdom. The new and perfect king, to come from the line of David, will carry the title 'Lord of Righteousness'.

Colossians 1:11-20
CONTEXT: The letter to Christians divided by faction and speculation, to recall them to unity in Christ.
IDEAS: Christ the only supreme head; our saviour; all creation through him; God was in Christ.

Paul wrote this letter to recall the church from divisive ideas to the centrality of Christ in their lives. He breaks into a great song of praise to Jesus, who was before all creation, the image of God on earth, our redeemer, and for ever supreme over all things everywhere.

Luke 23:33-43
CONTEXT: Jesus condemned and taken with his cross to Golgotha.
IDEAS: They have crucified my Lord; the work/cost of our salvation; profound truth in the mocking title.

On the cross of Jesus, the handwritten sign 'The King of the Jews', may have been intended as sarcasm, or mockery, or insult. But Luke knew, as we know, that Christ is indeed a king, and we are citizens of his kingdom.

Festivals

1 January: The Naming and Circumcision of Jesus

Numbers 6:22-27
CONTEXT: Miscellaneous legislation (from 5:1) thought to derive from the time the Israelites were in Sinai.
IDEAS: Holy Name; liturgical formulations; who 'blesses' who, how?; things in threes.

No Jew would pronounce the name of the Lord, either at home or in synagogue. Only the High Priest, in a formula of blessing, may use the sacred name.

Galatians 4:4-7
CONTEXT: Contrast between Jewish Law as a temporary 'guardian' and our status as adopted children of God.
IDEAS: Jesus born a Jew; Abba, the intimate name; children and heirs.

In contrast to the Jew, who dare not use God's name, Christians have learnt from the Jesus of human history that we are God's children, who can call on him by the most intimate of names.

Luke 2:15-21
CONTEXT: The Child is born and heaven cries glory.
IDEAS: What the shepherds saw; Christ born subject to the Law (Gal. 4:4).

In Luke's lovely nativity story, while angels and shepherds adore the holy child, his parents treat him like any other baby boy, circumcised and named eight days after his birth.

25 January: The Conversion of Paul

Note: The prescribed readings are either the passage from Jeremiah followed by that from Acts, or the Acts reading followed by Galatians.

Jeremiah 1:4-10
CONTEXT: Political/religious crisis – leading to the destruction of Jerusalem and deportation of many people.
IDEAS: God's knowledge and choice; a vocation implies the gifts to fulfil it.

Like Paul centuries later, Jeremiah found himself directly confronted by the God who challenges, calls and enables people to speak for him wherever he may need them to go.

Acts 9:1-22
CONTEXT: Persecution of the Jerusalem church (8:1b) and dispersion carrying the Gospel into the countryside; Paul a foremost antagonist (8:1a).
IDEAS: Sudden epiphanies; God's choices of leaders; Jesus's last appearance; Ananias's reluctance, and courage.

God sometimes calls unlikely men and women to his service. Even Saul, the vigorous opponent of those who followed the way of the Lord, may meet Jesus along his way. So Saul became Paul, a powerful witness to the Saviour of all.

Galatians 1:11-16a
CONTEXT: Paul justifying his independence from the Jerusalem church and its teaching which was still not free from Jewish observances.
IDEAS: True conversions; missionary styles; church structures and authority.

Paul is here strongly defending the authentic nature of his conversion, and his credentials as an apostle. He was commissioned by Jesus in a miraculous revelation.

Matthew 19:27-30
CONTEXT: Various things which must be renounced by a follower of Jesus.
IDEAS: Leaving everything behind; heavenly reward; Paul the 'last' apostle becoming 'first' in mission.

Jesus says that those who, for his sake, are prepared to give up everything of their former life, will find generous rewards in his kingdom.

19 March: Joseph

2 Samuel 7:1-16
CONTEXT: David has made Jerusalem the capital city of his kingdom. The Ark is restored.
IDEAS: Some things left for sons to do; God's plans; promise of greatness for a son.

King David wants to build a fine house for God, but is told instead of God's promise concerning his son Solomon, who will establish the kingdom and be treated by God as if he were his own son.

Romans 4:13-18
CONTEXT: In Paul's theology, Abraham is a primary example to us of the way God embraces as his children all who have faith.
IDEAS: Abraham father of all; promise to descendants.

Paul uses the example of Abraham's faith and trust in God to show how he came to be called the 'father', both of Israel and all who by faith are God's children.

Matthew 1:18-25
CONTEXT: The Gospel begins with the wonder of the Incarnation.
IDEAS: A unique pregnancy; angelic messengers; ancient hopes now become reality; Joseph's consternation.

In the four Gospels, only Matthew gives us this glimpse into the mind of Joseph, troubled by Mary's pregnancy, but hearing a word of assurance from God. He took Mary as his wife, and the child Jesus grew up in the care of Joseph and Mary.

25 March: The Annunciation

Isaiah 7:10-14
CONTEXT: King Ahaz of Judah threatened by an alliance of Israel and Syria.
IDEAS: God's voice through prophets; signs and wonders; the young woman (or 'virgin') and child a 'messianic' figure (we cannot be sure what Isaiah originally meant).

A young woman will give her son the name Immanuel, meaning 'God is with us'. Isaiah's words were meant as encouragement to King Ahaz in dangerous times, but for us they will always have the profound meaning fulfilled in Mary and the birth of Jesus.

Hebrews 10:4-10
CONTEXT: Old sacrificial systems once and for all done away with, in the sacrificial coming-to-earth and death of Christ.
IDEAS: Ps 40:6-8; Jesus's self-offering; sacrifice(s).

This writer sees Jesus as having been announced by a Psalmist. He would come to abolish the old sacrificial system by which humankind approached God, because in his own person he consecrates us all.

Luke 1:26-38
CONTEXT: Luke's beautiful Nativity story.
IDEAS: Davidic descent; names and titles; amazing news.

We hear now the strange and overpowering announcement by the angel Gabriel to Mary, and rejoice in her response of 'Yes' to God's will.

23 April: CWL: George

1 Maccabees 2:59-64
CONTEXT: The revolt under Mattathias against Antiochus and Syria 167BC, when the Temple had been desecrated (1:20ff).
IDEAS: Faith in desperate circumstances; God gives strength to fight evil; war in the name of religion.

Under the severest of persecution 150 years before Christ, the great leader and warrior Mattathias is here encouraging his three sons to draw strength from their trust in God.

OR *Revelation 12:7-12*
CONTEXT: The last battle at the end of time.
IDEAS: Leadership (of angels); evil must be fought against; ultimate victory.

Christ needs on earth those who will fight the good fight against evil and sin; John in this reading sees in heaven the final victory won, and Christ the vanquisher of all that is evil.

2 Timothy 2:3-13
CONTEXT: A pastoral charge from a senior leader to a church elder.
IDEAS: Images of the Christian life; endurance under hardship; eternal salvation.

This writer compares us to soldiers, athletes and farmers. The Christian vocation is never easy, he says, especially for a leader, but we can all affirm the enduring hope of our salvation through Christ our Lord.

John 15:18-21
CONTEXT: Jesus's final discourse to friends gathered for the last Supper.
IDEAS: Christians will always have enemies; distinctiveness.

Jesus warns his closest friends that discipleship does not mean popularity; indeed, true followers of him will always be persecuted in some way.

25 April: Mark

Proverbs 15:28-33
CONTEXT: Many and varied sayings, broadly secular.
IDEAS: Good news cheers; listen when reproved.

These ancient sayings speak about the joy of good news, and coming to fullness after failure. Mark, evangelist of good news, was one who once failed, but eventually joined the missionary team in Cyprus to proclaim the Gospel.

OR *Acts 15:35-41*
CONTEXT: Paul and Barnabas working in the church at Antioch.
IDEAS: Leaders visiting the churches; choosing collaborative teams; agreeing to differ.

There was a time when Mark had deserted Paul during his first mission to Greece. Now, planning another journey, Paul will not trust Mark but Barnabas does, and these two set out from Antioch for Cyprus.

Ephesians 4:7-16
CONTEXT: The unity of everyone within the church, and the Christian's calling.
IDEAS: All are gifted in diverse ways; the range of skills the church needs – and has; maturity.

Apostles, evangelists, teachers: these, writes Paul, are just examples of gifted people in the church. Every one of us has a special gift which we must recognise, then work and pray for our own learning and growing in the Christian truths.

Mark 13:5-13
CONTEXT: Jesus in Jerusalem as the climax nears – a collection of sayings about 'the end'.
IDEAS: Christians under trial – Mark's haste to write his Gospel; world in ferment; endurance.

Mark's Gospel was probably written in haste, at a time when it seemed possible that every Christian might be killed. This passage is from a series of Jesus's warnings of persecution, with his assurance of salvation through perseverance.

1 May: Philip and James

Isaiah 30:15-21
CONTEXT: Judah in alliance with Egypt against Assyria – although Isaiah has said God did not want the alliance.
IDEAS: Don't panic!; wait on the Lord; seeing God.

However much the people may panic at the foreign threat, Isaiah promises God's calm and peace. This passage ends with the same idea that Philip questioned Jesus about – whether we can see God.

Ephesians 1:3-10
CONTEXT: The letter opens with a section of praise for God's blessings.
IDEAS: God's eternal purposes and choices; his gifts to us in and through Christ.

This letter begins with a great hymn of praise to God for what he has done for us in Christ. In Christ, we are adopted as children of God, with the divinely-given wisdom and insight to understand God's purposes for us.

John 14:1-14
CONTEXT: Jesus's farewell discourses: promise of future bliss.
IDEAS: Our place prepared; seeing God in Jesus; prayer in Jesus's name.

Philip is the disciple who asks Jesus to be able to see God. The answer is that to know Jesus is to know God the Father, because they dwell deeply in each other, and Jesus is our way to all the truth of God.

14 May: Matthias

Note: The prescribed readings are either the passage from Isaiah followed by that from Acts, or the Acts reading followed by 1 Corinthians.

Isaiah 22:15-25
CONTEXT: Assyria invading Judah – a series of oracles against foreign nations, and an arrogant government officer.
IDEAS: Pride and a fall; a faithful servant promoted.

This is an Old Testament story of an arrogant man's downfall, and his replacement by a more honourable man who can be trusted with leadership. It has its parallel in the life of Matthias.

Acts 1:15-26
CONTEXT: The Jerusalem church begins to take shape following the Lord's Ascension.
IDEAS: The betrayal and fate of Judas; guidance from Scripture; human choices and God's choices.

With the suicide of Judas Iscariot, the church in Jerusalem decided that the number of leaders must be restored to the Twelve Jesus had appointed. From his other constant companions, Matthias was elected.

1 Corinthians 4:1-7
CONTEXT: Apostles, and all Christians, are servants of Christ.
IDEAS: Don't judge (condemn); no place for pride; all our gifts are God's.

We may wonder how Matthias felt when the church chose him to take the place of Judas among the Twelve. Paul writes here of the humility necessary for those called to be apostles and servants of Jesus.

John 15:9-17
CONTEXT: Jesus's farewell discourses – mutual indwelling of Jesus/Father/disciples.
IDEAS: Change in status; Christ's love is his commandment; friends of Jesus.

Matthias's status was changed by his election. Jesus tells his followers that all of us are changed from being servants to being his friends. It is he who chose us and equips us to be fruitful in work for him.

31 May: The Visit of Mary to Elizabeth

RCL only: *1 Samuel 2:1-10*
CONTEXT: Elkanah, the fruitful wife Peninnah and the barren Hannah – then the birth of Samuel.
IDEAS: The Lord does great things for me; a song of high revolt.

Samuel was born to Hannah when she had despaired of having a child. In thanks to God she sang this song of praise – from which there is no doubt Mary's song Magnificat derives.

OR *Zephaniah 3:14-18*
CONTEXT: Judah and her neighbours to be destroyed for disobedience – but a remnant will be preserved.
IDEAS: The Lord is here – his Spirit is with us; gathered together by God.

This prophet of the 7th century BC sees a time when all will be joy and peace, because God in his unceasing care will reveal the very real presence of the Lord with his people.

Romans 12:9-16
CONTEXT: Brief injunctions on Christian life, especially relationships within the church.
IDEAS: Love and humility, joy and peace, hope and endurance.

Be ready to mix with those who seem humble and unimportant, says Paul, in this short list of some of the ways Christians should behave. The key to it all is love.

Luke 1:39-49 [& 50-56]
CONTEXT: Angelic disclosures to Elizabeth and Mary of their miraculous pregnancies.
IDEAS: Two expectant mothers; perception and discernment.

Luke weaves together the wonderful stories of the sons born to Elizabeth and Mary. The mother of Jesus visits the mother of John, and the two are joined in the joy of what God is doing. Mary's hymn of praise and revolution is like that of Hannah in the Old Testament, who named her son Samuel meaning 'one who comes from God'.

11 June: Barnabas

Note: The prescribed readings are either the passage from Job followed by that from Acts, or the Acts reading followed by Galatians.

Job 29:11-16
CONTEXT: After a section in which God is praised, Job sums up his own past and present situations.
IDEAS: Being well-thought-of; diligence in works of mercy.

Job reflects on the good times, when he faithfully served God and neighbour and gained a good reputation. The same qualities were later attributed to Barnabas.

Acts 11:19-30
CONTEXT: The Judean (Jerusalem) church realising the Gospel is for Gentiles too.
IDEAS: Good news for all; church missionaries and emissaries; Barnabas integrates Paul into the community.

The Jerusalem church sent the highly-regarded Barnabas to examine the way the Gospel was being accepted by Gentiles for the first time. He was responsible for bringing Paul to Antioch, where they stayed and worked for some time.

Galatians 2:1-10
CONTEXT: Paul justifying how he came to faith and apostleship.
IDEAS: Resolving Christian differences; accepting the maverick!; varieties of mission.

Paul recalls that after he and Barnabas had led the church in Antioch for some time, they went together to Jerusalem to explain how it had become imperative for them to preach the Gospel to Gentiles.

John 15:12-17
CONTEXT: Jesus's farewell discourses – mutual indwelling of Jesus/Father/disciples.
IDEAS: Change in status; Christ's love is his commandment; friends of Jesus.

Barnabas's reputation was of one who faithfully carried out this commandment of the Lord, that the friends of Jesus are to love one another and be fruitful.

24 June: The Birth of John the Baptist

Isaiah 40:1-11
CONTEXT: The opening words of Second Isaiah, in Babylon during the captivity – offering hope of restoration.
IDEAS: Bad things come to an end – even God's punishments; prophetic voices; proclaim God's coming.

Israel must prepare for God's appearing, says the prophet, for he will bring about their return from exile. This announcement became for Christians a prophetic text about John the Baptist, who proclaimed Jesus and prepared the way for his coming.

Acts 13:14b-26
CONTEXT: A synagogue sermon in Galatia.
IDEAS: God's chosen people; all history led to Christ; now the Saviour has come.

Paul and Barnabas have travelled from Cyprus into Galatia. Invited to speak to the Jews there, Paul proclaims Jesus their Messiah. Throughout history God has prepared his people, and lastly came John, pointing them to Jesus.

OR *Galatians 3:23-29*
CONTEXT: Jewish Law does not apply within Christian freedom.
IDEAS: The Law did have its value; the intimate union of all faithful with God and each other, through baptism.

We are all new-born, says Paul. Our baptism has united us to God through Jesus Christ, in a way never possible by keeping the old religious laws.

Luke 1:57-66, 80
CONTEXT: Luke's interwoven narratives of Jesus and John – the birth of John.
IDEAS: Importance of names; last and great prophet; desert life.

The son born to Zechariah and Elizabeth in their old age is named John, which means 'God is gracious'. It will be John's prophetic calling to prepare people for the coming of the Son of God.

29 June: Peter and Paul

See next page for the readings if this day is kept for Peter alone
Note: The prescribed readings are either the passage from Zechariah followed
by that from Acts, or the Acts reading followed by 2 Timothy.

Zechariah 4:1-6a, 10b-14
NOTE: Some versions of the Bible transpose vv. 1-3 to follow 10.
CONTEXT: Re-establishing life in Jerusalem after the exile – visionary teaching of the new city and temple.
IDEAS: Biblical symbolism; the number seven = completeness; the two who serve (cf. Gal 2:7).

Paul would write later that he and Peter had different mission tasks, but the two together embraced both Jew and Gentile. Zechariah's rather strange vision uses the symbolism of two olive branches to mean the high priest and the king, whose combined work would bring about God's completeness – which Zechariah means by using the mystical number seven.

Acts 12:1-11
CONTEXT: The church growing in Jerusalem and Antioch.
IDEAS: Another Herod seeks to stop the movement; effective prayer; angelic appearances.

This reading and our Gospel concentrate on Peter. Herod Agrippa put him in prison, but the church prayed for him and God's messenger came to release him.

2 Timothy 4:6-8, 17-18
CONTEXT: The solemn charge laid on Christian ministers.
IDEAS: Preparing for death; a life God has used.

This letter expresses Paul's hope, near the end of his life, to reach safely that place with God to which all the righteous will come.

Matthew 16:13-19
CONTEXT: The disciples' difficulty in fully grasping Jesus's true nature.
IDEAS: Son of Man; Son of God; Peter's eyes opened; no publicity!

Simon is inspired to give Jesus his true title of Messiah, Saviour, and in return is given his new name of Peter, the rock.

29 June: Peter

See previous page for the readings if this day is kept for Peter and Paul
Note: The prescribed readings are either the passage from Ezekiel followed by
that from Acts, or the Acts reading followed by 1 Peter.

Ezekiel 3:22-27
CONTEXT: Ezekiel's calling – probably while in Babylonian exile.
IDEAS: Seeing/recognising the Lord; inspired words; hearing and rejecting.

Like Peter in our Gospel, Ezekiel is given a moment of recognition, when he knows the divine presence. This passage ends with a commission very similar to the one Jesus gave to Peter.

Acts 12:1-11
CONTEXT: The church growing in Jerusalem and Antioch.
IDEAS: Another Herod seeks to stop the movement; effective prayer; angelic appearances.

When Herod Agrippa began to try and crush the church, he put Peter in prison. But the church prayed for him and God's messenger came to release him.

1 Peter 2:19-25
CONTEXT: A letter of encouragement, probably to Christians under persecution. Concerning lifestyle.
IDEAS: Undeserved suffering; the example of Christ; what he achieved for us.

The letter of Peter is to Gentile Christians, and this reading seeks to encourage all who are humiliated or persecuted for their faith. Jesus, he says, is the supreme example of undeserved suffering, and we are to honour and follow the way of righteousness.

Matthew 16:13-19
CONTEXT: The disciples' difficulty in fully grasping Jesus's true nature.
IDEAS: Son of Man; Son of God; Peter's eyes opened; no publicity!

Simon is inspired to give Jesus his true title of Messiah, Saviour, and in return is given his new name of Peter, the rock.

3 July: Thomas

Habakkuk 2:1-4
CONTEXT: Babylon has conquered Assyria, but this brought no release to Judah. Habakkuk pleads for the people to renew their trust in God.
IDEAS: Watch and wait for the Lord; do not ever despair.

Thomas, after our Lord's resurrection, had to wait a week before he saw the risen Christ. This prophet speaks of watching and waiting for the Lord in confidence and faithfulness.

Ephesians 2:19-22
CONTEXT: The nature of the church, the Body of Christ.
IDEAS: Apostolic witness; physical/mystical body; none left out.

Paul writes to people who had not seen Jesus as his immediate disciples did, and assures them that by their faith they too are embraced in the kingdom building.

John 20:24-29
CONTEXT: The evening of Resurrection Day – Mary Magdalene the first witness – Jesus in the secure house.
IDEAS: Disciples together for safety; Jesus recognisable, wounded; seeing and believing.

The friends of Jesus, men and women, hid together in misery and fear when Jesus had died. But on that wonderful Sunday they suddenly knew his very real presence with them. However, one friend missed all the excitement.

22 July: Mary Magdalene

Song of Solomon 3:1-4
CONTEXT: An anthology of love poems and songs, perhaps allegorical – a song of a bride.
IDEAS: Searching for the loved one; finding and hugging.

In this very ancient and beautiful love poetry we can hear Mary Magadalene's very great love for Jesus, and her agonised search that early Sunday morning.

2 Corinthians 5:14-17
CONTEXT: Living for others, with openness, because of Christ's reconciling work.
IDEAS: Love compels; what the world thinks; all things new.

Love for Jesus leaves us no choice, says Paul. It takes us over completely, and directs our every thought and deed, as if we are newly-created.

John 20:1-2, 11-18
CONTEXT: Jesus has died and is buried; after the Sabbath, mourning can resume.
IDEAS: The empty tomb; Peter and (?) John rush in; Jesus unrecognised; Mary the apostle to the apostles; incredibly good news.

Mary Magadalene is remembered for ever as the first person to see the risen Lord. How wonderful for her, who loved him so much, to hear him lovingly speak her name.

25 July: James

Note: The prescribed readings are either the passage from Jeremiah followed by that from Acts, or the Acts reading followed by 2 Corinthians.

Jeremiah 45:1-5
CONTEXT: Jerusalem has fallen to Babylon, as Jeremiah warned. Baruch was Jeremiah's secretary and sometimes spokesman (cf. 36:6).
IDEAS: Self-aggrandisement criticised.

Jeremiah tells his secretary, Baruch, not to seek great things for himself, because God has other plans. James will be told much the same by Jesus.

Acts 11:27-12:2
CONTEXT: Barnabas and Paul 'plant' a church in Antioch, causing some concern in Jerusalem.
IDEAS: Help for needy Christians; church leaders persecuted; another Herod (Agrippa) cannot bear the new movement.

Paul and Barnabas had established a teaching mission in Antioch, but meanwhile Herod Agrippa began an attempted purge of church leaders in Jerusalem, of whom James was the first to be executed.

2 Corinthians 4:7-15
CONTEXT: Paul defending and justifying his apostleship.
IDEAS: God's power not ours; the hardships of vocation; words and works show forth Christ.

Paul writes that because God's grace is so great we are bound to speak out about it whatever the consequences.

Matthew 20:20-28
CONTEXT: Jesus and his company on the last journey to Jerusalem.
IDEAS: Mothers and sons; the kingdom beyond the End; serve, as Jesus served.

James is told not to seek greatness and honour either here or hereafter, but simply to set his heart on service like the Lord himself.

6 August: The Transfiguration

Daniel 7:9-10, 13-14
CONTEXT: The second half of this book, a series of visions written in the terrible times of Antiochus Epiphanes (170 BC).
IDEAS: Poetry of mystical experiences; 'Son of Man' and kingly power.

Daniel had a vision of heaven, where God's justice is supreme, and a very human figure is sent to earth in a cloud of glory to be king for ever.

2 Peter 1:16-19
CONTEXT: A reminder that the reality of God was revealed in Jesus.
IDEAS: Biblical truths – the witnesses and interpretations; God the Father's glory given to his son.

Peter was one of those present when the Lord was transfigured in a cloud of glory. This passage attests the reality of that event, to Christians of the second century.

Luke 9:28-36
CONTEXT: The mission of the Twelve – further experiences for the closest three of his miraculous power and true identity.
IDEAS: Revelations on hilltops; 'departure' (v. 31) = 'exodus', implying death; Law and Prophets – completed and fulfilled in Jesus.

Away from the demanding crowds, Jesus's true identity is disclosed to his three closest friends. In the presence of the figures of Moses and Elijah, a cloud of glory comes upon him and the voice of the holy one is heard.

15 August: The Blessed Virgin Mary

Isaiah 61:10-11
CONTEXT: Third Isaiah – post-exilic. Poems of warning and promise to the restored community. An 'anointed one' proclaims salvation (61:1).
IDEAS: Times to rejoice; wedding imagery.

These two verses are a short hymn of praise, in response to a divine message of God's imminent salvation.

OR *Revelation 11:19-12:6, 10*
CONTEXT: Angels and elders in heaven cry glory at Christ's reign, but in the world and the beyond evil is not yet vanquished.
IDEAS: No new joy without birth-pangs; symbolism of numbers and beasts; Mary and Jesus picturesquely represented.

John's highly symbolic language speaks of Jesus, born of Mary and within the whole history of Israel. As the people were once driven into exile, so the evil world forced Mary to flee and take refuge until the time appointed for the disclosure of God's Son.

Galatians 4:4-7
CONTEXT: Contrast between Jewish Law as a temporary 'guardian' and our status as adopted children of God.
IDEAS: Jesus born a Jew; Abba, the intimate name; children and heirs.

Because God has sent his son to be a human being, like us, born of a woman as we all are, we who believe in him now all have the status of children of our heavenly Father.

Luke 1:46-55
CONTEXT: Luke's intertwined narratives of the divine hand bringing Jesus and John to birth through Mary and Elizabeth.
IDEAS: Samuel (1 Sam 2:1-10); use of Magnificat in worship; God's revolutionary ways.

Mary breaks into a song of praise, in response to the angelic message that through her God would bring into the world his own Son, to reverse all the world's standards and be king for ever.

24 August: Bartholomew

Note: The prescribed readings are either the passage from Isaiah followed by that from Acts, or the Acts reading followed by 1 Corinthians.

Isaiah 43:8-13
CONTEXT: Second Isaiah – during the Exile. Encouragement, the promise of return and gathering in a newly-created Israel.
IDEAS: God needs – and enables – articulate witnesses; trust goes with understanding.

The prophet tells us that the work of God's servants and messengers is to witness to him, to expound and explain the truths of his being and his ways.

Acts 5:12-16
CONTEXT: The church in Jerusalem developing its way of life together.
IDEAS: How the world views the church; numbers growing; the Lord's work continues in the healing ministry.

The apostles in Jerusalem constantly proclaimed the resurrection of Jesus, and as the number of believers grew, so did the reputation of the church and the demands on it for the work of healing.

1 Corinthians 4:9-15
CONTEXT: Paul's plea against self-aggrandizement and faction.
IDEAS: Irony in criticism; complacency; hardships of the mission life.

There is no pride or glory in being an apostle for Christ, says Paul. In a strongly ironic tone he contrasts his life with that of comfortable Christians.

Luke 22:24-30
CONTEXT: At the last Passover Supper – wine and bread blessed and shared but still dissension in the group.
IDEAS: The way of humility and service; church entrusted with sustaining the kingdom work.

Jesus had to admonish his own chosen Twelve, when they began to argue about their own importance. His kingdom is one in which everyone seeks not to dominate but to serve, as he himself was the servant of all.

14 September: Holy Cross Day

Numbers 21:4-9
CONTEXT: The Israelites on the last stage of their journey to Canaan, the land of the Lord's promise. Progress both by detour (20:21) and victory (21:3).
IDEAS: Yet again blame the leadership; snakes (serpents) in Scripture; simply look (?ask) and be healed (cf Wisdom 16:7).

For the third time in the Bible, the Israelites on the pilgrimage to the Promised Land run out of food and water. This time there is no miraculous supply, only some relief from snake-bites when Moses made a serpent of bronze for healing. As Jesus reminded his hearers, whenever people raised their eyes to this sign, their illness was lifted from them.

RCL only: *1 Corinthians 1:18-24*
CONTEXT: Paul's corrective to congregational disputes.
IDEAS: God's wisdom versus human folly; human wisdom versus revelation.

To proclaim Christ nailed to a cross seems offensively foolish, says Paul, yet in reality it displays God's loving wisdom and mysterious saving power.

OR *Philippians 2:6-11*
CONTEXT: Paul in prison, writing to friends.
IDEAS: The humility of Christ and his exaltation.

Paul emphasises the humility of Christ, who although he was God, was obedient even to death on a cross. Therefore, he became our way to God and the focus of our worship, because Jesus Christ is indeed the Lord.

John 3:13-17
CONTEXT: Jesus in Jerusalem for Passover (a visit not referred to by the other Gospels).
IDEAS: 'Lifting-up' = crucifixion and glorification; faith brings eternal life.

Three times John's Gospel has Jesus speaking of being 'lifted up', with the double meaning of being raised for execution on a cross and raised to infinite glory. Faith in him means life for us.

21 September: Matthew

Proverbs 3:13-18
CONTEXT: A collection of ancient and traditional teachings, religious and secular; the call to the reader to pay attention to this distilled wisdom.
IDEAS: (God's) wisdom more precious than wealth; a different kind of prosperity.

Matthew proved this proverb true, when he turned away from making money to follow Christ in the wiser way where true riches and real prosperity are to be found.

2 Corinthians 4:1-6
CONTEXT: Paul's apostolic commission and the ministry of creative speaking/writing.
IDEAS: Change of life; clear teaching; Christ, not self.

Paul writes of having renounced all his past in order to follow the Gospel. The apostolic task is to proclaim Christ, serving him and serving the church.

Matthew 9:9-13
CONTEXT: Jesus's early miracles and teaching in and around Capernaum and Galilee.
IDEAS: He leads, we follow; the company Jesus keeps; knowing our sinfulness.

Jesus called Matthew from collecting taxes on behalf of the occupying Romans, to be one of the Twelve who shared most closely the work of inviting the sinful into the kingdom.

29 September: Michael and All Angels

Note: The prescribed readings are either the passage from Genesis followed by that from Revelation, or the Revelation reading followed by Hebrews.

Genesis 28:10-17
CONTEXT: Jacob journeying from Canaan to his homeland to find a wife.
IDEAS: God present at a pagan shrine; dream experiences; the two-way movement of angels.

It is a very ancient belief that gods reveal themselves to us in our dreams. Jacob, sleeping at a Canaanite shrine, dreamt of God's angels constantly moving between earth and heaven, and of God himself there alongside him.

OR *Revelation 12:7-12*
CONTEXT: John's visions of the end of time and God's final triumph.
IDEAS: Michael is Israel's champion (Dan 10:13); Satan active but defeated; Christ's rule in his kingdom.

The archangel Michael appears twice in the Bible, in mystical visions, as the champion of those who fight against evil. St John foresees the last great battle and the ultimate victory of God.

OR *Hebrews 1:5-14*
CONTEXT: The culmination of all God's self-revelation is in Jesus.
IDEAS: Angels are God's ministers; Christ supreme over them.

Angels are servants of God, as we are meant to be; and they give homage to Christ the Son of God just as we do.

John 1:47-51
CONTEXT: Jesus recruiting his apostles – Philip brings Nathanael.
IDEAS: The sceptic (v. 46) converted; Jesus's perceptiveness; echoing Jacob (see above).

Nathanael recognised Jesus as the Son of God. His adoration brought from Jesus the promise that he, and all of us, will see and understand what Jacob saw: God's angels mediating between earth and heaven.

18 October: Luke

Isaiah 35:3-6
CONTEXT: Assurance that Yahweh will destroy Israel's enemies, and restore her.
IDEAS: The Lord comes to strengthen and heal, people and places.

Luke, the doctor, tells us much about Jesus's work of healing. In Isaiah's poem of renewal, all the sick are healed and the weak made strong when the Lord comes to save his people.

OR *Acts 16:6-12a*
CONTEXT: Paul's second missionary journey – moving further westward in Asia Minor, as far as Greece.
IDEAS: God's guidance in mission; Luke joins Paul, Silas and Timothy.

This short passage contains the subtle change in Luke's story of the church in action. From telling us what 'they' did, on the mission of Paul and two others to the Gentiles, the word changes to 'we'. We can assume, then, that Luke joined the small group in Troas.

2 Timothy 4:5-17
CONTEXT: The solemn charge laid on Christian ministers.
IDEAS: A life God has used; loneliness and companionship; 'Father, forgive'.

The conclusion of this pastoral letter is very personal, and almost despairing in loneliness, but Luke is still there, and Paul is still aware of the Lord upholding him.

Luke 10:1-9
CONTEXT: Unique to Luke – see Ch 9: Mt and Mk both have parallels to sending Twelve. 70 (or 72 in some texts) lead the way.
IDEAS: 12 symbolise Israel, 70 equal Gentiles; mission is urgent, to prepare, bring peace, heal, proclaim the kingdom.

Luke's Gospel particularly stresses that the good news is for all people, not just for Jews. Only he tells us of Jesus sending disciples ahead of him, and the number probably symbolises all the nations then thought to exist.

28 October: Simon and Jude

Isaiah 28:14-16
CONTEXT: The alliance of Judah with Egypt against Assyria, which the prophet stren-
uously condemned; leaders have been false to the Lord.
IDEAS: Pact with the devil!; God lays corner-stone of rebuilding.

**Isaiah pronounces God's judgement upon those who give their loyalty to
the ways of the world – which will end in death. He has heard the Lord
say there will be a new corner-stone on which to build faith.**

Ephesians 2:19-22
CONTEXT: The nature of the church, the body of Christ.
IDEAS: Unity of Christians; apostolic witness; where God dwells.

**Buildings, firm foundations and corner-stones are common biblical
images for the community that shares a common faith. Paul uses the
metaphor to praise apostles and prophets, and to describe Christ himself
as the corner-stone on which everything rests.**

John 15:17-27
CONTEXT: Jesus's final discourses to friends at the Last Supper.
IDEAS: Christians called 'out of this world'; always persecution; Jesus's coming brings its
own judgement; witnesses.

**Jesus's first and primary witnesses were those whom he chose as constant
companions. In his last words to them, he encourages them to be distinctive, recognisable as belonging to him, despite the hatred they will
have to bear.**

30 November: Andrew

Isaiah 52:7-10
CONTEXT: Songs of the redeemed people – the Lord returns to restore.
IDEAS: Messengers of good news; come and see God at work.

Andrew was the messenger who took the news of Jesus to his brother Simon. Isaiah's poem, which Paul quotes in our second reading, tells of one who brings good news to the whole world, messenger of the deliverance God alone can give.

Romans 10:12-18
CONTEXT: Righteousness by Law or by faith – Jew and Gentile alike God's beloved.
IDEAS: One Lord for all; God needs news-bearers; Gospel reaching the entire world; mission.

Faith comes through hearing the word of the Lord, writes Paul, and that means people are needed to spread the Gospel. Messengers are needed in every corner of the world, to speak of Christ wherever they are sent.

Matthew 4:18-22
CONTEXT: Jesus's ministry begins, after his desert retreat.
IDEAS: Disciples called; God's choices; immediate responses.

Simon Peter and his brother Andrew, James and his brother John: these were the first four whom Jesus called from their daily work to be with him, learn from him, and share his mission work during his lifetime and beyond.

26 December: Stephen

Note: The prescribed readings are either the passage from 2 Chronicles followed by that from Acts, or the Acts reading followed by Galatians.

2 Chronicles 24:20-22
CONTEXT: A story not in the parallels of 2 Kings: Joash the king of Judah, the repair and neglect of the Temple; death of the priest Jehoiada, Zechariah's father.
IDEAS: 'Martyrs' before Christ; sudden inspiration; dying with a curse.

According to Israelite history, and as today's Gospel says, the priest Zechariah, in the 8th century BC, was the last to die a martyr's death. His crime was daring to criticise the king in the name of the Lord – but he was proved right.

Acts 7:51-60
CONTEXT: The growing church has provoked the religious authorities to strong action; Stephen brought to trial – Acts 7 is his lengthy harangue.
IDEAS: Stephen one of seven deacons (6:5); prophets were inspired; visions of glory; dying with forgiveness.

Stephen was the first martyr of the Christian era. The Jewish High Priest and the Council could not tolerate his preaching Jesus as the Messiah, and they stoned him to death even while he prayed – like his Master – for them to be forgiven.

Galatians 2:16b-20
CONTEXT: Paul's apostolic authority; the Gospel comes through the Jews but reaches Gentiles too.
IDEAS: Law and faith; dying we live.

Paul writes that to put our faith in Jesus is a kind of death, and out of this dying to rules and laws comes the freedom of an altogether new kind of life, no longer our own but Christ living within us.

Matthew 23:34-39
CONTEXT: A series of Jesus's biting criticisms of the religious legalists.
IDEAS: Entrenched theologies and ideologies; the fate of the prophet; Jesus's (God's) longing for all to accept his love.

Matthew knew only too well, by the time he wrote, that many Christians had followed Stephen in dying for their faith. So these words of Jesus had come true. We are given a glimpse of the divine yearning that everyone should greet the Lord with gladness.

27 December: John

Exodus 33:7-11a
CONTEXT: Israel at the Sinai camp – a renewed promise to Moses of God's purpose to bring them safe to Canaan.
IDEAS: Cloud signifying God's presence; face to face (but see v. 20).

John wrote that he was one of those few who had seen with their own eyes the incarnate Word of eternal life. It is said of Moses in this reading that the Lord God came to meet him face to face

1 John 1
CONTEXT: Prologue and opening of this tract or homily, whose main theme is the incarnation – the Word made flesh.
IDEAS: God heard and seen; joy of eternal life here and now; light and darkness; sin and forgiveness.

The eternal life from God has been seen and touched on earth in the person of his incarnate Word. Now we know God's pure light, and in it we are cleansed and forgiven.

John 21:19b-25
CONTEXT: Resurrection breakfast on the beach – restoration of Peter.
IDEAS: Peter's concern for John; none of us knows our (earthly) future or fate; Jesus's work goes on – the Word(s) fill the world.

The testimony of John comes to an end, and the supreme apostle of love reminds us of the truth of everything he has written.

28 December: Holy Innocents

Jeremiah 31:15-17
CONTEXT: The utter despair (of the exile) turned to incomparable joy in the return and renewal within God's loving care.
IDEAS: Sorrow comes to an end; new children compensate for those lost.

The Gospel quotes this lament, as a prophecy fulfilled when so many Jewish boys were slaughtered by Herod. But Jeremiah's word for the exiled people of his time promised a return from what was not death but merely separation.

1 Corinthians 1:26-29
CONTEXT: Paul's message to disputatious Christians, about wisdom and folly.
IDEAS: Strength and weakness; God's wisdom and ours.

The life of faith has its strange paradoxes, as Paul knew well. In all the intimidation of worldly power, God chooses the weak to show his true power working to bring down tyranny and save his people.

Matthew 2:13-18
CONTEXT: Unique to Matthew – the 'Wise Men' visitation and Herod's machinations.
IDEAS: God works through Joseph (as well as Mary!); refugees; tyrannical rulers.

The word of the Lord to Joseph was a command to flee for safety, so that Jesus would be preserved during the devastating slaughter of all the innocent boys whom Herod's soldiers could find.

Harvest Festival: Year A

Deuteronomy 8:7-18
CONTEXT: A discourse on the life of plenty in the Promised Land after the privations of the journey.
IDEAS: A land of plenty; remember God's leading – it is still he who provides.

The promise of the Lord to his pilgrim people was of plentiful harvests in their own good and fertile land. They were never to forget that it is God who both guides and provides.

OR *Deuteronomy 28:1-14*
CONTEXT: A ceremony of blessing and cursing, at the sanctuary established in Canaan.
IDEAS: Obedience makes blessings possible; God the source of all fertility.

When the Israelites settled in Canaan, they were promised God's blessings on town and country, people and animals, work and harvests; they must never forget that all things come from God.

2 Corinthians 9:6-15
CONTEXT: The collection made by the churches in Asia to help Jerusalem.
IDEAS: Cheerful giving; God's provision; liberality.

Paul uses the metaphor of seedtime and harvest, as he asks Christian people to be as generous with their gifts as God himself is the bounteous giver of all.

Luke 12:16-30
CONTEXT: Luke's collected incidents and teachings, to the general crowds.
IDEAS: The futility of acquisitiveness; God's riches; anxiety.

Jesus's parable illustrates the folly of spending energy piling up wealth, and his teaching should stop us worrying unduly about worldly needs. God know what we need.

OR *Luke 17:11-19*
CONTEXT: Luke has set this series of incidents and teachings in the context of Jesus's determined journey to Jerusalem.
IDEAS: Ritual uncleanness; remember to be grateful.

This incident of Jesus and the ten lepers whom he healed powerfully reminds us that we are always to thank and praise God for all his sustaining gifts.

Harvest Festival: Year B

Joel 2:21-27
CONTEXT: A late work in the stylised manner of earlier prophets; greatly dramatic, but exact historical circumstances not known.
IDEAS: Harvest bounty; presence of the Lord; universal spirit gift and salvation.

Although most of this prophetic writing is of doom and ruin, the poetry also has its inspiring affirmation of God's love, to be shown in abundant harvests that produce more than enough for all.

1 Timothy 2:1-7
CONTEXT: Pastoral charge concerning church oversight.
IDEAS: Pray for God's world; Christ our mediator.

Some of this passage is probably a quotation from an early Christian liturgy. We are urged to pray for the world and its leaders, that the church may live in peace and all find the truth of Christ.

OR *1 Timothy 6:6-10*
CONTEXT: Some final instructions to a church elder, following many detailed sections on church discipline.
IDEAS: Material/spiritual needs; life's direction and goal.

We are reminded by this letter not to grasp after more and more, but to be content with enough. There are great pitfalls that await the greedy.

Matthew 6:25-33
CONTEXT: Sermon on the Mount – collected teachings.
IDEAS: God the creator of birds and plants and people. Worries and frustrations – anxiety; God's concern for us; single-minded pursuit of the kingdom.

Jesus pronounces the natural world to be full of wonder, full of food and drink for its creatures and splendid to look at. We should praise God for his bounty, and try to set aside worries about our future.

Harvest Festival: Year C

Deuteronomy 26:1-11
CONTEXT: Prescriptions for social and ritual behaviour in the land of Canaan.
IDEAS: Harvest thanksgiving; firstfruits; thankfulness for God's work in (exodus) salvation; religious laws.

When you have gathered in your harvest, says the Scripture, you are to come into the house of the Lord and offer the firstfruits in worship and thankfulness for all the good things which come from God.

Philippians 4:4-9
CONTEXT: Final greetings and admonitions to dear friends.
IDEAS: Mutual concern; God knows our needs; think 'holy' thoughts.

Paul bids his friends never to be anxious, but always pray to God about what they need, and fill their minds with only good things.

OR *Revelation 14:14-18*
CONTEXT: The seven visions of the glory of heaven at the world's end.
IDEAS: God the divine reaper; all the earth a harvest.

In John's vision of the end of time, it will be like a harvest, when everything on earth is ripe and ready to be gathered in by God.

John 6:25-35
CONTEXT: People follow Jesus to Capernaum after 5000 fed.
IDEAS: Bread from heaven; Jesus the food for life.

Jesus had miraculously fed a great crowd from a little bread, but now he challenges them about their real need. God in his grace fed the wilderness people with manna, and Jesus gives us himself, true bread for eternal life.

Index to the Readings
Alphabetically by book